The Lioness and the Little One

The Liaison of George Sand and Frédéric Chopin

THE LIONESS
AND THE
LITTLE ONE

The Liaison of
George Sand and Frédéric Chopin

WILLIAM G. ATWOOD

New York
COLUMBIA UNIVERSITY PRESS
1980

Library of Congress Cataloging in Publication Data

Atwood, William G   1932–
The lioness and the little one.

Includes bibliographical references and index.
1. Sand, George, pseud. of Mme. Dudevant,
1804–1876—Relations with men—Fryderyk Franciszek
Chopin.   2. Chopin, Fryderyk Franciszek, 1810–1849.
3. Novelists, French—19th century—Biography.
4. Composers, Polish—Biography.   I. Title.
PQ2414.A8   843'.7 [B]   80-11288
ISBN 0-231-04942-0

Columbia University Press
New York   Guildford, Surrey

To the Memory of
Helen Morris
(1892–1970)

CONTENTS
�֍

INTRODUCTION

🌻

THE PRESENT BOOK, devoted to the liaison of George Sand and Frédéric Chopin,* originally began as a biography of the latter alone. My enthusiasm for Chopin's music developed early as a result of my studies with Dr. Wiktor Labunski, an excellent pianist as well as a compatriot and admirer of the Polish composer. In time this enthusiasm inevitably led to a curiosity about the life of the man behind the compositions. During my later college and medical school years, biographies of Chopin—more available, more portable, and less expensive than a piano—began to feed this new interest.

Naturally some aspects of Chopin's life intrigued me more than others and no period out of his brief thirty-nine years seemed as varied, as productive, and as perplexing as those nine that he spent with George Sand. Here was truly an attraction of opposites, a combination of complementary yet conflicting personalities. In musical terms theirs was a dissonant harmony, alternately strident and serene and yet, for the most part, strangely satisfying. Unfortunately the rapturous cadences of their first union ultimately gave way to a clashing coda of discordant tastes. The two lovers had, as Liszt observed, formed illusions and promises they could not fulfill.

* Because Chopin was in France during the period of his liaison with Mme Sand, I have elected to use the French spelling of his name, i.e., Frédéric instead of the Polish Fryderyk. With other Polish given names I have been somewhat arbitrary but for the most part I have chosen the French versions, especially in the case of those Poles living or visiting in France at the time, e.g., Chopin's sister was known to George Sand and her family as Louise rather than Ludwika, and Grzymała was generally addressed by his French contemporaries as Albert rather than Wojciech.

"When the dream is over," he wrote in his biography of Chopin, "that nature which is the most deeply impressed and the most firm in its hopes is the one that is shattered and wasted."[1] There is no doubt that Chopin was "shattered" by the disintegration of his relationship with Sand. His creative life ended with this rupture and he himself survived it by only two years.

With this brief summary of events it is easy to make Chopin into a pathetic victim. Certainly the energetic and irrepressible Mme Sand, whom Balzac once called the "Lioness of Berry," often overpowered her pale, tuberculous companion, her "petit Chopin," the "little one" she came to regard more as a son than a lover. The story of their relationship, Curtis Cate has suggested, might well be entitled "From Passion to Pity."[2] But was Chopin merely another unsuspecting prey, exploited by the insatiable Mme Sand who reputedly snared her lovers and pinned them down like butterflies, only to resurrect them later as heroes for her novels? It is true that Chopin did not entirely escape this fate (viz., George Sand's novel, *Lucrezia Floriani*).

Today, thanks to the superb scholarship of Bronislas Sydow and his associates, Suzanne and Denise Chainaye, and Irène Sydow (who have collected Chopin's correspondence), and the even more Herculean efforts of Georges Lubin (who is still retrieving the incredibly prolific outpourings of George Sand's pen) we have a more balanced perspective on the intimate lives of this celebrated couple.

If the fragile Chopin still deserves our sympathy because of his weakness and vulnerability, George now commands out admiration because of her strength and tolerance. For all the transparency of her overstated self-justifications, she was a generous person who gave liberally, not only of her money but of her emotions, to those she loved. This, indeed, proved to be one of her greatest faults: she was *too* indulgent, most obviously and most disastrously with her own children—and she always considered Chopin as her "second son." It is not to the musician's credit that he abused her patience and goodwill. In the long run, he proved more peevish than her spoiled son, Maurice, and more petulant than her willful daughter, Solange. To posterity his genius may serve as an excuse, but then we today live only with the music and not, as did George, with the man. The music may be divine but the man was all too human.

As much as M. Lubin's collection of Mme Sand's correspondence has contributed to our understanding of the author's life, it cannot alter the fact that her literary talents were limited. She herself would be the first to admit that much of her writing was motivated purely by financial need. She seldom revised what she hurriedly scribbled—partly because her publishers' deadlines gave her no time for such luxury and partly because, as she freely confessed, she hated to reread what she had written. The result was many potboilers and a number of turgid, religio-socio-historico-politico-philosophical expressions that gained her little popularity in her time and less respect in ours. Her initial success stemmed largely from her early, semi-autobiographical works like *Indiana* and *Lélia,* while today's public favors her *romans champêtres.* Dealing with the lives of her beloved Berrichon peasantry, these latter novels have a touching beauty. In them she endows her characters with a vivid reality, empathizes with their downtrodden plight, and ennobles their simplicity with a human dignity. These lovely portrayals are worth thousands of her pompous pontifications.

As a literary figure, George Sand may have been neglected in this century (at least outside of France), but even allowing for this, when one compares her artistic ability to Chopin's, few would contest his superiority. And yet, in any examination of their lives, George, the lesser genius, triumphs as the greater human being—greater in her range of interests (stretching from needlework and cooking to politics and literature), greater in her physical stamina (two of her lovers were tuberculous and one syphilitic, yet she escaped the ravages of both diseases), and greater in her emotional endurance (as witnessed by her resilience in the face of a father's death, a mother's hostility, numerous financial crises, and a host of romantic traumas). But most of all George triumphs as a great humanitarian—at least in her ideals if not always in her accomplishments.

She served repeatedly as a champion of the underdog and liked to call herself a "communist" which, of course, was a calculated exaggeration of her liberal sentiments. Today it is popular to stress her concern for women's rights. But if the label of "communist" is too extreme, that of "feminist" is too narrow. While she protested the bondage of women, who were lumped together with children as "minors" under the Napoleonic Code, her concern for all those many countrymen of hers (male and female) who were disenfranchised by the bourgeois regime of Louis Philippe was still more compelling. Her vision was broad, one of equality for *all* people, a vision which essentially transcended sexual distinctions.

Unfortunately, like many of her romantic colleagues, Mme Sand tended to be more rhapsodic than analytic. The expression of her ideals was often vague and amorphous. Perhaps this may be a reflection of viewing too many facets of human potential to focus exclusively (and clearly) on a limited few. Perhaps the diversity of her background (being the descendant of both royalty and riffraff) and the breadth of her experiences (ranging far beyond those of the average nineteenth-century woman) may have made it difficult for her to assimilate thoroughly all that she encountered.

In some ways it is the example of Mme Sand's life that expresses her idealism more lucidly than do her writings. While she worked and wrote with dedication to make the timeworn motto of Liberty, Equality, and Fraternity a reality for all Frenchmen—and indeed, all mankind—she realized that these privileges carry responsibilities and only those who accept the latter are entitled to the former. Certainly her life was burdened with responsibilities—responsibilities that she not only accepted willingly but sought actively. And Chopin must be included among these. Throughout a career that is often condemned as licentious, George exhibited an altruism and a self-discipline for which she is seldom given credit. There is no doubt that she was—and always wanted to be—unbridled, but this for her did not mean the freedom to rampage through life without constraint. On the contrary, she sought to impose her own control over her destiny, and this she ultimately did with admirable effect.

Much of this insight into George Sand's character is the result of the complex portrait of her which is emerging from M. Lubin's persistent research. Happily, with regard to the years of her alliance with Chopin, this material is already available to us and we are now in a position to appreciate a number of the more worthy qualities of this remarkable woman. These new dimensions of her personality, along with her many other flamboyant traits, already well-touted, eventually confirmed my decision to concentrate on that portion of Chopin's life which he shared with the mistress of Nohant.

To the best of my knowledge, there are few detailed works devoted exclusively to the fascinating union of this paradoxically paired couple. While numerous biographies of one or the other of these individuals exist, I have always sensed varying degrees of bias in their treatment of the relationship between the two. The biographers of Mme Sand tend to highlight Chopin's peevish and parasitic dependence on their heroine, while the Chopin biographers often see George Sand as a self-righteous, domineering hypocrite whose supposed affection for Chopin was little more than an "ego trip" for herself. I have no desire to force Sand and Chopin into preconceived molds (such as proto-feminist or latter-day Oedipus) and have tried to avoid the snares of over-romanticizing or over-psychoanalyzing their personalities and actions. Post-mortem psychoanalyses are risky and usually finish by revealing more about the author than his subject. In drawing as much as possible from Sand's and Chopin's private correspondence as well as other contemporary sources, I hope to let the characters and their era tell us their own story with a minimum of interpretation on my part. Nevertheless I realize that any writer inescapably gives a certain slant to his work merely by the choice of materials he includes, no matter how factual they may be.

As one of the readers of this manuscript observed, Chopin's and George Sand's life together was not the flaming *vie passionelle* that is often imagined. Despite the romantic milieu in which they existed, both, were serious-minded individuals, as sensible as they were sensitive. They organized their lives to enhance their productivity as artists, which resulted in an orderly existence that was generally quiet and routine. But, because each was "overwhelmed" with what Liszt called the "fatal, beautiful gifts of genius,"[3] they tended to expend less effort on the more mundane, human aspects of their relationship. It is in this sphere of their lives—as lovers and companions—that the drama develops. Their productivity as artists speaks for itself. Their humanity is what I hope will come alive for the reader of this book.

The Lioness and the Little One

I GLADLY ACCEPT your proposition," George Sand wrote Franz Liszt on October 22, 1836. "Get me a room and let's set up house as before."[1] The "proposition" to which George referred was an invitation from the pianist and his mistress, the countess d'Agoult, to join them in Paris. "Come stay with me, rue Neuve-Lafitte, Hôtel de France," Marie d'Agoult insisted. "It is quite nice and not too expensive. I have a room and my salon will be at your disposal any time of day to receive your friends. This way we will be sure to see plenty of you."[2]

Two days after her reply, George was installed in the Hôtel de France with her two children: Maurice, age thirteen, and Solange, age eight. Their room was just a floor below that of Franz and Marie. The countess, who had literary aspirations, was more than glad to have George share her salon. But underneath her apparent congeniality lurked a certain ambivalence. As a writer George had gained a reputation which Mme d'Agoult envied and, in affairs with men, she had achieved an independence the countess greatly admired. All this tended to nurture in Marie d'Agoult a secret rivalry which bordered on jealousy. At times it was difficult to hide her resentment, but knowing Liszt's fondness for the masculine-mannered novelist, Mme d'Agoult tried her best to remain cordial.

Throughout the fall and early winter of 1836 the countess regularly included Mme Sand in the lively salon which she and Liszt had established in the Hôtel de France. There George met a host of personalities from the musical and literary world. Recalling the countess' friendship that year George wrote in her mémoires that "it was in her lodgings or through her that I made the acquaintance of Eugène Sue, the baron d'Eckstein, Chopin, Mickiewicz, Nourrit, etc. . . ."[3]

It is somewhat paradoxical that among these many new acquaintances the one who was to exert the greatest influence on Mme Sand's life seemed to create a very slight impression on her at the time of their introduction. George never made any further allusion to the circumstances under which she met Frédéric Chopin, and the latter, with his typical reticence, seems to have remained silent on the subject through his life.

In contrast, others who were less directly involved exhibited a far greater volubility. Out of the fabric of speculation, boasting, and mere gossip woven around the event, it is virtually impossible now to trace the actual threads of truth. But since the countess d'Agoult, by George's own admission, was responsible for her introduction to Chopin, there would seem to be little doubt that Liszt also must have been involved* and, according to the pianist, it was George who first expressed a desire to meet Chopin. Her interest had been whetted by all she had heard of him, especially from Liszt himself, who claimed that he often spoke "of this truly exceptional artist in Mme Sand's hearing." Through him she heard praise of Chopin's "ability and more of his poetic genius: she knew his works and admired their amorous sweetness. She was struck by the abundance of emotion permeating this poetry and by the heartfelt outpourings in a tone so lofty and nobly distinguished."[4] No wonder she was anxious to meet this extraordinarily gifted young man of twenty-six!

But the introduction did not prove easy to arrange since Chopin was not at all eager to make the acquaintance of the

---

*Certainly Liszt later had much to recount about this auspicious occasion which his mistress had arranged. Unfortunately his irrepressible personality could no more resist embellishing an historical fact that it could a musical phrase and much of what he wrote is therefore suspect. (Many of the embellishments were probably contributed by his later mistress, the Princess Carolyn Sayn-Wittgenstein, who, in fact, wrote much of his biography of Chopin.) Yet despite Liszt's literary excesses, he was a participant in the events that took place, and his account of them possesses at least some veracity of feeling if not of fact.

famous novelist who, at thirty-two years of age, had already gained quite a notorious reputation. To Liszt's chagrin he discovered that Chopin actually "seemed to fear this woman more than other women" (p. 158). The fact that she smoked cigars and often wore men's clothing must have given him an intimidating impression of coarseness and aggressiveness. Yet, in reality, Mme Sand's physical appearance was not the least bit menacing. She was "very small," according to Mme d'Agoult, and "looked even smaller when dressed like a man. In such an outfit she had a casual air and even a youthful, virile grace. Neither the outline of her breasts nor the prominence of her hips betrayed her feminine sex. Nothing—be it the tight-fitting black velvet redingote, the high-heeled boots, the tie wrapped around her rather plump neck, or the man's hat cocked cavalierly over her thick locks of short hair—could detract in any way from her uninhibited manner or the nonchalance of her bearing. She gave the impression of quiet strength. . . . Her dark eyes, like her hair, had something very strange in their beauty. . . . There was a calm and yet disturbing quality about them."[5]

Mme Sand tended to be rather unorthodox, not only in her dress but also in her behavior. "Like a Delphic priestess she said so many things that others could not say,"[6]—or, at least, would not dare to say. In many ways the romantic avant-garde truly found in her their oracle. Such a woman, it would seem, could only antagonize a man like Chopin who was so restrained, so fastidious, and above all so conventional.

Even Mme d'Agoult, who had boldly flouted convention in her liaison with Liszt, found George a bit difficult to comprehend on their first encounter. "Was it a man, a woman, an angel, or a demon? Did she come from heaven or from hell?"[7] the countess had wondered. Predictably, Chopin would assign her to the latter realm. Those infernal clouds of cigar smoke billowing from her would surely settle over him like a pall of disgust and blind him to anything attractive in her. Sensing an inherent conflict in their personalities, Chopin "avoided her and delayed their meeting."[8]

How Liszt and his countess finally succeeded in bringing two such divergent individuals together is peculiarly omitted from the pianist's flowery "reminiscences." In light of Chopin's unconcealed aversion to Mme Sand it is surprising that he later invited her to his apartment. Perhaps he was curious to see this strange anomaly whose eccentricities made her the talk of Paris. But more likely it was the insistent urging of the Liszt-d'Agoult household. Whatever the reason, on Friday, November 5, Chopin asked her to a small soirée in his rooms on the Chaussée d'Antin. Franz and Marie were there, as well as others. George, with the anticipated cigar in her mouth, chatted at length on weighty philosophical matters while Chopin clowned lightheartedly with his guests. Both seemed unusually relaxed since Chopin was ordinarily quite sedate and George rather silent in the presence of strangers. A few nights later, on November 9, they met again at a dinner in the home of some of George's friends, Charlotte and Manoël Marliani.

If Chopin did not find Mme Sand personally appealing in these early meetings, he was, at least, impressed by her fame and boasted to his family, "I have made the acquaintance of a great celebrity: Mme Dudevant, known by the name of George Sand." But his basic impression remained unchanged. "Her appearance," he added in his letter, "is not to my liking and doesn't please me at all. There is even something about her which puts me off. . . ."[9]

Apparently Mme Sand did not return to Chopin's apartment until the following month when Liszt coaxed his friend into giving an impromptu musicale on December 13. George, it seems, wanted to meet the novelist Eugène Sue and another prominent writer, the marquis de Custine, both of whom Chopin knew. By this time she considered herself on close enough terms with her host to take the liberty of inviting Heinrich Heine on her own. "If you can arrange it this evening between 9:00 o'clock and midnight," she urged, "come meet us at Chopin's. . . . We are having a very choice and intimate little get-together. Join us if you like."[10]

Despite the short notice, an impressive collection of Paris's artistic elite assembled that night in the Chaussée d'Antin, including the popular operatic composer Giacomo Meyerbeer, the German pianist Ferdinand Hiller, the great romantic painter Eugène Delacroix, and the prominent Polish literati Julian Ursyn Niemcewicz and Adam Mickiewicz.

The salon in which this company gathered was lit by only a few candles clustered around the large Pleyel piano which was the focal point of the room. In the velvet glow of the quivering candlelight the guests found themselves transported into one of those transcendental realms so ravishing to the romantic mind.

> Corners left in darkness seemed to remove the limits of the room and to extend it into the shadows of space. In a play of light and shade, clothed in a whitish slipcover, a piece of furniture could be seen, vague in outline; it stood like a specter come to hear the sounds that had called it forth. The light concentrated around the piano, fell on the floor, gliding over the surface like a spreading wave and mingling with the flickering gleamings of the hearth where, from time to time, orange-colored flames, short and broad shot up like curious gnomes, summoned by words in their own tongue.[11]

The music that evening was as magical as the setting. When the famous tenor Adolphe Nourrit sang, "the effect was indescribable." After he had finished some Schubert lieder the audience sat spellbound. Later Liszt performed and Chopin improvised on several themes, running his fingers over the keyboard in a startling glissando after each improvisation to jolt his listeners back into reality. At the end of the evening Chopin and Liszt joined talents in a performance of Moscheles' four-hand Sonata in E-flat Major. As always Chopin insisted on playing the bass while Liszt executed the treble with a scintillating display of pyrotechniques that left the listeners "breathless."

Throughout the performance Liszt kept an eye on Mme Sand who sat "deep in an armchair, her arms on a console . . . curiously enrapt and becomingly subdued" (p. 96). Another guest, the Polish composer Joseph Brzowski, also watched Mme Sand that evening: ". . . dark, dignified, and cold," she sat entranced by the music, "her dark hair parted in the middle, falling in curls on both sides of her face, and secured with a ribbon around her brow." In her "regular features, calm, or rather inanimate in their expression . . . one could only perceive intelligence, reflection, and pride." Against the background of men who surrounded her she stood out sharply. Both the manner in which she dressed and the way in which she behaved attracted attention. The outfit she had chosen was "fantastic," Brzowski remarked, "(obviously proclaiming her desire to be noticed). . . ." It was a Turkish costume, "composed of a white frock with a crimson sash and a kind of white shepherdess' corsage with crimson buttons."[12] Sitting by the fireplace she wore a solemn expression as she casually puffed away at her cigar in the hushed atmosphere of the dimly lit room. Although she seldom spoke, "she was charming in her turkish dress and smoked her head off,"[13] another guest commented. After the music was over, Chopin passed around ices and the crowd broke up into small groups for conversation. But "George Sand, glued to her sofa, never quitted her cigar for a moment."[14]

What this enigmatic woman was thinking as she sat smoking and gazing into the fire can only be imagined. Doubtless she was aware of a certain fascination she had begun to feel for her sensitive young host, the frail-looking musician with the aquiline nose and aristocratic bearing. But she had already trodden the path from fascination to infatuation so often that such an experience was scarcely novel for her any longer. On the other hand neither was it merely casual this time. Although George had enjoyed music since childhood when she used to crawl beneath her grandmother's harpsichord, it seems to have been more than the musician's talent that now attracted her. Chopin's fragile appearance, his retiring manner, and his constant cough betrayed a delicate, vulnerable creature, capable of arousing Mme Sand's deepest sentiments. "I need to suffer for someone," she once confessed to a former lover, "I need to use up that excess energy and sensitivity inside me. I need to nourish that material solicitude whose nature it is to look after a tired and suffering being.[15] It was, in many respects, a mother's fulfillment that George Sand had been searching for throughout most of her thirty-two years.

In a little over three decades this woman had lived an incredibly full life, rich in almost every human experience except that of a mother's love. Fatherless when she was only four, she had been raised by a grandmother whose austere eighteenth-century background radiated little warmth to the sensitive child so abruptly thrust into her care. Sent off to a convent school in her early adolescence, she had been taught to love God and struggled desperately to make Him fill the void in her lonely life. But theological abstractions could never take the place of human affection. When George finally got to know her mother later on, she found her harsh, domineering, distant, and unfeeling.* The two women were worlds apart in temperament and seldom able to comprehend each other's needs. At last George fled in desperation from the mother who had disappointed her into a marriage which disgusted her. As the baroness Dudevant she found conjugal love as disillusioning as the religious passions of her adolescence. Yet once free of marital obligations she could never seem to satisfy the insistent demands of her complex, emotional nature with any of the numerous lovers that became a part of her life. Fiercely independent, she would never bring herself to accept a love that subjugated her. Unwilling to be dominated, she more than once turned to younger men whom she could protect and support in exchange for filial devotion. Still, none of these had truly fulfilled that intense desire for the perfect communion of souls which she constantly sought. There was, she eventually concluded, only one truly satisfying rela-

---

* To George's credit, she never repaid her mother "in kind." With a strong sense of filial obligation and a remembrance of a more loving relationship which had existed between the two in her earliest years, she was quite generous to her mother in later life.

tionship: "Glory is empty and matrimony insufferable," the successful novelist proclaimed to a friend in the summer of 1836. But "maternity," she asserted, "brings inexpressible delights."[16]

Could it be that Mme Sand's maternal instinct was again aroused that evening as she sat before the fire in the candlelit salon on the Chaussée d'Antin? In Chopin's slight frame one could sense more of the youth than the man, in his exquisite talent there was an intimation of sadness, and in his eloquent reticence George was more than willing to listen for the voice of a lonely child crying out for a mother's love and assurance. The urge to alleviate such a craving was almost a compulsion with Mme Sand who tended to give of herself all too often with a readiness that many considered profligate.

If Chopin no longer seemed repelled by George Sand, he was certainly not in the least attracted to her. The bohemian milieu in which she moved was altogether alien to the cultivated circles of the aristocracy which he adored. These differences in taste extended well beyond the mere conventions of dress and manners and into the sphere of morals where the scent of scandal clung heavily to Mme Sand's private life. With a scornful insouciance she shrugged off public opinion. What people thought about her didn't matter, she quipped, as long as "they don't say that I have two men in my bed on the same day."[17]

During the month of December 1836 George was to limit that particular privilege to only one young man—Charles Didier, for whom she rushed back to the Hôtel de France after Chopin's party on the thirteenth in order to keep a midnight rendezvous. However, she seemed upset that night and was not her usual self. "There was a pleasant enough intimacy between us," Didier wrote in his journal the next day. "But underneath it there was something gnawing away. As day approached she had a horrible bout of despair."[18]

Whether or not Chopin seriously disapproved of George Sand's behavior, his impeccable sense of decorum must surely have been disarmed by the blatant indiscretion with which she flaunted her private life before the public. His personality was such that "in music as in literature and the ways of life everything verging on melodrama was torture to him. He was," as Liszt so astutely observed, "repelled by the furious and frenzied face of Romanticism."[19]

Chopin's few brief contacts with George Sand in 1836 had so far not allowed him to glimpse the more disciplined side of his new acquaintance. Beneath her flamboyant façade there was a sense of order and responsibility without which her incredible productivity could never had been achieved. These qualities would some day also enhance Chopin's own productivity during the years they eventually shared with each other. From George, Chopin was to derive the strength and security which would lead to the richest flowering of his musical genius. And without her both his physical and artistic faculties quickly faded and died.

However, no one could have foreseen this in December of 1836, and even if Mme Sand had succeeded in arousing Chopin's interest that autumn after their first meetings there was little opportunity for such an interest to ripen into intimacy. Less than a month after that last evening in the Chaussée d'Antin, George Sand returned to her country home at Nohant for the winter.

I T IS DIFFICULT to say whether Nohant belonged to George Sand or George Sand to Nohant. Legally speaking it was only in the preceding six months that the estate had come back into her full possession. Prior to that it had been under the control of her husband, the baron Dudevant, since their marriage in 1822. Although she had left him in 1831 she did not recover her property until many years later after a long series of sordid court proceedings which nearly made her despair of ever regaining the lovely old home where she had spent so many of her childhood years. Nohant she regarded as her "nest" where she hoped someday to "be able to die in peace."[1]

The large eighteenth-century house which George Sand inherited from her paternal grandmother, Mme Dupin de Franceuil, had been built in the reign of Louis XVI. Its yellowish-gray exterior combined a severe symmetry with a gracious elegance. In its somber formality the old chateau somehow retained an inviting warmth. The repetitious façade of shuttered windows with their rippling panes of glass was broken by the smooth curve of the arch over the front door. Two large wings with gracefully rounded windows projected on either side of the house while a series of small dormers pierced the steep slant of the dark, slate roof. To the front of the property a high wall preserved the privacy of Nohant in spite of the nearness of the village square with its rustic church and quaint cottages. Within this wall the tree-shaded driveway curved leisurely up to gray-panelled doors of the entrance. In the rear, a green expanse of lawn opened onto a garden through which gravel paths meandered casually in sharp but agreeable contrast to the rigid austerity of the house.

Nohant had been and always was to be, for George Sand, a retreat in whose quiet precincts she could relax and renew those forces that would carry her through the turbulent years of her restless life. It symbolized tranquillity which often brought her happiness, at times boredom, and occasionally a melancholy loneliness bordering on despair. But for the most part Nohant provided her with an abundance of joy. There, in her youth, she had known what it was to run free across the meadows or ride horseback through the fields, carefree and full of laughter. Only at Nohant could George enjoy such simple rural pleasures along the peaceful banks of the river Indre. Brimming with youthful effervescence she once described her country life to the countess d'Agoult: "I start on foot at three in the morning, with the firmest intentions of returning at eight; but I get carried away. I forget myself along the brooks, I run after insects and don't get home until noon, absolutely roasted to death. The other day, I was so exhausted that I went right into the river with all my clothes on. . . . Sometimes, after coming out of the water, I throw myself down on the grass in a meadow with my clothes still soaked and take a siesta."[2]

Not only was it a delicious sense of tranquillity that George Sand experienced at Nohant, but also a reassuring feeling of stability. Her grandmother Dupin, who originally bought the property, was perhaps the one most responsible for this, and the aura of her presence still lingered over the house in which she had raised her grandaughter. An august personage of the French Enlightenment, Mme Dupin was born in 1748, the illegitimate daughter of the maréchal de Saxe and a beautiful nineteen-year-old bourgeois girl, Marie Rainteau. The maréchal himself had been the illegitimate product of a union between Friedrich August, elector of Saxony, later king of Poland, and the ravishing Aurore de Koenigsmark. It was said that George Sand not only inherited the latter's name but also her "great dark velvety eyes" and much of her intellectual brilliance. In addition, she acquired from her that strong maternal instinct which, passing from generation to generation, became an obsession with all the women in George's family. Aurore de Koenigsmark, despite the profligate nature of her son, Maurice, willingly sacrificed her jewels to further his ambitions. But her maternal dedication was frustrated by Maurice's amorous indiscretions which eventually cost him a potential dukedom and the promise of a throne. With only the title of comte de Saxe, granted him by his father, Maurice migrated to France, where his half-sister, the dauphine, wife of Louis XV's son, obtained a position for him in the service of the king. For his heroism in the battle of Fontenoy he was created a maréchal and received a vast estate with a yearly pension of 50,000 livres.

Following the birth of a daughter by his mistress, Marie Rainteau, the maréchal soon abandoned both mother and child, having come to realize that Marie unfortunately shared his own passionate predilection for freedom over fidelity, a familial characteristic which was to loom prominently in George Sand's own life.

Deserted by the maréchal, Marie Rainteau sought the protection of more than one subsequent lover while her daughter, Marie-Aurore, found a home and allowance through the generosity of her aunt, the dauphine. Ultimately the young girl married an infantry captain, Antoine de Horne, whom George Sand, in her *Histoire de ma Vie*, later elevated to the nobility with the title (never granted him in life) of "comte de Horne." Unluckily both the marriage and the groom were very short-lived, leaving Marie-Aurore a widow at an early age. Returning to her mother's home she became attracted to her Aunt Genevieve's lover, M. Louis-Claude Dupin de Francueil, receiver general for the duchy of Albret, and in 1777 they were married; she was thirty and he sixty-two. For the following ten years they lived happily and extravagantly. Whatever physical passion the marriage may have lacked was more than compensated for by the paternal qualities which

Marie-Aurore discovered in her "old husband" or "papa" as she often called M. Dupin.

The couple had only one child, a son, Maurice, born in 1778 in the castle of Chateauroux. Mme Dupin from the outset was inordinately fond of this son and, following the death of her husband in 1788, he became the focus of her life. The revolution erupted a year later and "citizeness" Dupin found herself in a precarious situation. Though she was neither especially rich nor well-connected, her sympathies gradually became aligned with the upper classes when fanaticism took control of the revolution. She gave financial assistance to the aristocratic emigrés and "illegally" concealed some of her more precious possessions for which she soon found herself in prison. After her release, she and her son, along with the latter's tutor, the abbé Deschartes, sought a more secure, quiet existence in the province of Berry, where Mme Dupin purchased an estate in August of 1793. The property was called Nohant and had once been the site of a fourteenth-century castle. Of this nothing but a single tower remained, while the large house which Mme Dupin and her son inhabited dated only from the latter half of the eighteenth century.

Here, in a peaceful setting, Marie-Aurore was able to live in relative calm. However, as Maurice grew up, he found the peacefulness of Nohant less to his taste than to his mother's. In his restlessness he shattered the serenity of their provincial life by fathering an illegitimate child with one of the servant girls. The child, christened Hippolyte, always went by the surname of Chatiron although Maurice acknowledged him and provided for his support. Marie-Aurore, being an adaptable woman, adjusted to the presence of the new grandson and even grew fond of him. What later proved far more difficult for her was Maurice's determination to leave Nohant and become a soldier. But the greatest blow was yet to come: one day Maurice returned home with a bride! While Mme Dupin could stand being separated from her son, she could not endure having to share him—especially when her competition proved to be the daughter of a lowly birdseller on the Paris quays. "You don't love me any more," she berated Maurice. "If only I had died, like the others in '93, I would have remained in your heart as I was then and would never have had a rival.[3]

Her new daughter-in-law, Antoinette-Sophie-Victoire Delaborde, was a so-called dancer, who had proffered the careless disorder of her existence to an assortment of "protectors." By one of these she had had a daughter several years earlier. In 1800 when she first met Maurice Dupin, she was, in fact, little more than a professional camp follower, but one at least with the fortunate distinction of getting herself a general. Considerations of wealth and rank, however, soon gave way to those of youth and passion in the fickle head of Sophie-Victoire, who shortly afterwards abandoned her old general for his handsome young aide-de-camp.

In 1803, when Maurice realized that his new mistress was pregnant, he finally decided to marry her. Still whirling her way through life with blithe abandon, Sophie-Victoire could scarcely find time to pause, even for the birth of her second daughter, Amantine-Aurore-Lucile, on July 1, 1804. In a rose-colored dress, the young bride was dancing a quadrille with some friends while Maurice accompanied them on his violin. Suddenly her husband saw her face contract in pain and, throwing down his violin, he rushed to help her. As the startled dancers stared in astonishment the excited couple vanished into an adjacent room where, moments later, Mme Dupin gave birth to a swarthy baby girl with big brown eyes.

Even though Maurice named his new daughter Aurore in honor of his mother, the elder Mme Dupin refused to have anything to do with the child for many years. As a result the little girl spent her early life in the impoverished atmosphere of her mother's attic apartment in Paris while her father was away at the Napoleonic wars. In 1808 when Aurore was four, her mother, again pregnant, embarked on an exhausting trip to rejoin her husband, now an aide-de-camp to Murat in Madrid. There Sophie-Victoire gave birth to a boy. The return trip to Nohant in June was hot, dusty, and especially fatiguing for the children, who came down with alarming fevers. Aurore recovered but the infant succumbed. Tragedy then fell upon tragedy and shortly afterwards Maurice himself was killed when a spirited stallion he had brought back from Spain dashed him on some stones as he was returning home one night from La Châtre.

Aurore's grandmother now found herself lodged in the same house with the daughter-in-law she could never bring herself to accept and the granddaughter she could not bring herself to reject. Friction and frustration followed until Sophie-Victoire decided to leave for Paris in order to care for her illegitimate older daughter, Caroline. Aurore was then left alone at Nohant under her grandmother's supervision. It was during these years that the young girl grew to love the Berry countryside and developed her lifelong attachment to Nohant. There she learned to shoot, to ride, and to hunt. Since she could pursue these sports much more easily in men's clothes she often took to wearing them as a matter of convenience. Galloping across the open fields in her long redingote, cap, and boots she was often mistaken for a man, both amusing and shocking her neighbors.

On Christmas day, 1821, the death of her grandmother put a sudden end to these pastoral pleasures. They could have continued had Aurore followed her grandmother's wishes and gone to live with her cousins, the count and countess de Villeneuve, who owned the chateau of Chenonceaux. But she chose instead to return to her mother's apartment in Paris. The choice was unfortunate, for her mother, as she grew older, became shrewish, coarse, vindictive, and at times irrational. " 'Oh my child,' " her grandmother warned her shortly before she died, " 'what a time you will have if you fall into her hands! You don't know your mother and I don't want you to know her. God preserve you from ever knowing her.' Alas," Aurore realized too late, "the premonitions of this fine lady were only too well founded."[4]

Indeed life with Sophie-Victoire eventually became so intol-

erable that Aurore eagerly welcomed an escape from it
through marriage. One day, while eating ices with some
friends outside the Café Tortoni in Paris, she was introduced
to a young man, Casimir Dudevant, the illegitimate but recognized son of the baron Dudevant, a Napoleonic peer from the
province of Gascony. With his grotesquely long nose, Casimir
was not handsome. In fact, as Heinrich Heine put it bluntly,
he had "the face of a grocer, completely undistinguished" with
a "tepid, commonplace, banal, empty, porcelain-like expression."[5] Nevertheless to Aurore he seemed the protector for
whom she had been looking, "so good, so honest, so disinter-
ested."[6] The fact that he did not press his suit very passionately rather pleased the eighteen-year-old girl who, from the
outset, seemed to regard Casimir as more of a comrade or
brother than a lover. On September 17, 1822, with Mme Dupin's consent, the young couple was married in a civil ceremony at the town hall of the first arrondissement in Paris, and
later the same day in the Church of St. Louis-d'Antin.

As the wife of M. Dudevant, Aurore could at last return to
Nohant with the sanction of society and her family. But little
by little it grew clear to Mme Dudevant that she and her husband were cast in very different molds. Aurore shared few of
Casimir's habits or tastes, which were largely restricted to
hunting, local politics, and the wine bottle. In the evenings she
tried to instill in him an interest in literature, philosophy, and
music. But Casimir had a distinct aversion to music, philosophy didn't interest him, and literature only put him to sleep.
He did, however, provide his wife with one source of endless
pleasure throughout the rest of her life: a son, Maurice, born
the year following their marriage. Like the preceding
Maurices in her family, this son was to become the object of an
obsessive maternal devotion. The love which Mme Dudevant
might have concentrated on her husband, had Casimir been
more compatible, came to be channeled in her son's direction.
A few months after his birth, Aurore wrote a friend, "My little
Maurice absorbs my attention so much that for him I forget
everything else that is nearest and dearest to me . . . if you

only knew how one idolizes and slaves for one's child" (p. 114).

So much did Maurice become the pivot of her lonely life that in 1828 Mme Dudevant went so far as to state, "If I should lose Maurice nothing on earth could console me in the seclusion in which I live. He is so necessary to my existence that without him I would have no interest in anything" (p. 444). He "is my faithful companion, he goes and comes with me and sleeps with me. He is my chaperon and my husband" (p. 470).

Notwithstanding the enormous attention which Mme Dudevant expended on her son, her reserve of maternal affection remained so great that she eventually sought other outlets for it. These she found in the tenants of her estate and the local Berrichon peasantry whom she came to regard as her personal charges. In a sense she adopted them and found great satisfaction in tending to their needs and providing for their pleasures.

In her new role of benefactress to the community she wrote her mother in 1826, "I am devoting myself to medicine, not for my own sake since I don't care much about it, but for my peasants' sake" (p. 348). By the following year she could already "reset broken noses, patch up cut fingers, mix various medicinal potions and brews, prepare plasters, and even, when necessary, enemas" (p. 388).

Yet, in spite of the enjoyment which Mme Dudevant derived from these duties, life at Nohant grew more and more tedious for her. Certainly she found great happiness in her son, but "freed from all real anxieties and troubles," she reflected, "married to an excellent man, and mother of a beautiful child, surrounded by everything which could cater to my tastes," she still found that she was "bored with life" (p. 269). The real fault, she eventually concluded, must lie with Casimir and she confronted him with this conclusion—but to no avail. Although he often tried to please and comfort his wife, Casimir simply could never comprehend the woman he had married. From that time on Aurore began to look elsewhere for the love and understanding which was lacking in her husband.

In 1826, on the death of his father, Casimir became the baron Dudevant. This accolade, however, brought little satisfaction to his young baroness, who, after all, was the great-great-granddaughter of a king.

The birth of a second child, a daughter named Solange, took place in 1828, but failed to alter the ever-increasing alienation of Mme Dudevant from her husband. Indeed it is now generally accepted that the father of this child was not actually Casimir, but rather a young man named Stéphane Ajasson de Grandsagne, the "half-consumptive, half-mad" son of an impoverished noble family from the neighboring town of La Châtre.

By this time Aurore had not only grown to feel that Casimir was a failure as a lover and a husband; she also had begun to realize that he was not even very competent as the administrator of her estate. He seemed to have little financial judgment and what he did possess was often clouded by alcohol. It especially disturbed Aurore to think that the baron's financial bunglings might someday jeopardize the future of her children and even risk the loss of Nohant. She could tolerate a great deal but never this. "I am above all a mother," she warned Casimir, "and I can be firm enough when it is necessary. You will find me always ready to excuse you and to console you, but I intend to make myself clearly heard in all matters that concern the welfare of my children" (p. 583).

Then one day in July of 1830 Mme Dudevant met a handsome nineteen-year-old boy as "lovable and light as a hummingbird from the perfumed plains" (p. 742). With him she was to launch a new life and a new career. His name was Jules Sandeau and his impact on the disgruntled young baroness was instantaneous.

By December of that year the last shreds of affection which Aurore might still have felt for her husband disintegrated completely. Shortly before Christmas, Mme Dudevant accidentally came across a copy of her husband's will and with an unscrupulous disregard for the instructions on its cover, which read, "To be opened only after my death," she deliberately tore off the seal and began to read. "Good God!" she exclaimed in horror as her eyes scanned its contents. "What a will! Full of curses and nothing else! In it he had gathered together all his hatred and anger against me, all his reflections as to my perversity and all his feelings of contempt for my character" (p. 737). Casimir's opinion of her, she was stunned to discover, was just as low as hers of him. To continue the farce of their marriage now seemed utterly impossible.

The following month Aurore packed her wounded pride along with a few possessions into a coach and, curling up on the back seat with a sackful of stuffed turkey hens for a pillow, she set out for Paris. On January 6 she arrived there to find Sandeau anxiously waiting for her. Giddy with the exhilaration of her new love she burst out: "To live! How delicious, how wonderful, even in spite of irritations, husbands, boredom, debts, relatives, scandals, heartbreaks, and petty quarrels: To love, to be loved! It is such happiness. It's divine" (p. 921).

She did, in fact, return to Nohant periodically to see her children and to wheedle more money out of Casimir. Paris, she found, was a very expensive city to live in.

At about this time Mme Dudevant again took to wearing men's clothes frequently. They required so much less effort than the elaborate feminine fashion of the era, and dressed as a man she could come and go along the boulevards, in the theaters, and elsewhere with an independence not ordinarily accorded to a woman. Furthermore, men's clothes were much more economical and no matter how modestly she tried to live, her expenses always seemed to exceed her income.

The longer she remained in Paris the more she realized that without financial independence she was not really free to do what she wanted. Since Casimir was not inclined to be particularly generous with his wayward wife, Aurore finally decided to try her hand at writing, purely as a matter of necessity. Her initial efforts met with a cool reception. One editor even told her quite bluntly, "Don't bother producing books. You're better off producing children."[7] Eventually, she and Jules together were able to publish several articles in the *Revue de Paris* and later in *Figaro.*

In the fall another of their joint efforts was published, this time a novel, *Rose et Blanche,* which had a moderate success. By the spring of 1832 Aurore finished still another novel on her own which so impressed Sandeau that he insisted she publish it under her name alone. This created a problem, for neither her mother nor the dowager baroness Dudevant would countenance the use of their family names. Since Aurore and Jules had previously written under the *nom de plume* of "J. Sand," Mme Dudevant was persuaded to retain the name of Sand. Why she chose the first name of George is less certain. Accounts vary. Some say that she made the choice capriciously as the day of her decision happened to be St. George's Day (April 23). Another version claims that she liked the rural connotations of the word "George" (whose Greek and Latin roots—*georgikos* and *georgicus*—refer to things agricultural) and associated the name with the happy pastoral life of the Berry countryside she adored.* Whatever the real reason for her choice, she now christened her new literary alter ego "George Sand." The title of the novel was *Indiana* and soon both the book and its author were known all over Paris. Poor Sandeau, Heinrich Heine commented years later, he "could never make himself as distinguished with all his name as she did with the half of it. . . ."[8]

In George Sand, Aurore Dudevant had created more than a pseudonym; she had fashioned a literary personality, and in order to make it live she infused her own vibrant spirit into its image. It was almost as if Mme Dudevant herself had died in this act of creation. In her own words, she announced that summer: "In Paris Mme Dudevant is dead. But Georges [*sic*] Sand is reputed to be a hale and hearty gay blade."[9] From this

---

* Initially Mme Sand spelled her new name in the French manner, "Georges," later anglicizing the spelling to "George." This change may have been the result of influences carried over from the English convent school she attended as an adolescent in Paris.

time on the new author tended to refer to herself in the masculine gender and some of her contemporaries even felt that she had gone so far as to take on the appearance and manners of a man. "I don't care for Mme Sand," one commented. "She is a pretty boy but not much of a woman."[10] Others even went so far as to deny that she was, in fact, either male or female but said she was simply a "being." As for George herself it was a matter of little concern. "Take me for a man or a woman," she said indifferently, "whichever you prefer."[11]

While Aurore Dudevant had been passionately in love with Jules Sandeau, George Sand now regarded him merely as an immature child in whom she no longer had any romantic interest. Sandeau took it very badly. "He is shattered . . ." George noted, "and will be miserable for a long time to come but after all he is terribly young" (p. 272). Then, with an almost defiant tone, she added, "He will never have the right to keep me from being a mother to him" (p. 273). Poor Jules! He had responded to George's lure as a lover only to find himself enmeshed in a maternalistic web he had not anticipated. As time passed this was to prove a recurrent theme with Mme Sand who could never bring herself to distinguish very clearly between sons and lovers.

After her break with Jules, George turned more intensely to her writing. Later in the same year of 1833 she published her highly autobiographical novel, *Lélia*. Only when she had finished it did she fully realize the true identity of the character she had described. "I failed to understand one thing clearly enough," she admitted with some surprise, "that is, that I am without any doubt completely Lélia" (p. 374)—the restless, searching Lélia who was never to find true satisfaction or total fulfilment with any of the men she loved.

During 1833 Marie Dorval, an outstanding actress with a charming personality, began to exert a strange magnetism over George Sand. The two women had known each other for several years, but it was only at the time of Mme Sand's rupture with Sandeau that her interest in Marie Dorval became an obsession. She idolized the actress, considered her "the love-liest of women," and confessed outright that she dreamed of her constantly. "To love you so deeply and have to spend so many days away from you, Marie, makes me very sad" (p. 258), George wrote her in February of that year. "I don't feel I have lived those days when I don't see you, my dear" (p. 248). Marie seemed to have literally mesmerized her, and by March George was all but desolate apart from her. "I can't see you today," she wrote her at that time. "No such luck. But Monday in the morning or evening—either at the theater or in your boudoir—I must come kiss you or I'll go mad" (p. 286).

Unfortunately after one such passionate billet-doux Dorval's lover, the count de Vigny, concluded that George was a les-bian and forbade his mistress to see her anymore. From then on the relationship between the two women cooled somewhat but nothing ever destroyed George's adoration for the actress up to the very day of Marie's death sixteen years later.

During the same year, 1833, George embarked on a brief affair with the author, Prosper Mérimée. But after eight days of "the most unbelievable foolishness of my life," she reported that "the experiment failed completely" (p. 375).

Later, when friends tried to introduce her to Alfred de Musset she balked. "He is such a dandy," she protested. "We wouldn't get along together" (p. 277). Nevertheless her pub-lisher, Buloz, mischievously seated her next to Musset at a din-ner party shortly afterwards and the result was an agreeable surprise. Mme Sand found the dandy a very intelligent and sensitive person underneath his sophisticated façade of airy charm.

Over the following months she and Musset saw each other often. From their earliest conversations they talked of a trip to Italy, and in December they departed. Misfortune accom-panied them from the outset. The coach in which they left Paris immediately had a collision, Alfred became seasick on the voyage from Marseille to Genoa, and on their arrival in Italy George came down with a fever. Finally they reached

Venice, where they installed themselves in what is now the Hotel Danieli. Within a short time Musset also contracted a fever and began to have wild hallucinations. Desperate, George called in a young Italian doctor, Pietro Pagello, who eventually cured Musset's illness and conquered George's affections.

By the end of March Musset had recovered sufficiently to return to Paris. He was aware of the relationship which had developed between George and Pagello, and ultimately brought himself to accept it stoically, even graciously. "Poor George! Poor dear child," he wrote her in one of his more lucid moments. "You deceived yourself. You thought you were my mistress, but you were none other than my mother. . . . It was incest we committed."[12] He was right, George concluded. "I loved you like my son. It was a mother's love," she replied, "(and I am still bleeding from it)."[13]

She did not exsanguinate, however; instead she settled down with Pagello in a small apartment where she lived a quiet bourgeois life for the next few months. From a literary point of view it was a most productive period during which she wrote the first of her *Lettres d'un Voyageur,* completed her novel *Jacques,* and jotted down many of the notes for her later Italian stories. At first she was happy; life with Pagello seemed so idyllic after Musset's stormy departure when she needed a period of emotional convalescence. Little by little, however, she found it increasingly stultifying. She craved a more challenging environment and more intellectual companionship. But most of all she missed her children. As soon as she was able to muster sufficient funds from her publisher and her husband she returned to France.

In order to see the children she had to return to Nohant— and Casimir. Both her property and her income still remained under her husband's control, and Casimir had not changed. As usual, the only thing which did not seem to be entirely under his control was himself. His temper was extremely volatile and could erupt suddenly and irrationally. One October evening in 1835, just after leaving the dinner table, the baron unleashed a display of violence which convinced George of the necessity of obtaining a definite separation. The episode began with Maurice playing around his father's chair in the salon. When George saw that this was irritating Casimir she told Maurice to leave the room. After he had gone there was a sharp exchange of words. George accused Casimir of being drunk at which he ordered her to leave the room also. "I won't go," his wife replied, "You forget that this is my house as much as yours."[14] In a rage, the baron at first tried to strike her and then, running to a nearby room, he snatched up his hunting gun and threatened to shoot her. Fortunately there were guests present who restrained him, but Mme Dudevant's resolve to leave her husband once and for all was now unshakeable.

Early in the spring of that year, George had consulted a lawyer in Bourges about the arrangements for a separation. The lawyer's name was Louis-Chrysostom Michel. "The first thing that struck me on seeing Michel initially," George recalled, ". . . was the extraordinary configuration of his head. He seemed to have two heads stuck together." With "his fine pale countenance, his magnificent teeth, and his myopic eyes which . . . peered across his funny-looking spectacles, he presented a unique appearance of being actually young and old at the same time."[15] In reality he was thirty-seven. An ardent admirer of George Sand's *Lélia,* he quickly extended his admiration from the book to its author, who reciprocated his sentiments, and within a matter of days the two were lovers.

Although Michel may have appeared somewhat ludicrous as a lover he proved more than able as an advocate and was a great help to George in securing her separation. After months of agonizing and humiliating courtroom battles, an out-of-court settlement was finally reached. The baron acquired jurisdiction over Maurice as well as the proceeds from George's property in Paris, the Hôtel de Narbonne. Mme Dudevant, in exchange, retrieved her beloved Nohant and the custody of her daughter. The misery of marriage and the distastefulness of dissolving it had now convinced the disillusioned baroness that she would never again complicate a misalliance with matrimony. "For my part I would rather spend the rest of my life in a dungeon than marry again."[16] This emphatic declaration did not mean, however, that she now intended to seek serenity in celibacy, but merely that from then on her mistakes would never again be marital ones.

Some time later, following the death of Casimir's stepmother, a revision of the original settlement granted Mme Dudevant the custody of her darling Maurice. With this it would seem that her life should have been completely happy. But Mme Sand found her struggles were by no means over. She had both of her children again but Casimir still had half of her income. To meet her expenses she had to work harder than ever. Religiously she turned out her daily quota of pages even though she realized that the demands on her purse often exceeded the supply of her inspiration.

Off and on she found a brief respite from her efforts in the form of a handsome young Swiss poet, Charles Didier. And in August of 1836 she forsook her work altogether to join Franz Liszt and the countess d'Agoult for a brief vacation in Switzerland. On returning to Paris that fall she took up residence in the Hôtel de France directly below the rooms occupied by her companions from the summer. It was a fortunate arrangement, for in the small salon which Marie d'Agoult had improvised, George found herself in the midst of a stimulating milieu of artists, writers, and musicians, among whom she first met Frédéric Chopin.

ఇక CHAPTER THREE ఇక

IF CHOPIN GAVE little thought to Mme Sand after their introduction in the fall of 1836, it was because his attentions were concentrated on a young Polish aristocrat named Maria Wodzińska. Nine years his junior, Maria was the daughter of count Wincenty Wodziński, a former Polish senator and owner of a 50,000-acre estate in Służewo, not far from Warsaw. Chopin had first met Maria when she was only ten. Her three older brothers, Antoni, Casimir, and Felix, lived and boarded with Chopin's parents during their student days at the Lyceum in Warsaw. From the beginning music provided the common ground on which Frédéric and Maria built their early friendship—a friendship which would, one day, evolve into romance.

In September 1835 Chopin visited the Wodzińskis, who were then living in Dresden. There he suddenly became aware that Maria, who was now a very mature sixteen, no longer appeared the child he remembered from Warsaw. Her handsome features glowed with a rich Mediterranean warmth, inherited from Italian ancestors who had migrated to Poland in the sixteenth century with Buona Sforza. Her sparkling dark eyes, her straight black hair, her olive complexion, and resonant contralto voice were lovely vestiges of this background. What nature had endowed her with, Maria had cultivated. An accomplished pianist, she appeared several times in charity concerts in Geneva and, as a painter, she was unusually gifted in portraiture and watercolor sketches. At least twice Chopin served as her model during the fall of 1835 and the following summer. Her interest in poetry was to win her the admiration of the Polish poet Słowacki, who wrote the poem "In Switzerland" for her. Besides her artistic achievements Maria also possessed all those delicate, little social graces essential to a young lady whose family moved in the aristocratic circles of European society with such figures as Queen Hortense of Holland and Prince Louis-Napoléon, the future emperor of France.

This, at least, was the radiant Maria that Frédéric saw, the Maria that enchanted and captivated him, even if it may not actually have been the Maria of reality. Others who were not looking on the young girl with the eyes of a lover have described her features as irregular, plain, and rather full-lipped, her personality as coquettish, and her artistic accomplishments as dillettantish. Perhaps love transformed her, for Mlle Wodzińska had certainly won Chopin's heart.

Intoxicated with his lovely Maria, Frédéric remained in Dresden until the end of the month. On the eve of his departure he played a farewell waltz* for her and inscribed the manuscript: "Pour Mademoiselle Marie."[1] Attached to it were a few bars of the E-flat Nocturne (Op. 9, no. 2) and a note with the words, "Soyez heureuse" (May you be happy). Spontaneously, Maria took a rose from a nearby bouquet and gave it to him. Both were profoundly moved. Maria wrote:

> Saturday, after you left us, all of us were sad. Our eyes were filled with tears as we wandered around the drawing room where you had been only a few moments before. Father came back in a short while and was upset at not getting to say good-by to you. Mother was in tears and talked constantly about her "fourth son," Frédéric (as she calls you). Felix looked very glum; Casimir wanted to joke as usual, but that day none of his remarks seemed funny because he was half choked up. . . . You were the subject of all our conversations. Felix asked me to play your waltz, (the last thing we received and heard from you). It gave us great pleasure—to them in hearing it, to me in playing it. . . . Nobody ate dinner. Everyone kept looking over at your usual place at the table. . . . Adieu (quite simply). A childhood friend doesn't need to stand on ceremony. . . . Adieu.[2]

* The Waltz in A-flat, Opus 69, no. 1. Though written in 1835, this waltz was not published until 1855, six years after Chopin's death, hence the opus number 69.

Back in Dresden the following summer, Chopin became even more enamored than before. He was too timid to confess it, however, until the night before he left, when he finally mustered up the courage to express his love. At twilight on September 9 he proposed to Maria. She accepted, but Mme Wodzińska insisted that their engagement be kept a secret until count Wodziński had given his consent. Chopin agreed.

Months were to pass while he waited in vain for word of the count's approval. He had not expected an immediate reply, since Mme Wodzińska had indicated that she would need some time to broach the matter to her husband. In her very first letter after Chopin's departure, however, there was a suggestion of misgiving concerning the whole affair. "How I regret that you had to leave on Saturday when I was too sick to think about 'the twilight hour' " (i.e., the still secret engagement) she had written him. "We didn't talk about it as much as we should have. We could have discussed it at more length the next day. . . . Don't think that I am going back on anything I said. Not at all. It is just that we should have decided on what course to follow" (p. 197). Then she included in her letter some disturbing remarks. Referring to Maria she commented cryptically: "Who knows how she will be a year from now?" (p. 198). "Nevertheless," she continued, "you can be sure I am on your side." And she closed by saying, "I bless you with all my heart like a loving mother" (p. 199). Maria's own warm post-script had been heartening: "We are inconsolable over your departure; the three days since you left have seemed like centuries. Do you feel the same way? Do you miss your friends a little? Yes, I can answer for you and I don't think I'm wrong; at least I need to think I'm not. I tell myself that this 'yes' comes from you (because that is what you would say, isn't it?). . . . Adieu, *mio carissimo maestro*. Don't forget Dresden now and Poland a little later on. Adieu, au revoir. Ah, if it could only be sooner!" (p. 201).

Then, little by little, Maria's notes became less frequent, their tone less intimate, and their effect less encouraging. When letters did arrive they did not contain the news Frédéric was anxiously awaiting. Instead, they were full of trivial gossip and innumerable requests. "If you have a chance," Mme Wodzińska would write, "Maria begs you to send her some new novels. The stores will certainly be flooded with them by the new year" (p. 203). A typical postscript of Maria's would add: "Thanks so much for the autographs. Please send us some more. (Mother told me to ask you)" (p. 205). And, as always, there were incessant admonitions for Frédéric to take care of his health: "Why haven't you said a word about wearing the woolen stockings with your slippers or going to bed before eleven . . . let me repeat: take care of yourself and all will go well" (p. 204). These admonitions of the countess were of far greater significance than they perhaps appeared, since Chopin's health constituted one of the major obstacles to obtaining count Wodziński's sanction for the marriage. Undoubtedly financial and social considerations also troubled the count. Although he never mentioned it openly, he must have wondered whether the musician could possibly guarantee a young bride the security and status to which Maria was accustomed.

The longer the count delayed his reply, the more apparent it became that he was not really in favor of the marriage. As the waiting period stretched out from month to month Maria herself showed less enthusiasm, and the countess grew more and more apathetic in her correspondence. "It has been a long time, quite a long time since we received your letter" (p. 210), Mme Wodzińska apologized in January 1837, and Maria added lackadaisically, "You can see that I am lazy about writing since postponing my thanks until our next meeting absolves me from writing more now" (p. 212). When, though, were they to meet again? No direct mention of the engagement was made in most of their correspondence and no definite plans for the future were ever discussed.

A vague indifference began to pervade their letters. Maria, who confined her communications almost exclusively to footnotes, now scarcely found time to add even these. "I can only write a few words . . ." (p. 219) she would scratch hastily at the bottom of one of her mother's letters.

In February an epidemic of influenza swept Paris, and Chopin fell ill with a fever accompanied by a severe cough and a siege of blood-spitting. His doctors were not entirely sure whether his symptoms were due merely to influenza, or perhaps to something more serious, such as consumption. The silence of Służewo did little to speed his recovery, and he was at last advised to leave Paris for the sake of his health. His old friend, Titus Woyciechowski, invited him to go to Germany. And, out of the south came overtures from Nohant, where Mme Sand hoped she might entice her new acquaintance. In a letter to Franz Liszt that March she wrote, "Marie [d'Agoult] tells me I might hope for Chopin: tell him that I not only ask but beg him to come with you, that Marie can't live without him, and that I adore him."[3] Later, through Mme d'Agoult, she sent an even more emphatic message: "Tell Chopin," she wrote, "that I idolize him" (p. 765).

Frédéric considered her invitation and discussed the matter with Liszt. "The old boy wants to go there," the latter wrote Marie d'Agoult in February. "He is always talking about it."[4] As late as the end of May, Chopin was still thinking of accepting George's invitation and even wrote Maria's brother, Antoni: "I may be spending several days at George Sand's."[5] But whether due to physical inertia, indecision, or a hesitancy to place himself under obligation to Mme Sand, Chopin remained in Paris. His thoughts, however, were constantly in Służewo. In April, after having heard nothing from Maria or her family for some time, he wrote Mme Wodzińska: "Surely my letter of a month ago must have reached Służewo. . . . At times I really don't know what to say. How I wish I were with you today at Służewo. I could say more then of what I feel than I can write" (p. 216). But there was no opportunity to say anything, for the Wodzinskis did not come to Paris that summer as they had intimated—nor did they invite Chopin to visit them in Poland. Furthermore they continued to evade all reference to the engagement.

In June, Chopin inquired wistfully, "Is the summer beautiful in Służewo? Can you sit in the shade under the trees and paint? . . . It is already getting uncomfortable for me here in Paris. My doctor has ordered me to go to Ems [a health spa], but I don't know yet where I'll go or when" (p. 223). No reply came.

Gradually Chopin's disappointment turned to despair. Weak and dejected, he allowed Camille Pleyel, the piano manufacturer, to talk him into a trip to England. Another friend, Julian Fontana, wrote ahead to make arrangements for him in London. The following is Fontana's letter to Stanislas Koźmian at 28 Sherrard St., Golden Square, London:

Paris, July, 1837

Dear Stanislas,
   I am writing you on behalf of Chopin who is about to leave . . . I know you will render him every friendly service if you can help him in any way. . . . He is coming for a short stay—a week or ten days—to get a breath of English air. He does not wish to meet anyone, so I beg you to keep his visit a secret, otherwise he will have all the artists after him. . . . If you know of a good hotel in your neighborhood give Chopin the address.[6]

On July 11, 1837, Chopin and Pleyel arrived in London, where they installed themselves on a lavish scale in Leicester Square. As Fontana had predicted, Koźmian turned out to be an excellent guide and a most helpful friend. "Without him, I would be lost in London."[7] Frédéric wrote.

Apart from Koźmian, however, little about England or the English pleased Chopin. The climate certainly did not agree with him, and he complained about the soot-filled air, the dreary dampness, and the muddy streets. "The only way to have a good time here is not to stay too long," he grumbled. Still ailing and depressed, Chopin was scarcely in a mood to appreciate London or its inhabitants. "Oh the English," he gasped, "their homes, their palaces, their carriages, their wealth, their ostentation, their styles, their trees—everything from soap to razors," he fumed, "everything here is so remarkable and yet so monotonous; it is all so proper, so over-scrubbed, and yet still as black as his lordship's rear end! (p. 225).

Trying to remain incognito, Chopin did not perform in public at all except for one night when he attended a dinner given by Mr. James Broadwood,* in his home at 46 Bryanston Square. There he was introduced simply as "Mr. Fritz" and attracted no special attention until after the meal when he succumbed to the temptation to try Mr. Broadwood's piano. At that point, his inimitable style gave him away and several of the guests immediately recognized him.

As for the remainder of his London excursion, Mme Moscheles reported that "he did not go out and wished no one to visit him for the effort of talking told on his consumptive frame. He heard a few concerts and disappeared."[8] Even his good friend Mendelssohn, who was in London that summer, did not know of Chopin's visit until he had already gone. "They say," he heard later, "that Chopin came here unexpectedly two weeks ago, but didn't see anyone. One evening he played magnificently at Broadwood's then hurried off again. It seems he is quite unwell and very miserable."[9]

If anything, he was even more miserable when he left London than when he arrived. Just before his departure he received a crushing letter from the countess Wodzińska, making it all too painfully clear that Maria would never be his. Her family had decided to remain in Poland all summer and Chopin, therefore, could no longer expect the opportunity of seeing her any time within the near future—if, indeed, ever.

Resigned, he replied to Mme Wodzińska on his return to Paris: "Your last letter followed me to London, where I dawdled away last month. I thought of going to Germany via Holland, but I came back home as it was getting late in the season and I will probably stay here in my room for the rest of it. I hope your next letter, Madame, will be less gloomy than your last one" (p. 227).

---

*The noted English piano manufacturer; he was the London counterpart of Camille Pleyel.

His only reference to "Mlle Maria" was a reminder to write her brother, Antoni, who was fighting with a regiment of Polish lancers in Spain. Certainly the remainder was a propos; no one could have been more acutely aware of Maria's indifferent writing habits. Apart from that, there was little more to add now that the promises of "the twilight hour" would never be fulfilled. It would hardly be correct to say their "engagement" had been broken; its existence had, in fact, never really been acknowledged. Chopin did not see Maria again.

In 1841 she married count Joseph Skarbeck, the son of Chopin's godmother and a distant cousin of his mother. Frédéric learned of the marriage through his sister, Louise, who wrote, "May God grant them happiness and forget the rest."[10] The marriage proved to be an unhappy one and eventually ended in a papal annulment, some years later. Subsequently Maria remarried and became Mme Władysław Orpiszewski, which she remained for the rest of her life.

The last words she had written Chopin in 1837 were "Adieu. Remember us"[11]—and he always did. After his death a small bundle wrapped in pink ribbon was found in his apartment. It contained all Maria's letters along with the rose she had given him in Dresden. Across one of the envelopes was scrawled "Moja Bieda"—my sorrow.

e⅜⅜ CHAPTER FOUR ⅜⅜

MME SAND WAS disappointed that she could not lure Chopin to her chateau in the spring of 1837, but she lacked neither company nor activity while she was there. Her recent visit to Paris had provided her with many new friends and interests. There she had come in frequent contact with two men whose attraction for her was of a philosophical rather than a physical nature: the abbé Hugues Félicité Robert de Lamennais and Pierre Leroux. In her opinion they were "the two greatest intellects of our century."[1] Through Liszt she had met Lamennais in 1835, and Sainte-Beuve had introduced her to Leroux the same year.

The abbé Lamennais had begun his career as an ardent champion of catholicism, but he felt that the Church was losing contact with the masses. Caught up in the currents of romanticism, he had an idealistic conception of the "common man." He was a liberal who advocated universal suffrage, the abolition of censorship, and freedom of education for all. Believing in the supremacy of the Church, he tried to incorporate his social doctrines into the framework of catholicism with the aim of fusing a theocracy and a democracy into one state. "God and Liberty; the Pope and the People"[2] was his motto. Conservative elements in the Church, however, considered his views unorthodox and succeeded in thwarting his goals. Unable to inject democracy into the Church, Lamennais decided to inject religion into democracy. He broke with Rome and proclaimed that from henceforth he regarded the people as "the new Messiah." Yet he did not become a revolutionary or an atheist; he recognized the necessity of order and authority in government and social action, and, though working outside the Church, he still regarded religion as the source of that authority, so much so that his enemies derided his philosophy as an attempt to flaunt the cross with the red cap of Liberty.

In Lamennais, Mme Sand found an articulate expression of her own social idealism, which up to then had been only a vague and amorphous instinct in her life. She flung herself at the abbé's feet, "ready to give herself up completely," the countess d'Agoult observed, "ready to be swallowed up by his opinions, to become an instrument of his thought."[3] Her enthusiasm, indeed, proved to be as irrepressible as it was unsolicited, and the master soon found his new disciple a source of great embarrassment. The voraciousness with which she assimilated his theories was equalled only by the versatility with which she adapted them to her own unique interpretations. Within a short while her association with the abbé began to generate a great many rumors, none of which ruffled her in the least. She made no effort to suppress the gossip and even relished the idea of provoking a scandal over it. "I am seeing the abbé de Lamennais quite often," she told a friend that winter, "and am crazy about him. This has caused a lot of talk which would seem rather odd to you if you could see how old he is and what he looks like! People are even saying that I am going to settle in Paris to keep house for him. What a wonderful idea! We would run a magnificent household together!"[4]

The abbé himself, however, was not so enthusiastic at being the object of Mme Sand's obsession, and when she started to utilize his journal, *Le Monde,* as a mouthpiece for her conception of woman's mission in modern society, he grew quite alarmed. In her *Lettres à Marcie,* he permitted her to advocate equality of the sexes in love, but when she proposed to publish her views on divorce and "the role of passion in a woman's life," he recoiled in horror. Abruptly dispensing with her assistance, he left his avid apostle stunned and perplexed. "After he had urged me on," George complained, "he found that I was progressing too fast for him."[5] "There is still more of the priest in him than I had supposed."[6] Having decided that he had become too much of a poet and prophet to be practical, she nevertheless retained a great respect for this powerful personality throughout her life.

What Mme Sand had absorbed from Lamennais was a philosophical orientation that prepared her for the man she was to call a "new Plato, a new Christ," Pierre Leroux. In Leroux she imagined that she had found her moral and intellectual salvation. His "philosophical demonstrations . . . have completely resolved my doubts and provided the basis of my religious faith."[7] Much of her later thinking and writing was, indeed, colored by his influence. But while George floated through her new empyrean of metaphysical thought, she was careful to keep her feet solidly on financial terra firma by finishing her latest novel, *Mauprat*.

At the end of January, 1837, Mme d'Agoult arrived at Nohant for a visit. She was expecting—without apparent enthusiasm—her second child by Liszt, and in this rather disgruntled mood she wryly observed the frenzied activities of her hostess. George, at this time, was writhing in the final throes of her convulsive affair with Michel. Despite this distraction she continued to write at a frantic pace. "Poor great woman!" Marie commented, "The sacred flame which God has kindled in her can find nothing outside to devour, and so consumes all that remains within her of faith, youth, and hope. Charity, love, and sensuality, those three aspirations of the soul, the heart, and the senses, have overpowered this fatally gifted nature and led her into doubt, deception, and satiation. Bottled up within her, they make her life a martyrdom. . . . Oh my God, grant to George the serenity of a Goethe."[8]

It was truly a period of torture for George. Michel was losing patience with her. His wife, his children, and his business affairs made it too difficult for him to manage a mistress who lived miles away. But the more he tried to retreat from George, the more she pursued him. She saw the inevitability of a separation but could not accept it. "I was well aware when I gave myself to you, that the course of worldly affairs would always pull us apart," she wrote him that January. "I realized that the ambitious spend only an hour a day on love and that love is only a day in their lives."[9] "You'll never understand why, how, or to what extent I love you. I really don't know why I waste all this ink trying to explain. . . . I would have followed you through heaven and hell as Dante followed Virgil." Slowly, however, she became resigned to Michel's indifference. "I don't know what fatal attraction came over me," she went on to write him. "I thought I knew and I think I understand now. May God's will be done . . . the trees don't complain of the wind which batters them nor the earth of the mountains which crush it" (p. 660).

Then, as summer approached, George, tired from her tribulations, suddenly experienced an unexpected release from her anguish. Explosively at dawn on June 11, 1837, she jotted in her journal: "How gay the blue and white of this paper seems! How filled with birds the garden sounds! How fragrant is this sprig of honeysuckle in my glass: Piffoël, Piffoël,* what a terrifying calm there is within your heart! Has the flame really been extinguished?"[10] Happily it had.

In May the countess d'Agoult returned again to Nohant, this time with Liszt. The weeks that followed were full of sunlight and happiness for Mme Sand. Chopin, it is true, was not there to augment her rapture, but perhaps this was just as well, for the countess d'Agoult, like her hostess, had taken more than casual notice of the attractive young Pole. "Chopin is an irresistible man," she let George know that spring. But then with one of her typically caustic remarks she added, "there is nothing of any permanence about him but his cough."[11] And yet she had not failed to observe that when he did cough it was always with "an infinite grace" (p. 216).

Had Chopin accepted Mme Sand's invitation to Nohant that summer, he would have found himself in an atmosphere pervaded with music. George had bought an expensive Pleyel

---

*Since the previous summer in Switzerland with Franz Liszt and Marie d'Agoult, George had been dubbed "Dr. Piffoël" while her two companions were nicknamed collectively the "Fellows." Individually, Franz was also referred to as "Crétin" and Marie as "Mirabella" or the "Princess."

piano in anticipation of Liszt's visit and placed it in the
countess d'Agoult's room on the first floor. The enjoyment she
derived from it was well worth the investment. "Beneath my
window," she wrote that June, "under the screen of linden
leaves which covers it, is that window out of which float sounds
the whole world would love to hear." [12]

Those balmy summer days in Berry were full of activity and
passed quickly for George. Sometimes she and Marie would
leave the house before dawn to wander beside the river,
through gray clouds of mist that rolled eerily off the surface
of the Indre. Later in the day they would ride or hike across
the neighboring countryside, indulging in lively conversations
which darted erratically from the frivolous to the philosophical.

In the tepid evenings a languid aura would settle over Nohant and engulf the inhabitants in its mood. While Liszt seated
himself at the piano in the shadows of the countess's room the
others would gather outside on the lawn and listen spellbound
for hours to his improvisations. No sooner had he touched the
keys than "the breeze dropped, dying of exhaustion in the
long grasses. . . ." The air was perfumed with the delicate
scent of lilacs and "a deep calm settled over the garden" (p.
61). Even the nightingales succumbed, George claimed, and
their voices faded away into the twilit foliage. Silently the
countess would glide about the terrace, her filmy white gar-
ments floating in the moonlight as it filtered through the linden trees. At times she would pause and "rest on a swaying
branch which scarcely bent beneath her weight any more than
if she had been a ghost" (p. 62). Behind her the tall motionless
spruces looked like dark specters against the night-blue of the
sky. On the steps of the doorway to her terrace, George sat in
rapt attention while the exquisite melodies wove a spell of
delight and sadness about her. Their strange and mournful
harmonies enveloped the hushed garden in a delicious mystery. "All my sorrows are turned to poetry, all my instincts
become exalted" (p. 46), she whispered to herself in those
magic moments.

In the midst of all this beauty, however, something deep within her was disturbing Mme Sand's happiness. While Liszt's music elated her, she found that it could sometimes touch a "note of anger" in her as well. "Hatred is devouring me," she confessed in her journal, but "hatred of what? Oh God, will I never find anybody worth the effort of being hated?" (p. 46). Seeing Liszt and Mme d'Agoult together made her envy their affection. "Ah, if only I were loved!" (p. 45) she exclaimed sadly. "No one but God deserves to be loved," Liszt told her pontifically. "That may be," George conceded, "but when one has loved a man it is indeed difficult to love God" (p. 8). Michel had left a certain void in her life that summer which had not yet been filled and which accounted for much of her restlessness and discontent.

This unhappy situation was soon ameliorated by the arrival in June and July of a series of handsome and talented young men including the actor Bocage, the poet Didier, and the playwright Félicien Mallefille. The mistress of the house brightened up considerably with their appearance. But Liszt, looking beneath the surface, sensed that George would really have preferred the "zentil Zopin," as he facetiously alluded to their absent friend, the "pretty Chopin." Didier, it is true, soon came to annoy his hostess; Bocage on the other hand rather appealed to her,* but it was to be Mallefille who would finally rekindle her passions.

From the sidelines Mme d'Agoult observed this procession of young admirers as they passed through Nohant, and it may well have been jealousy which prompted her to quip maliciously to Didier that George had finally become "incapable of both love and friendship."[13] Certainly nothing could have been farther from the truth; George still had an astonishingly boundless capacity for the one as well as the other.

In August an abrupt shock jolted the quiet atmosphere of Nohant: Sophie-Victoire Dupin fell ill and died within a short while in Paris. "I have lost my dear little mother!" George

---

* Sand and Bocage became lovers briefly, a fact which later greatly upset Chopin.

wrote a close friend on the twenty-fourth of that month. "Her death was as sweet and as calm as possible, without any agony or even any awareness of the end. She simply went off to sleep, thinking she would wake up a little later."[14]

Despite their stormy relationship, George was deeply affected by her mother's death. "Poor little woman! Clever, intelligent, artistic, petulant, generous, slightly unstable, and selfish over little matters but good when it came to the important ones. She caused me much suffering," George had to admit, "and my greatest problems were due to her. But she made up for this in recent times and I had the satisfaction of seeing that she finally understood my character and behaved with complete fairness to me in the end" (p. 175).

The family buried Mme Dupin in Montmartre. At the graveside George could not contain her grief. "My poor mother . . . is no more!" she cried. "She rests in the sun beneath the lovely flowers around which the butterflies flutter without the least thought of death. I was so struck by the gaiety surrounding her grave in the Montmartre cemetery on such a beautiful day that I wondered why our tears should flow so freely . . ." (p. 190).

As the sparkling sunlight fell across the grassy slopes of the little cemetery high above Paris, George stood sadly beside the grave and wept—not only for the mother whom she had come to bury, but for the one who had, in fact, not lived at all. "I never had a mother or a sister to dry my tears,"[15] she once wrote a friend many years before, and throughout the rest of her life Mme Sand tried to give to others that maternal affection which she herself so often craved and seldom found.

CHAPTER FIVE

THE SUMMER OF 1837 ended unhappily for both George Sand and Frédéric Chopin. August found one grieving over the death of a parent while the other mourned the loss of a love. Maria Wodzińska no longer existed for Chopin except as a memory. His dreams of marriage had proved a mirage. The vision of happiness, centered around a home and family, began to fade, and in the emptiness that was left there remained a bitter loneliness.

In an effort to forget Maria, Chopin turned to his work. Most of his days were filled with teaching, a financial necessity as always for him. Some of his pupils were serious but many, from the upper echelons of society, were dilettantish and could have driven the most devoted teacher to exasperation. However, during the fall of 1837 Chopin experienced a peaceful oblivion in these routine pedagogic duties.

Only in the creation of music, though, did his spirit find its true consolation. As Liszt observed, "He unburdened his soul in composition as others do in prayer, pouring out those effusions of his heart, those unexpressed sorrows, those indescribable griefs that devout souls spill in their talks with God. He told in his works what they tell only on bended knee: those mysteries of passion and pain which man has been permitted to understand without words because he cannot express them in words."[1]

Chopin could accept the blows of fate with stoical resignation but the wounds cut deeply. Inside him they festered and eroded until they all but sapped both his emotional and physical strength. Maria had left a profound scar in his existence, one which would always be slightly painful. The Wodziński family was so enmeshed in his past, so intimately associated with his youth, his family, his Warsaw, and his native land that its rejection of him seemed to gnaw away at the roots which nourished his being. Despondent, he gave vent to the death he felt within himself through the somber cadences of the majestic Funeral March. Much of his past and a little of his spirit died that year, but in death they underwent a musical transfiguration, leaving a more beautiful monument to the memory of Maria Wodzińska than she perhaps deserved.

From July 1836, just before his abortive "engagement," Chopin published nothing until October 1837, when his second volume of Études, Opus 25, appeared. These were dedicated to the countess d'Agoult and, for the most part, had been written much earlier, although they only came to press for the first time that autumn. Many of the other compositions which emerged out of the disappointing year of 1837* possess a haunting melancholy which reflects the anxiety and sadness Chopin suffered then. There is a bittersweet sorrow in some of them, a quality which the Polish call *żal* to express "all the tenderness and all the humility of a resigned and unmurmuring regret. . . ."[2]

An offspring of the romantic era, the twenty-seven-year old Polish composer probably derived a certain amount of gratification in acting out the tragedy of unrequited love *à la* Werther. After all, his was an epoch that extolled sensitivity to an exquisite degree which may sometimes be a little beyond twentieth-century comprehension. However, even if Chopin did indulge himself in a mood of "sweet sorrow" during much of this period, his musical output was not entirely morbid and plaintive. Some of his compositons were, in fact, quite spritely (cf., the Mazurka in D, Op. 33, no. 1).

---

*That year saw the completion of the two Nocturnes in B Major and A-flat Major, Opus 32 and the beginning of a third in G Minor, Opus 37 no. 1. Chopin also composed several of the Mazurkas of Opus 30 and Opus 33 that year along with a song, "My Darling," which may have been written for Maria. The Scherzo in B-flat Minor, Opus 31 and the Impromptu in A-flat Major, Opus 29, which were also written in 1837, have a vigor and playfulness respectively that may indicate a degree of emotional rehabilitation.

As Maria's image was receding into the shadows of "the twilight hour," the outlines of another feminine silhouette came into focus on Chopin's horizon that fall of 1837. In October George Sand returned to Paris, and one of the acquaintances she made a specific point of renewing was that of Chopin. The latter did not remain unmoved by her flattering overtures. His impressions of the "pretty boy" were mellowing. In his journal that month he wrote: "I have seen her three more times. It seems like only a day. She gazed deep into my eyes while I played . . . such dark strange eyes she had. What were they saying? She leaned against the piano and her eyes seemed to caress mine. I was overcome. My soul seemed to find its haven in the smile of those remarkable eyes. Her face was masculine, its features heavy, almost coarse, but those sad, strange eyes! I longed for them . . . my heart was conquered. . . . She understood me . . . I have seen her twice since . . . one time alone. She loves me! Aurore! What a charming name! Like the dawn it banishes the darkness!"[3]

Chopin, however, was not the only one to find Mme Sand fascinating that fall. Back at Nohant, the bearded young Creole, Félicien Mallefille, who was looking after the Dudevant children, also had an eye for their mother. A writer of plays and novels, he was not only an employee but a colleague of Mme Sand, and very soon her lover as well. When Marie d'Agoult first introduced him to George, the latter had considered him "outrageously ugly, vain, and stupid." But her opinions, though emphatic, were not irrevocable, and when Mallefille appeared at Nohant during the summer of 1837 he received a cordial welcome—so cordial, in fact, that he was persuaded to stay long after the other guests had departed. His status was soon made permanent when he agreed to serve as tutor for Maurice and Solange. In this new capacity he also found himself called upon to act as traveling companion to their mother and accompanied her on pleasant excursions to the Franchard gorges and the Pyrénées.

Mme Sand's sortie to Paris in October interrupted this new liaison only briefly, and after she returned to Nohant she and Mallefille settled down to a peaceful provincial winter. Writing

Liszt and Marie d'Agoult in December of 1837, she described their prosaic existence: "My private life has nothing of much interest to merit your attention. It is quiet and industrious. Mallefille heaps dramas on top of novels, Pelion on Ossa, while I pile novels on top of short stories, Buloz on Bonnaire . . . Maurice, caricatures upon toy soldiers and Solange, chicken legs on top of wrong notes. So much for the strange, heroic life we lead at Nohant."[4]

It did indeed appear strange to Mme d'Agoult, who could not help recalling her friend's first impressions of Mallefille. "Do you remember our arguments over him?" she reminded George, ". . . how ugly he was, how stupid, silly, vain, and intolerable? He seemed to arouse your wrath like one of those furies that Homer described in Juno and Venus. I really had to say to you *mezza voce* that one either learned to live with other people's petty vanities or else had to live alone. In reality the most difficult thing of all is to live in peace with one's own vanity."[5] Then with a perceptive pungency she added, "How your enthusiasms do evaporate, how the stars in your heavens go plunging to the earth! Poor Mirabella,* some day her turn will come too, won't it?" (p. 824). Her remark was truly prophetic, for the countess d'Agoult soon fell from Mme Sand's favor, as did her young protegé, Mallefille. But if the latter's star was soon to decline, it at least shone brightly enough during the remaining winter months of 1837–38.

Another star also shed its light briefly at Nohant that winter. This particular one, however, was strictly a literary luminary and cast no romantic rays whatever. In February, Honoré de Balzac, who was visiting nearby in Frapesles, wrote Mme Sand, "I have learned, my dear illustrious one, that you are still ensconced in Berry. I have always wanted to make a pilgrimage to Nohant . . . and I would not like to return [to Paris] without having seen the Lioness of Berry in her den or the Nightingale in her nest. There is both a strength and a gracefulness about you which I admire more than in anybody else."[6]

---

*One of George Sand's nicknames for the countess d'Agoult.

Although George had not always had the warmest regards
for this prolific rival of hers, she granted the request, and on
February 24, Balzac arrived to view the "curious animal" that
inhabited Nohant. He was an enormous man whose ego easily
matched the proportions of his physique. Nevertheless he and
the petite mistress of Nohant found each other quite amusing
during their brief but animated encounter. Writing his intimate friend Mme Hanska, Balzac recorded his impressions
of his visit with a candor that was brutally blunt at times.

My dear little countess,
   I learned that George Sand was at her home in Nohant, not
far from Frapesles, and I went there to pay her a visit. . . .
Since you are a remarkably curious woman or, rather, a
curiously remarkable woman I am going to tell you about my
visit.
   I arrived at the chateau of Nohant the Saturday before Lent
around seven-thirty in the evening and found comrade George
in her dressing gown, smoking a cigar after dinner, all alone beside the fireplace in a huge room. She wore some pretty yellow
slippers that were fringed, some rather seductive stockings, and
a pair of red trousers. That should give you some idea of her
tastes.
   As to her physical appearance she has a double chin like a
clergyman. She doesn't have a single white hair despite her
frightful misfortunes; her swarthy complexion hasn't changed,
her lovely eyes still sparkle, but she has an almost stupid appearance when she is thinking. This is because—as I told her after
studying her carefully—all her expression is in her eyes.
   She has been at Nohant a year now, very unhappy and working like a horse. She leads a life similar to mine. She goes to bed
at six in the morning and gets up at noon. As for me, I go to
bed at six in the evening and get up at midnight. But naturally,
I conform to her habits here and we have chatted away for the
past three days from five in the evening after dinner up to five
in the morning, with the result that we know each other better
now from those three chats than during the previous four years
when she used to come to my place while she was in love with
Jules Sandeau and then tied up with Musset. . . .
   There she is, buried in her remote retreat, condemning both
marriage and love, since in both she has suffered nothing but
deceptions. Her type of man has not been easy to find. That's

the whole problem, and she will continue to have a hard time finding him since she is not a lovable woman. She is a boy, an artist; she is great, generous, devoted, and basically chaste. She has the characteristics of a man: *ergo* she is not a woman. Talking with her so intimately for three days I no more felt that tingling of the skin that one should feel with a woman . . . than if I had simply been chatting with an old chum. She has great virtues but those which society fails to understand properly. . . .

She is an excellent mother, adored by her children; but she dresses her daughter, Solange, like a little boy and that's not good. . . . She smokes far too heavily and carries on a little too much like a princess. . . . She knows and acknowledges those things which I have thought of her without having told her so: that is, she has neither the power to create nor the gift of constructing a plot nor the ability to arrive at the truth nor the art of pathos; but without knowing the French language she has *the style;* that much is true. . .

All in all, she is a man, so much the more so because she wants to be one; because she has given up the role of a woman and is no longer one. A woman attracts and she repels and since I am very much a man, if she makes that impression on me, she will certainly make the same impression on other men like me; she will always be unhappy. Right now she is in love with a man who is inferior to her [Mallefille] and in such a relationship there is nothing but disenchantment and deception for a woman of her fine nature. A woman should always love a man who is superior to her or else be so well deceived that she thinks he is.

I have not escaped with impunity here at Nohant. I have taken up a terrible vice: she has made me smoke a *houka* and some *Latakieh;* I have suddenly become addicted. . . ."[7]

While much of Balzac's visit was devoted to serious discussions with his fascinating hostess, the two also indulged in a bit of gossip. As Balzac commented to Mme Hanska, George was becoming disillusioned with the countess d'Agoult. Their friendship had been constructed on a very fragile base and was held together only by the most tenuous bonds. Now it was beginning to disintegrate. In one of her more underhanded maneuvers, Mme Sand suggested a plot for a novel to Balzac, one which she herself lacked the nerve to write. Two of the characters were clearly meant to represent Liszt and Mme d'Agoult, and the portrayal of the latter was decidedly unflattering. Balzac welcomed the suggestion and set to work on it shortly afterwards.

When the novel, entitled *Béatrix,* finally appeared a year later in 1839, George had some qualms about her duplicity and feared that Marie might suspect her role in its origin. Worried, she wrote Balzac, "I count on you to clear me of any blame if it ever occurs to her to accuse me of spreading malicious stories."[8] A letter soon arrived absolving George of any collusion, and with this written proof of her "innocence" Mme Sand could now sit back smugly and smile at the success of her little conspiracy. A friendship had been destroyed, however, and there was to be no further intimacy between George Sand and Marie d'Agoult.

ᏇᏇᏇ CHAPTER SIX ᏇᏇᏇ

I N T H E S P R I N G of 1838 Mme Sand had to go to Paris for a revision of the terms of her separation from Casimir. She had not seen Chopin since the preceding October, but she had hardly forgotten him. At the beginning of the year she wrote, tongue-in-cheek, to Mme d'Agoult: "Piffoël may go to Paris at the end of January, especially if Berlioz' Mass is going to be given a second time as the papers have announced. Piffoël will give *Sopin* [*sic*] an affectionate handshake for *Cretin's** sake and also for *Sopin's* own sake *because Sopin is very zentil.*"[1] Piffoël did not get to Paris then as she had planned, but her spring excursion to the capital in April brought her once more in contact with the young Polish musician who seemed so charmingly—and so challengingly—aloof.

Through the winter Chopin had continued to teach and compose, and on several occasions had even been induced to perform in public despite his well-known aversion to this. "I am not fitted to give concerts," he once complained to Liszt. "The public frightens me, I feel suffocated by its panting breath, paralyzed by its curious glance, mute before those unknown faces."[2] None of these fears, however, communicated themselves to his audiences and, as a critic at one of his performances that winter exclaimed: "His success was enormous! . . . The atmosphere was electric. Whispers of ecstasy and astonishment which are the bravos of the soul, filled the concert hall at all times. Onward Chopin, onward! Let this triumph convince you; no longer be selfish; share your exquisite talent with all. . . . When anyone asks who is the greatest pianist in

*Nickname for Franz Liszt.

Europe, Liszt or Thalberg, let all the world be able to reply, like those who have heard you play: it is Chopin!"[3]

Not only as a pianist, but as a composer as well his fame was spreading rapidly. Schumann, reviewing Chopin's compositions in Germany, was full of praise. The second set of études he described as "a testimony of bold, intrinsic creativity, truly poetic images, not without some small flaws here and there, but on the whole powerful and moving."[4] Two of Chopin's Nocturnes (Op. 27) he considered "the most heartfelt and glorious creations that can be imagined in music" (1:317). The Scherzo in B-flat Minor he regarded "as quite comparable to a poem by Lord Byron," and as for the Mazurkas of Opus 30, he claimed that "Chopin has elevated the mazurka to a small art form" (3:36).

In regard to his performance, Schumann was equally effusive: "Imagine an aeolian harp with the whole gamut of tones and think what it would sound like if stroked by the hand of an artist to produce all sorts of fantastic flourishes over a steady deep ground bass with a gracefully flowing melody audible above it, and you will have a vague idea of his playing" (2:103).

Heinrich Heine, too, was lavish in his praise: "We must grant Chopin genius in the fullest sense of the word. He is not merely a virtuoso, he is also a poet . . . he comes from the land of Mozart, Raphael, and of Goethe." Throughout Europe artistic circles were raving about Chopin at this time while Parisian society literally worshiped him. "Chopin is the favorite of that elite who seek in music the most exquisite enjoyment of the soul," Heine wrote. "His fame is of an aristocratic kind. He is perfumed with the praise of good society and is himself as aristocratic as his person."[5] Even Mme d'Agoult commented then that Chopin was "the only pianist I can listen to who does not bore but actually moves me deeply."[6] How moved Liszt would have been to hear his mistress' candid critique!

Quite apart from his artistic ability, Chopin was an extraordinary creature, dignified in appearance and discreet in behavior. "His whole being was harmonious. . . . The blue of his eye was more animated than dreamy. . . . The delicacy and transparency of his complexion caught the eye, his blond hair was silky, his nose slightly tilted, his bearing distinguished, and his manner had such an aristocratic stamp that he was instinctively treated like a prince. His gestures were many and graceful, the tone of his voice was always subdued and often dampened, he was small of stature and frail of limb. His entire appearance called to mind the morning-glory, swaying on stems incredibly fine and their cups so divinely colored, but of such a tenuous texture 'that the least touch would destroy them."[7]

Artistically divine and divinely delicate! Mme Sand found him truly captivating that spring. "Someone adores you," she scribbled coquettishly on a scrap of paper signed "George." "I, too! I, too! I, too!" Marie Dorval scrawled enthusiastically underneath.[8] Through April and May while George remained in Paris, she saw Chopin a number of times. As a rule their meetings took place in intimate surroundings, usually at Mme Marliani's or count Grzymała's, sometimes in the company of others, sometimes alone. Friendship soon progressed to flirtation. Kisses were exchanged. Sentiments were kindled, and it appeared that circumstances might plunge the two precipitously into passion had not Chopin abruptly halted this progression. A bit chagrined, George acceded for the moment, but later complained to Grzymała about Chopin's preference for a platonic rather than a physical relationship. "I want you to know," she wrote him toward the end of May, "that only one thing about him [Chopin] displeased me":

that is, that he had the wrong reasons for abstaining. Up until then I considered it fine that he refrained out of respect for me, out of timidity, or even out of faithfulness to another. All that would have been a sacrifice and consequently something that required purity and strength. . . . But at your house, just as he was leaving us, as if he wanted to conquer some temptation, he said two or three words which did not agree at all with my ideas. Like a prude he seemed to scorn whatever was not refined

about the human body and to blush because of temptations he
had had. It was as if he were afraid of soiling our love by being
carried away any farther. That way of looking at the final embrace has always been repulsive to me. If that last embrace is not
something as holy, as pure, and as dedicated as the rest, there is
no virtue in abstaining from it. . . . Is there ever a love without
a single kiss, and a kiss of love devoid of sensuality? To *scorn the
flesh* cannot be wise or useful except for those who are nothing
but *flesh;* but with the person you love there is no such word as
scorn, only the word *respect* which should be used when one ab-
stains. At any rate those weren't the specific words he used. I
can't remember exactly what he said but I think it was that *certain actions* could spoil the memory. Now wasn't that a stupid
thing for him to say? Did he really mean it? Who is the unfortunate woman who has left him with such impressions of physical
love? Did he have a mistress who was unworthy of him? Poor
angel. They should do away with all women who defile in men's
eyes the most respectable and holy thing in all creation, that
divine mystery, the most serious act in life, the most sublime
thing in the universe. . . . It is this manner of separating the
spirit from the flesh that makes convents and brothels necessary.[9]

In spite of her frustration, Mme Sand had by no means lost
her attraction to Chopin. As indicated by a note to Delacroix,
she continued to see him up to the last minute before her
departure for Nohant in the middle of May.

My dear Lacroix,
   I am leaving tomorrow at five in the morning and certainly
wouldn't want to go without saying goodbye. . . . As a temptation to make you drop in this evening I will tell you that Chopin
is going to play for just a few of us who will be gathered casually
around the piano. That is when he is truly sublime. Come at
midnight if you are not too sleepy and if you run into anyone I
know, don't say a word because Chopin has a terrible fear of
outsiders. *Adieu.* If you don't come, at least remember me affec-
tionately.

George (p. 407)

Back at Nohant George found herself in a state of confusion. The flood gates of emotion had opened, and she was

about to be inundated. She knew well the risks involved in attempting to run the rapids of romance again—but she had never yet drowned in Cupid's currents. Somehow, though, she could not make up her mind whether to let herself be carried away again or not.

One reason for her hesitation was Mallefille. How would he take it if she were to leave him? And if she did, would Chopin be willing to take his place? In the midst of her indecision she wrote her dear friend, countess Marliani:

> Darling,
>   I received your wonderful letters. However, I have been slow in replying because as you know the weather changes so during the season when one is in love. One says so often "yes," "no," "if," "but," all in a week's time. In the morning it seems that this is absolutely intolerable but then by evening one thinks nothing could be more delicious. Therefore I can't write you anything definite until my barometer registers something at least clear-cut if not stable. I really don't have anything to complain about, but that is not exactly the same as being happy. . . . (p. 417)

George was truly in a dilemma. Did she dare abandon Mallefille when Chopin still remained so enigmatic? Why had Frédéric drawn the line so suddenly in their relationship a few weeks earlier? Over and over she pondered the possible explanations: Was it prudery? Was it bashfulness? Or was he simply not interested in her at all? She was aware of Maria Wodzińska's existence and feared she might still have a rival in her. If that were the case maybe it would be best if she withdrew altogether. On the other hand if she didn't withdraw, what would be her chances of success? The tension within her was mounting to an intolerable pitch. She had to know.

In the warm spring sunlight the Berry countryside was bursting into bloom. Yet not a single daisy in the fields around Nohant could tell George Sand whether Chopin really loved her or not. What the daisies could not tell her, though, she suspected Chopin's good friend Albert Grzymała might, and in order to find out she sat down with pen and paper to write him. The resulting letter is one of monumental length and colossal gall. To read it in its entirety requires a degree of patience no less formidable than Mme Sand's prolixity. The following excerpts highlight the main questions which troubled George in her anxious state of mind toward the end of May, 1838.

"It would never occur to me to doubt your loyalty when it comes to matters of advice," she began flatteringly.

Don't ever have any fear of that. . . . Let's deal with the situation straightforwardly once and for all because everything that I do in the future will depend on your final answer on this subject. Listen to me carefully and reply clearly, definitively, and to the point. This person [Maria Wodzińska] that he wants or should or thinks he should love, is she the right one to make him happy or would she actually increase his suffering and his woes? I am not asking whether he loves her or whether she loves him or if she means more or less to him than I do. . . . I simply want to know which of *the two of us* he ought to forget or abandon for his own peace of mind, for his own happiness. . . . I have no desire whatever to play the role of the wicked witch. . . . I will put up no struggle at all against his old childhood friend if she is a sweet and pure young thing. If I had known that there was another commitment in our child's life I would never have tried to breathe in the fragrance of those flowers intended for another altar. By the same token he would have fled from my first kiss had he known that I was the same as *married* [to Mallefille]. We did not deceive each other at all. We let ourselves be carried away by the passing wind and swept off to another world for a bit. But it is nonetheless necessary that we come back down to earth after our celestial flight through the Empyrean. Poor birds, we have wings but our nest is on the ground and when the songs of angels call to us from on high, the cry of our family pulls us back below. As for me, I am not willing to give myself up to passion although deep within my heart there is a flickering glow which threatens to burst into flame. My children will give me the strength to resist anything which would take me away from them or the way of life which is best for their education, their health and their well-being. . . . Besides there is that excellent creature [Mallefille] *perfect* in every respect as far as goodness and honor go. . . . He is like a piece of melted wax, however, on which I place my seal and when I decide to change the imprint, I can easily do so with a little bit of care and patience. Right now, though, that is not possible and his happiness is something I regard as sacred.

Well, so much for me. Involved as I am, tied down without the freedom to go too far, I cannot expect our *little one,* in his turn, to break the chains which bind him. . . . I am afraid our love can only survive under those conditions in which it originated, that is to say, from time to time when the right winds whisk us into each others' arms, we will fly out among the stars again only to leave each other and come back to earth, for we are the children of earth and God has not destined us to end our pilgrimage together. . . .

My obligation, therefore, has been mapped out for me as you can see. And yet there are two ways in which I can fulfill my duty: the one would be to stay as far away from C[hopin] as possible, try to stay out of his thoughts, and never allow myself to be alone with him. The other would be just the opposite, to be with him as much as possible without compromising M[allefille]'s confidence, to remind him gently of my presence in his relaxed and contented moments, and to clasp him chastely in my arms at those times when the celestial winds happen to sweep us up and whirl us through the air. I will adopt the first method if you tell me that the *lady in question* can give him pure and genuine happiness, can take care of all his needs, can regulate and systematize his life and bring calm to it . . . then I swear to you I will try to make him forget me. I will take the second course if you tell me one of two things: either that his domestic happiness can and should be designed with several hours of chaste passion and tender poetry or that domestic happiness is not possible for him, that marriage or any such involvement would be death to this artistic soul, and that he should be kept away from it at all costs and even helped to overcome his religious scruples. . . .

If his heart, like mine, can manage two completely different loves, the one which would act as *the body* of life, the other as *the soul,* so much the better. . . . (pp. 428–33)

But the truth of the matter was that George herself did not really find it easy to carry on the dual love-life she was suggesting. Despite her protestations she was, in fact, losing interest in Mallefille. "Since he returned to Paris (you must have noticed it)," she continued in her letter to Grzymała, "instead of awaiting his return impatiently and being unhappy

away from him, I suffered less and breathed more freely . . ."
(p. 436).

Caught in an awkward position between her attachments to
one man and her attraction to another, George found herself
in a romantic quandry. In the past the answer had always
seemed to simple to her. "I have trusted a great deal to my instincts, which have always been noble," she told Grzymała. "I
have sometimes been deceived about people, but never about
myself" (p. 434). Now, however, she was confused and uncertain about her real feelings.

"I am not a fickle creature," she protested in defense of her
shifting sentiments. "I am, on the contrary, so much in the
habit of loving exclusively whoever really loves me, so slow to
become aroused by passion's flame, and so accustomed to living with men without even thinking of my femininity, that I
was truly a little bewildered and upset by the effect which this
person [Chopin] produced on me. I have not yet recovered
from my astonishment and if I had any pride I would be very
humiliated at having let my heart fall straight into infidelity
just at the moment when I thought my life was to be calm and
stable forever" (p. 435). "This is a frightful letter," George admitted in closing. "It will take you six weeks to get through it.
It is my *ultimatum* . . ." (p. 438).

As he read the last words of this incredibly long-winded appeal for advice, poor Grzymała must have staggered under its
relentless barrage of verbiage. George's lengthy and disconcerting revelation had led him down into the most obscure
caverns of her psyche where the only source of illumination
seemed to radiate from her own self-constructed halo of sanc-
tity. If there was a large measure of scheming in George's
calculations, however, there was also a genuine element of sin-
cerity in her concern for Chopin's happiness.

We do not know Grzymała's reply to this letter, but whether
it encouraged or discouraged Mme Sand, it certainly did not
deter her. At the beginning of June she wrote again: "I will be
back in Paris on Thursday to tend to some business matters.
Come and see me and try not to let the little one [Chopin]

know. We will surprise him. . . . As in the past, I will be staying at Mme Marliani's" (p. 445).

By now Chopin too was becoming quite agitated as he felt his own equilibrium being threatened by the waves of emotion arising within himself. In a state bordering on panic he also turned to Grzymała for help. "I absolutely must see you today, even if it has to be at midnight or later," he scribbled urgently. "Don't be upset. You know I have always valued your opinions. It's a matter of some advice I must ask you for."[10]

But there was little time for advice and even less to reflect upon it. George's arrival was imminent. In vain Grzymała attempted to guard her intended surprise. "I cannot be surprised," Chopin told his friend. "I saw Marliani yesterday and he informed me of her arrival. I shall be at home until five o'clock, giving lessons the whole time. (I've already finished two.) What's going to happen? God only knows. I really don't feel at all well. . . . Let's have dinner together somewhere." A time and place were chosen: "Tomorrow, Thursday, at 5:45 or 6:00 o'clock at the Café Doré . . . in a private room," Chopin specified. "We'll go from there to the Marliani's" (p. 254).

As the two friends planned, they dined that night on the corner of the rue Laffite and the boulevard des Italiens and left afterwards for the Marliani's to see George, who by then had already arrived in Paris.

"The dawn [l'Aurore]," Chopin commented, making a pun on George's real name, "was lost in the mists yesterday. I hope," he added optimistically, "there will be some sun today" (p. 254).

AS LISZT NOTED, Chopin seemed to fear Mme Sand more than any other woman and had been reluctant at first to have anything to do with her. His reluctance arose, to a certain extent, from his natural reserve, a feature of his personality which was especially evident where women were concerned. It also stemmed (perhaps to an even larger extent) from the conservative Catholic heritage of his family, so far removed in its outlook from the liberal attitudes of George Sand's antecedents. Little in the background of Chopin's life had prepared him for the woman he had now encountered.

Nicholas Chopin, Frédéric's father, was an energetic, industrious man who came from French peasant stock; his wife, Justyna Krzyżanowska, a quiet, devout woman, belonged to an impoverished Polish family of aristocratic connections. Without being narrow-minded or prudish, both had a firm sense of propriety which they instilled in their children, not so much by indoctrination as by example. Warmth and happiness pervaded their home life in spite of frequent financial adversities, and the atmosphere which they created for their children emphasized both the value and the pleasure to be derived from close family relationships. The strong sense of familial solidarity among the Chopins contrasted sharply with the loose family ties and frequently absent marital bonds among George Sand's forebears. The likelihood that people such as Chopin's parents could ever understand, much less appreciate, someone like Mme Sand seemed so remote that it must have given Frédéric cause for reflection. By involving himself with George he ran the risk of alienating his family, and even if he did not lose their respect he would, in any case, be renouncing many of the ideals and traditions which they lived by.

It is ironical that while George Sand was descended from a king of Poland on the paternal side of her family, Chopin's father and paternal ancestry were entirely French—at least as far back as his great-great grandparents, Catherine Oudot and Francois Chopin, who came from the province of Lorraine. In 1787 Frédéric's father, Nicholas, emigrated to Poland for reasons that are not entirely clear. There he eventually became tutor in French to the children of count Frédéric Skarbek, who lived with his family on an unpretentious estate in the village of Żelazowa Wola, just outside of Warsaw. In the one-story, whitewashed manor house with its shingled roof, Nicholas Chopin met the reticent but attractive young housekeeper, Justyna Tekla Krzyżanowska, a distant relative of his employer. He sat across from her at the dinner table and frequently after their evening meal the young tutor would play his flute or violin while Justyna joined him at the piano or sang to his accompaniment. On June 2, 1806, this happy relationship culminated in marriage.

After their wedding the young couple moved into a small three-room apartment in a modest outbuilding on the estate. Under its crude, timbered ceiling, which also sheltered the bakery and kitchen for the manor house, were born the first two of the Chopins' four children: Louise, on April 6, 1807 and Frédéric Francois on March 1, 1810. The latter was baptized on April 23, 1810, his godparents being Nicholas Chopin's two young tutees, count Frédéric Skarbek and his sister, countess Anna Skarbek.*

At that time Żelazowa Wola was under Saxon jurisdiction, which made the new son of Nicholas and Justyna Chopin a subject of Friedrich August I, King of Saxony, who, by a twist of fate, was the distant cousin of a small five-year old French

---

*The name Frédéric was chosen in honor of the child's godfather, who was represented at the christening by a proxy, François Grebecki. Chopin's middle name may have been selected because of this proxy. However, François was a common family name among the Chopins.

girl named Amantine-Aurore-Lucile Dupin, living then at her grandmother's estate, Nohant, south of Paris. On October 1, 1810 Nicholas Chopin was appointed professor of French at the Warsaw Lyceum, located in the Saxon Palace, where the family was assigned new living quarters. There in 1811 a third child, Isabelle, was born, followed by a fourth, Emilie, in 1813.

Although the Chopins could not provide a luxurious environment for their children, they did provide a cultivated one in which music was an important element. At an early age Louise began to study the piano and by the time Frédéric was six it was apparent that he, too, exhibited an unusual interest in music. Seeing this, the Chopins soon decided to give him formal lessons along with their daughter.

In the summers of 1824 and 1825, Frédéric's parents, worried over his frail appearance, sent their son off to the country to visit a schoolmate in the little village of Szafarnia. There he was placed under a strict regimen of health measures. But despite these precautions the young boy began to show more and more of the ominous signs of consumption which his family had feared. By February 1826 he was writing another of his school friends, "They have put leeches on my throat because my glands are swollen."[1] His sister Emilie, who had also contracted the same disease, grew quite sick that year and died the following April. Her loss was an overwhelming shock to the close-knit family, whose grief was so great that Mme Chopin never ceased to wear mourning for the rest of her life.

In the wake of this tragedy, Frédéric began to devote more of his time to music, having enrolled in the Principal Music School of the Warsaw Conservatory, where he studied under its director, Joseph Elsner. In September 1828 he made a brief trip to Berlin, caught glimpses of Spontini and Mendelssohn, and heard a number of concerts and operas which allowed him for the first time to extend his musical horizons beyond the limits of his native land.

After his graduation from the conservatory in 1829, Frédéric was encouraged to continue his studies abroad. But lack of finances made this difficult. Nevertheless his family managed to send him to Vienna for a few weeks that summer. There Chopin was astonished at the reception he received. "I really don't know why it is that I seem to amaze the Germans," he wrote his parents, "and I, in turn, am amazed at their amazement. . . . Haslinger [a prominent music publisher in Vienna] advises me to play in public. Everyone here insists that it would be a great loss to Vienna if I left without being heard. It is all so inconceivable to me" (p. 100).

No sooner had Chopin agreed to perform than arrangements were made for his debut on August 11, 1829, in the Kaerthnerthor Theater. His reception was enthusiastic for the most part, with only minor reservations. But there was one significant criticism at that concert which was to plague him throughout his entire career: "According to the general opinion," he was informed, "I play too quietly, or rather too delicately for audiences like those here in Vienna, who are accustomed to pianists that bang the instrument to pieces." Chopin, however, eventually resigned himself to such comments. "It is impossible to escape without some kind of 'but'," he remarked stoically, "and I prefer that to having it said that I play too loudly" (p. 107).

Shortly afterwards, a second concert was a far greater success. The *Allgemeine Musikalische Zeitung* insisted that the young man was indeed a "master of the first order. . . . The remarkable delicacy of his touch, his indescribable technical agility, his consummate shading of tone with the deepest of feeling, his incredible clarity of execution, and his delightfully inimitable compositions reveal a unique virtuoso who appears unheralded on the musical horizon like the brightest of meteors."[2]

After having seen Berlin and Vienna, Chopin began to feel that Warsaw had little to offer him as far as his musical career was concerned. "You wouldn't believe," he exclaimed to his friend Titus Woyciechowski, "how dreary Warsaw seems to me these days. Without my family to hold me here I wouldn't stay."[3] There was, in fact, another reason why Chopin lingered, and this he would confide only to Titus. "I have already found my ideal, to whom I have been faithfully devoted for six months, although I haven't said a word to her" (p. 132). The young girl, Constantia Gładkowska, was a lovely and talented vocal student at the Conservatory. To her romantic but inhibited admirer she had become the symbol of feminine beauty: virtuous, noble, pure, and, like all ideals of perfection, unobtainable—in fact, as far as Chopin was concerned, even unapproachable. His repressed ardor found expression only through music. It was she "whose inspiration is responsible for the *Adagio* of my concerto* and the little waltz [Op. 70, no. 3 in D-flat] which I just wrote this morning" (p. 132), he told Titus.

When Chopin finally finished the rest of his concerto, he performed it at his formal Warsaw debut in the National Theater on March 17, 1830. As in Vienna, he was a great success, but there was again the same criticism: "The audience in the parterre complained that my playing was hardly audible" (p. 146). Nevertheless the enthusiasm of the public was sufficient so that within five days Chopin gave a second performance. The applause and praise following this were so phenomenal that the pianist was urged to give a third concert. After the agonizing efforts of preparing two programs, however, the thought of a third had no appeal for him. "You can't imagine," he confessed, "what a torture I go through the three days before I have to play in public" (p. 148).

More interested in his compositions than in the career of a virtuoso, Chopin now devoted his energies to finishing a second concerto, which he had already begun. By August the new work was completed and on October 11, 1830 it was performed by the composer at his third and final concert in Warsaw.

After this, Chopin was firmly resolved to leave Poland. "I have already bought a trunk for my trip," he wrote Titus, "my

---

*Concerto no. 2 in F Minor. Although this is the first concerto Chopin wrote, it was published after his later Concerto in E Minor. Hence, it is always labeled "no. 2" despite the fact that this is chronologically incorrect.

clothes are ready, my manuscripts have been corrected, my handkerchiefs hemstitched, and my trousers tailored. All that's left is to say goodbye, and that's the worst (p. 204).

Finally, on November the second, he set out with Titus for Vienna, where the two arrived on the morning of November 23, 1830. Scarcely had they got settled when events occurred in Warsaw that suddenly changed all their plans. On the twenty-ninth of that month there was an uprising in the Polish capital against the oppressive Russian regime which controlled the nation. Titus, strong, vigorous, and decisive, immediately set out for Warsaw to aid his countrymen, but Chopin, paralysed by indecision, paused, reflected, eventually set out, then wavered, and ultimately returned to Vienna in an agonizing state of guilt, confusion, and exhaustion.

His parents insisted that he remain where he was. He certainly lacked the physical qualifications of a good soldier, and his return to Poland would only mean the useless sacrifice of his talent and career. He accepted their admonitions but was miserable. "From the day on which I learned about the events of November 29," he wrote, "I have become increasingly upset and despondent" (p. 251). "What is happening to you?" he asked his family in desperation. "I don't do anything but dream of you. This rain of blood, will it ever stop?" (p. 261).

He soon found that the atmosphere in Vienna was not at all sympathetic to the Polish cause. Time and again he sensed the hostility that surrounded him. The Austrians, who had previously participated in the partition of his homeland, were not generally well disposed toward the Poles. "The good Lord made one mistake," he overheard one day in a restaurant, "that of creating the Poles" (p. 243). "There is nothing worth bothering about in Poland" (p. 244), was the scathing retort.

Despite his unhappiness in Vienna, he lingered on. Spring came and found him still there, angry and depressed. On April 4 he appeared at a morning concert in the Redoutensaal, and again in June he made a public appearance at a benefit concert in the Kaerthnerthor Theater. These affairs, however, brought him little attention. Musically, he was stagnating in Vienna, and by the end of the month he had definitely decided to leave for Paris. Only two problems held him back. He had neither money nor a passport.

Apologetically he wrote his parents. "I will undoubtedly have to take more money from Peter's bank than Papa anticipated. I do the best I can but, Dear God, I don't have any other choice unless I set out on my trip without enough in my pocket. . . . Forgive me!" (p. 275). Regarding the passport he met with nothing but endless obstacles. "They promise me a passport every day," he complained, "and every day they send me on another wild goose chase trying to get back the one I had to leave at the police station. Today they tell me my passport has been lost! Not only that, they won't even bother to look for it. So now I have to apply all over again for a new one. We Poles have to put up with all sorts of strange things these days. I am all ready to go but I can't budge. I will take Bayer's advice and have them give me a passport for England. However I will go to Paris" (p. 264).

Finally on July 20, 1831, he and a friend, Alfons Kumelski, set out by coach for Munich. Vienna had been a great disappointment to the young musician, who now left it with few regrets. "While I have been here," he commented, "I have learned nothing that is really Viennese. Why, I can't even dance a waltz properly. What more is there to say?" (p. 276).

In Munich, Frédéric had to delay his trip for several weeks while he waited for funds from his father. As soon as possible, he resumed his journey and reached Stuttgart by early September. He had not been there long when word reached him of the fall of Warsaw. After nine months of bitter struggling, Poland had at last been crushed by the Russians on September 8, 1831. The effect of this news on the sensitive, homesick young traveler was indescribable. He was feverish with anxiety which he could express only in choked, explosive phrases, confided to his diary. What he wrote was agitated and incoherent, the expression of a futile, helpless, almost sickly rage. Visions of horror overwhelmed him, terrified him, and drove him into a frenzied state that all but left his mind unbalanced.

"The suburbs are destroyed, in flames!" he imagined wildly.
"Oh God, do You exist? Yes, You do but You don't avenge us.
Haven't there been enough Russian crimes? Or are You a
Russian too? My poor father! My poor dear father, is he starv-
ing? Perhaps he doesn't have enough to buy food for my
mother. Perhaps my sisters have become victims of the unleashed fury of the Russian soldiers. . . . Oh, Father, what
comforts for your old age! Mother! Sweet suffering Mother"
(p. 281). "And here I am doing nothing, just sitting around
emptyhanded. All I do is sigh from time to time and pour out
my despair on the piano!" (p. 283). "Alone! Alone!" he
sobbed, "Ah, no one can imagine my misery!" (p. 281).

Weak and shaken, Chopin eventually collected his few
belongings and set out, once more, on the last lap of his journey. In the third week of September he reached Paris.

Almost immediately his spirits revived. "Paris is everything
you could wish for,"[4] he exclaimed. It was, indeed, a city of
remarkable beauty, incessant activity, endless variety, and incredible excess. "You find the height of luxury and the depths
of filth, the greatest virtue and the worst vice, all side by side
here," he informed his recent companion, Kumelski. "At
every step there are posters about ven[ereal] disease—noise,
uproar, bedlam, and smut, more than you can imagine. . . .
You can go around in winter dressed in rags and still move in
the best of circles" (p. 15).

The Parisians astonished him. "Such strange people," he
remarked. "After dark you hear someone shouting out the
titles of the latest pamphlets, and for a sou you can buy three
or four pages of printed trash such as "The Art of Getting
and Keeping Lovers," "Priests in Love," "The Archibishop of
Paris and the Duchess of Berry" and a thousand other ob-
scenities of the same sort, very cleverly written sometimes" (p.
56).

During his first week in Paris, Frédéric settled in a room on
the fifth floor of a lovely old house on a pleasant tree-shaded
street, No. 27 Boulevard Poissonière. He was delighted with it.
"You can't believe how marvelously I am situated," he wrote

excitedly. "I have a little room, exquisitely furnished in mahogany, with a little balcony on the boulevard from which I can see all Paris from Montmartre to the Panthéon . . . many people envy my view but not my stairs" (p. 16).

Artistically, Paris of the 1830's was experiencing the flowering of the romantic movement. New forms of expression were blossoming forth in all the arts with such a rapidity that their growth often seemed wildly out of control. Because these new forms did not fit into the classical molds, many regarded them as undisciplined and considered the "flowering" of romanticism, in all its lush profusion, as the creeping overgrowth of a jungle which threatened to choke out all civilized expression in the arts. A storm of controversy rained down upon the new movement, but its effect was only to provide a richer, more fertile environment in which the seeds already planted would flourish. The result was that this period witnessed, as well as nourished, a crucial development in the realm of the arts, a development which was to make Paris one of, if not *the* most stimulating, provocative, and exhilarating cities in all of Europe.

In the single year of 1831 when Chopin arrived in Paris, Victor Hugo published his *Feuilles d'Automne* and *Notre-Dame de Paris;* Balzac, his *La Peau de Chagrin;* Musset, his *Contes d'Espagne et d'Italie;* and Stendahl, *Le Rouge et le Noir.* At the Porte St. Martin Theater, Dumas' *Antony* and Victor Hugo's *Marion Delorme* were playing. In the Salon of 1831 Delacroix submitted six paintings including his outstanding *28 Juillet* (Liberty leading the people). The Opéra-Comique was presenting operas by Cherubini, Weber, and Auber, while the Opéra staged one of the greatest Romantic extravaganzas of all time, Meyerbeer's *Robert le Diable.* The Italian Theater, though it produced little that was noteworthy in 1831, was directed by the renowned Rossini. The Conservatoire, under the direction of the aging Cherubini, held its usual annual concerts, featuring performances of Beethoven, Rossini, and Weber, among others. On the concert stage Franz Liszt was dazzling and electrifying his audiences while Hector Berlioz,

though not in Paris in 1831, was preparing compositions in
Rome that winter which were to overpower, perplex, and
sometimes please the Parisian public during the ensuing decades. Two newcomers, who were not yet in the artistic lime-
light, had just arrived in Paris that year: a brilliant young German poet, Heinrich Heine, and an energetic young
Frenchwoman from Berry, the baroness Dudevant.

It was not until February that Chopin was able to make his
musical debut in Paris, at the "salons de MM. Pleyel et Cie,"
No. 9, rue Cadet. The concert hall glittered that night under
the sparkling crystal chandeliers, ringed with hundreds of
candles and silhouetted against the ceiling by rows of flickering sconces on either side of the room. The four enormous
mirrors to the right of the audience reflected their elegant
finery along with the soft, rich drapery of the windows opposite them. The assembled crowd consisted largely of Polish
emigrés, many of whom were aristocratic and most of whom
were appreciative. Their tickets had cost them ten francs
apiece. Mendelssohn and Liszt also attended, full of enthusiastic admiration for their new colleague.

While the subsequent criticism in the *Revue Musicale* was on
the whole favorable, Chopin felt that he had not really taken
Paris by storm and became discouraged. Homesick, he confined his social life to the small colony of Polish exiles who
circulated in and around the Île Saint Louis and the faubourgs
St. Germain and St. Honoré. On Mondays he could always be
seen at Prince Adam Czartoryski's and on Thursdays at the
weekly soireés given by count Ludwik Plater. In such circles he
was eventually introduced to the baron James de Rothschild,
whose wife was immediately captivated by him and asked to
become his pupil. In no time, wives and daughters from all
over the *haut monde* of Paris were following her example.
Overnight Chopin found that his social success had guaranteed his financial future. Soon he was giving up to five or six
lessons a day for which his pupils discreetly placed twenty
francs on the mantelpiece as they left.

His income now soared beyond his expectations, but then so

did his expenses. In the fall of 1832 he explained to one of his friends, "You will undoubtedly think that I am on my way to making a fortune. Don't be deceived. My cabriolet and white gloves cost more than I make" (p. 85). Whatever the cost, though, Chopin considered it essential to equip himself with all these luxuries in order to maintain his new status. Within a short while he moved to a finer apartment in the Cité Bergère and soon afterwards to even more elegant accomodations at No. 5 (and later No. 38) rue de la Chaussée d'Antin.

In Warsaw the Chopins were delighted with their son's success but somewhat worried about his reaction to it. "My dear son," his father wrote him, "a young man can easily go astray if he does not discipline himself. With a talent and disposition like yours it could easily go to your head" (p. 106). His extravagance especially upset them and they warned him repeatedly to save money.

Despite these warnings Frédéric continued to play the dandy, running up accounts all over the city—at Chardin-Houbigant the perfumier, Rapp the shoemaker, Feydeau the hatter, and Dautremont the tailor. His wardrobe was elaborate, expensive, and impeccably elegant. A friend, observing him in Paris at the time, commented, "He turns all the ladies' heads and makes all their husbands jealous. He is *à la mode*. No doubt we shall all soon be wearing gloves *à la Chopin*" (p. 129). Behind his frivolous façade, however, remained the sensitive young artist, and to those who had the opportunity of knowing Chopin at closer range, the finer qualities of his nature were readily apparent.

In the spring of 1834, Ferdinand Hiller invited Frédéric to accompany him to the Music Festival of the Lower Rhine held at Aix-la-Chapelle in May. Although Chopin was eager to go, it was only at the last minute, when he induced Pleyel to buy one of his waltzes (the Waltz in E-flat, Op. 18) for five hundred francs, that he was financially able to make the journey. His father's admonitions on frugality had obviously not been heeded. At Aix, Chopin and Hiller ran into Mendelssohn, who came down from Düsseldorf, where he was then director of the orchestra. The three young men remained inseparable during the whole of the festival, and when it ended, Mendelssohn persuaded his two companions to return to Düsseldorf with him for a brief visit.

During the winter of 1834–35 Chopin played in public a number of times, appearing with Hiller, Liszt, and Berlioz, among others. Despite the favorable reviews in the Paris journals he felt he had not been well received. In his opinion the thunderous impact created by his colleagues' music made the gossamer delicacy of his own pianistic style seem flimsy and ineffectual. The following year he avoided the concert stage altogether and subsequently he limited his public performances, realizing that his intimate manner was not well suited to vast halls and large audiences.

In composition he confined himself almost exclusively to the piano, for which he wrote numerous waltzes, scherzos, ballades, nocturnes, polonaises, mazurkas, études, and other works. While Schumann hailed him as a "genius" and Liszt spoke reverently of the "Church of Chopin," the composer was subject to considerable criticism from some of his other contemporaries. Oddly enough, several of his severest critics were those friends who most admired him as a person and a pianist. For example, Mendelssohn found the mazurkas "so mannered they are hard to stand."[5] And Moscheles complained of the "artificial and forced modulations" of the études. "My fingers struggle and tumble over such passages," he wrote.[6] "On the whole," he concluded, "I find his music often too sweet, not manly enough, and hardly the work of a profound musician." (p. 295).

During the summer of 1835 Chopin learned that his parents intended to spend several weeks in Karlsbad, and immediately set out to meet them there. It had been five years since they had last seen each other, and their reunion was full of emotion. "Our joy is indescribable," the three wrote his sister, Louise and her husband in Warsaw. "We keep embracing each other over and over again. What more can we do? What a pity you are not with us."[7] Those few happy weeks together would have seemed all the more precious had Nicholas and Justyna Chopin realized they would never see their son again.

After leaving his parents, Frédéric did not go directly back to Paris but stopped in Dresden for that fateful visit with the Wodziński family which was to open the painful chapters of his "engagement" to Maria.

It was shortly after the "twilight hour" of this brief romance that Chopin met George Sand, who was not only willing to console him for his lost love, but also eager to provide him with a new one. The rambling rhetoric of her interminable letter to Grzymała, written from Nohant in May of 1838 made these intentions unmistakably clear. Less than a month later she was back in Paris and Chopin was in a dilemma. He knew instinctively how his family would feel if he became involved with Mme Sand, and he could easily anticipate the reaction of his friends in the fashionable faubourgs. But love, delicious and intoxicating, was beginning to dissolve his scruples, release his inhibitions, and cloud his vision. He no longer seemed to notice the great differences in background, personality, and interest between George and himself. Or, if he did, perhaps he intuitively perceived how these differences often served to complement rather than combat each other. In either case, the young musician, proud, sensitive, shy, and vulnerable, was now about to surrender himself to the very woman he had once found so coarse and repugnant. What would have appeared unlikely, if not impossible, in the fall of 1836 was about to take place in the summer of 1838. "It's not faith, it's love that moves mountains,"[8] George once observed, and she seemed to have been right.

WITH HIS SINISTER black mustache, worthy of Mefistofeles himself, Félicien Malle-fille hovered, like an ominous cloud over the dawn of Chopin and George Sand's new romance. Firmly ensconced at Nohant in his role of tutor to the Sand children, he remained intensely devoted to their mother with a passion bordering on ferocity. Fully aware of his mistress's admiration for Chopin, he took it to be merely a matter of artistic adulation and treated her new friend with the greatest respect. In fact, he even went so far as to write an effusive letter to the musician, in which he enclosed a poem, written under the spell of one of Chopin's compositions. "My dear friend," he began innocently,

> Some time ago, during one of those evenings when you were surrounded by a group of especially appreciative friends, you abandoned yourself completely to your inspiration and played that *Ballade Polonaise* of which we are so fond. Recognizing the hands which alone could make it speak, the melancholy genius, enclosed within your instrument, had hardly begun to relate its mysterious sorrows when we all fell into a deep reverie. After you had finished, we remained silent and thoughtful, still listening to the sublime song even though its last note had long since vanished in the air. What were we all dreaming about? What thoughts had been aroused deep within us by the melodious voice of your piano? It is impossible to say, for each individual envisions different things in music, just as one does in the clouds. . . . As for myself, lost in the darkest corner of the room, I wept as I pictured in my mind's eye those desolate images which you evoked in my imagination. On returning home I tried, in my own manner, to recreate them in the following lines. Read them with indulgence and if I have not in-

terpreted your *Ballade* as it should be, accept the offering as a proof of my affection for you and my sympathy for your heroic homeland, Poland.[1]

Shortly afterwards, in order to see Chopin more freely, Mme Sand contrived to send Mallefille to Le Havre with her son. But her maneuvering did not prove to be as subtle as she had hoped. Mallefille was hardly as gullible as she had assumed and far less malleable than she had expected. He was not long in recognizing his mistress's duplicity, and, having the "hot passions of a Creole," he could not easily accept the presence of a rival with unruffled composure. Earlier that summer he had fought a duel over George's affections on much slimmer grounds of suspicion than now confronted him. It was not surprising therefore that his fury should erupt to even greater heights when he finally discovered the true nature of the relationship between Chopin and his mistress. Quickly George realized how much she had overestimated her powers of deception and grew alarmed to find her romantic little masquerade turning into an explosive melodrama.

Seething with rage, the walleyed, love-crazed Mallefille stationed himself across the street from Chopin's apartment each day, waiting for George to make an appearance. It was not long before his vigil was rewarded and he caught sight of her coming out the door. With pistol in hand he lunged forward and would have wreaked his vengeance if a large wagon had not providentially lumbered down the street just then and separated him from his victim. Terrified, George grabbed up her skirts and ran to the nearest corner, where she flung herself breathlessly into an empty hackney coach. Within seconds the carriage careened out of sight, its driver flailing wildly at his horses while Mallefille stood helplessly behind, fuming and frustrated.

Badly shaken by this experience, Mme Sand did not dare encounter Mallefille face to face again. She did manage to communicate with him, however, through Pierre Leroux. Stunned but by no means speechless, she sharply informed her would-be assailant that women "do not belong to men by brute force and that nothing is gained by slitting throats."[2]

In the weeks that followed, more tumultuous scenes occurred, leaving all the unhappy participants acutely distraught. The one to suffer most in the end proved to be the love-stricken Creole, Mallefille, whom ensuing events actually reduced to physical illness. Only Mme d'Agoult seemed to find the whole episode deliciously amusing: "Poor Mallefille!" she chortled as she wrote a friend of hers, "There he is, bedridden with his vanity, doomed forever to be *dis*-abused, *dis*-illusioned, *dis*-enchanted and all the other *dis-'s* in the world. And can you imagine why? Oh dear, it's really a priceless story."[3] In her malicious way, Mme d'Agoult viewed her old friend's predicament as more hilarious than heartrending. Comic though it seemed to her, the disconcerting truth of the matter was that a tragic ending could well have followed in the wake of those violent events. Mme Sand, who was all too clearly aware of this, soon decided that it would be foolish to remain in Paris, where Mallefille's smouldering jealousy constituted a perpetual threat to herself and to Chopin as well. In addition, she had other reasons for wanting to leave the city that autumn: both she and her son had suffered a great deal the past year from attacks of rheumatism, which were especially aggravated by the harsh winters in Paris and Berry. She knew, furthermore, that the cold months ahead would surely take their yearly toll on Chopin's weak chest and chronic cough. A warm climate somewhere in the south would benefit all three of them and provide a convenient escape from the menace of Mallefille.

She broached the matter to Chopin, and together the two of them discussed the idea with several of their closest friends who were well acquainted with the difficulties of their situation. Mme Marliani's husband Manoël, the Spanish consul to Paris, and a Majorcan friend of his, Francisco Frontera,* recommended the Balearic Islands as ideally warm and comfort-

---

* A musician who preferred to be called simply "Valldemosa," the name of his native village.

ably remote—in other words, perfectly suited to their purposes.

No sooner had this project begun to take shape, however, than Chopin, with his obsessive concern for propriety, began to have qualms. He was deathly afraid of scandal and worried about the gossip their little adventure would generate among his aristocratic pupils and the distinguished salons in which he circulated. He was also concerned about the effect it would have on his family back in Warsaw. Plagued by these fears he began to reconsider the whole affair, but George remained firm in her decision to leave—with or without Chopin. Perhaps the very firmness of her decision finally influenced her vacillating companion to go along with her as planned.

Ironically enough, it was George who afterwards came to worry about public opinion as much as Chopin had in the beginning. In her memoirs which appeared over a decade later, she discreetly omitted any reference to the awkward triangle that had precipitated their amorous flight. "As I was making my plans and preparations to leave," she declared retrospectively in one of those characteristic revisions of reality with which her memoirs abound,

> Chopin, whom I saw every day and for whose genius and character I felt the tenderest affection, said to me several times that if he were in Maurice's place he would soon be cured himself. I mistakenly believed him and I arranged for him to come on the trip, not in place of Maurice but along with Maurice. His friends had insisted for a long time that he should spend some time in the south of Europe. He was considered to have tuberculosis. Gaubert,* however, examined him and assured me that this was not so. "You will find this out for yourself" he told me, "if you give him some air, exercise and rest." Others, knowing quite well that Chopin would never make up his mind to leave Paris and the way of life he led there (unless someone whom he loved, someone who was devoted to him took him away), strongly urged me not to discourage that desire which he had so appropriately and so unexpectedly manifested.[4]

* A physician friend of George Sand.

No doubt George realized that she would have to assume much of the responsibility for the success of their excursion, but she was hardly prepared to shoulder the full burden that was to fall on her.

> Even had I gone alone with two small children in a strange country," she wrote, looking back, "I would certainly have had my hands full without adding an additional emotional strain and medical responsibility. But Chopin was in such good health at that time that nobody was worried about him. Except for Grzymała, who had ample doubts on that subject, all of us were completely confident. All the same I encouraged Chopin to brace himself as best he could, since it was virtually impossible for him to entertain the thought of leaving Paris, his doctor, his friends, even his apartment and piano without a certain horror. He was a man of such rigid habits that any change no matter how small constituted a terrible ordeal in his life. (p. 436)

Ultimately George succeeded in calming Frédéric's fears by painting visions of balmy skies and sun-drenched seas. They were "off to an enchanted isle" she convinced him. Majorca was to be that "poetic haven" for them where they could "live without cares, without aggravations, without obligations, and above all," she emphasized happily, "without newspapers."[5]

Meanwhile the abandoned Mallefille was adjusting quite admirably to his rejected status and coming to accept it with quiet resignation. He has "calmed down" now, Mme d'Agoult reported shortly afterwards, and "George has packed herself off, chasing after true love under the shade of the myrtle trees of Palma! You really have to agree," she exclaimed with irrepressible delight, "that is a much prettier story than anyone could possibly make up."[6]

In reality the lovers had not sailed away to the Mediterranean quite as blithely as Mme d'Agoult's breezy description would imply. In 1838 the Balearic Islands were quite remote from Paris and could not be reached without an arduous, time-consuming trip for which a host of complicated details had to be planned in advance. Arrangements for transportation had to be made, apartments dismantled, mailing instructions provided, and an assortment of friends, pupils, and tradesmen notified. All this, of course, had to be handled with the utmost discretion in order to satisfy Chopin whose fastidious precautions created innumerable delays.

Naturally the matter of primary importance was that of money. In order to finance their ambitious expedition the couple discovered that a sizeable sum was going to be required. For the past two years or more Chopin had been working on a series of twenty-four preludes which was to include one work in each of the major and minor keys. The task was still unfinished, but he succeeded in persuading Camille Pleyel to advance him 500 francs for the group of compositions on the promise that he would complete them in Majorca. The balance of 1500 francs which he was to receive for the entire collection would be paid to him then. Knowing how urgently Chopin needed the cash, Pleyel took advantage of the situation to insinuate that the Preludes be dedicated to him. With circumstances as they were, the composer could hardly refuse.* Even with the income from these new works, Frédéric realized that he would still probably be short of money and secured an extra 1,000 francs from the banker, Auguste Léo† and a thousand more from a lender named Nouguès.

To Grzymała and another close friend, the pianist Julian Fontana, Chopin confided the secret of his journey and requested that the two of them look after his mail. Fontana was further delegated to oversee his financial affairs and take

* Chopin had at first intended to dedicate the Preludes to Joseph Christoph Kessler, a pianist whom he had known in his Warsaw days. The original manuscript, now in the National Library in Warsaw, bears the inscription: "24. Preludes for the pianoforte, dedicated to my friend, J. C. Kessler by F. Chopin." However, in March of 1839 the composer wrote Fontana that Pleyel could have the dedication to either the Preludes or the second Ballade (F Major, Op. 38). "If Pleyel insists on the *Ballade,* dedicate the *Preludes* to Schuhmann [sic]." At that time he specifically stated that Kessler was to have "nothing" (p. 320). However, Probst (Chopin's agent for the German publishing house of Breitkopf and Haertel) either failed to be notified of this change of plans in time or deliberately sent the manuscript on to the Leipzig publishers without waiting for Chopin's final authorization. (Chopin suspected the latter.) Hence the German edition remained dedicated to Kessler while the French and English editions substituted Pleyel's name as Chopin wished.

† A relative of the pianist, Ignaz Moscheles.

care of any problems that might arise in regard to his apartment.

Still fearful of gossip, Frédéric decided to leave Paris independently of the Sand family. Traveling at a different time and by a separate route, he was to meet Mme Sand and her children in Perpignan. If he failed to arrive there within a certain time, George was to proceed on without him. This time limit was apparently devised by Mme Sand, who no doubt had misgivings as to whether Chopin would, in fact, arrive at all. By now she knew him well enough to realize that at the last minute he might lose his nerve and not have the courage to carry out his intentions.

Looking over her own financial situation, George discovered that she too would have to raise some money for the impending journey. From the sale of her manuscript *Sept Cordes de la Lyre* she was able to obtain 5,000 francs. At the same time she acquired an advance of 1,000 francs for the reprinting of an earlier novel, *Simon*. This made a total of 6,000 francs, which seemed more than adequate for the trip since Manoël Marliani had assured her that she would need only 1,500 francs to reach Palma. Nevertheless, as a further precaution, a Spanish friend of the Marlianis, Señor Gaspar Remisa, provided her with a letter of unlimited credit on the banking house of Canut y Mugnerot in Palma.

Once in Majorca, George planned to continue work on a new quasi-philosophical, quasi-religious novel which she had already begun, entitled *Spiridion*. In addition she promised to provide a revised version of *Lélia* for her publisher. With such a full program of work outlined for herself in Majorca, it seemed that Mme Sand should have more than ample funds to care for her family during their absence from France.

Because of the Carlist war, which was ravaging much of Spain then, it was difficult to obtain passports to that country in 1838. But through their friend, Manoël Marliani, at the Spanish consulate, George and Frédéric were able to circumvent this problem with little difficulty.

Finally, on October 18, all preparations were completed and George left Paris to be followed in several days by Chopin. Accompanying her were her two children—Maurice, now aged 15, Solange, 10—a maid, Mme Amélie, three enormous yellow leather trunks full of books and clothes, and six bags bursting with a host of miscellaneous items which she feared—and with good reason—would not be available in Majorca. All this she managed to squeeze into the diligence that stood waiting for her in the courtyard of the Messageries Générales de France on the rue St. Honoré. Within a short while the carriage was jolting down the streets of the city, heading toward the open country. Inside, Mme Sand settled back in her seat and leisurely pictured the happy months that lay ahead for her in Majorca. In her mind's eye she had a vision of "some faraway quiet retreat where there would be no notes to write, no newspapers to peruse, no callers to entertain; where I would always wear my dressing gown, where every day would last for twelve hours, where I could shake off the duties of polite behavior, break away from the mental turmoil by which we French are all tormented, and devote a year or two to a little historical research and to studying the grammar and syntax of my own language at the same time as my children."[7]

By noon of the first day the diligence had reached Plessis-Picard, where George stopped to visit an old cavalry friend of her father's, Colonel Duplessis and his family. It was the Duplessis's who, years earlier, had introduced George to her future husband, the baron Dudevant, outside the Café Tortoni in Paris. However, in spite of the unintentional disservice which the family had rendered her in this introduction, Mme Sand retained the warmest affection for them and always referred to Colonel and Mme Duplessis as "father" and "mother."

From Plessis the Sand Family detoured by way of Melun, Chalon, and Lyons in order to visit other friends. Because of Maurice's health they traveled slowly, stopping every night to rest at an inn. From Lyons they took a steamer down the Rhône to Avignon and proceeded on to Nîmes in order to see Jules Boucoiran, a former tutor of the Sand children. At last, on October 30, they arrived in Perpignan, where George was hoping to meet Chopin.

எ CHAPTER NINE 羰

FOR TWENTY-FOUR anxious hours Mme Sand waited restlessly in Perpignan, expecting Chopin's arrival. She had ample justification for her anxiety since Frédéric had continued to be plagued by indecision until the last moment before his departure. When he finally mustered up his courage to meet George, so little time was left that he was barely able to reach Perpignan by the date agreed upon. In order to do so he was forced to travel by mail coach, the fastest but most exhausting means of transportation. Riding in the coach with him was Don Juan Mendizábal, the Spanish statesman and former President of the Council of Ministers in the government of the Queen-Regent, María-Cristina. He was a mutual friend of Chopin and George Sand, to whom he had given a number of letters of recommendation for prominent Majorcan families. It was Mendizábal who had ordered the confiscation of the monasteries in Spain only a few years earlier, and who was thus indirectly to provide the young lovers with the romantic retreat in Valldemosa where the two remained for the greater part of their stay on the island.

On the evening of October 31, Chopin finally arrived in Perpignan. George was relieved to see him and more than surprised to find him "fresh as a rose and rosy as a beet—in good health besides, having withstood his four nights on the mail coach heroically."[1] On the following day the two set out for Port-Vendres, seven and a half leagues from Perpignan, where they arrived by diligence on a beautiful November morning shortly before noon.

While waiting for the boat to Barcelona, Mme Sand wrote countess Marliani:

Darling,

I am leaving France in two hours. I am writing you from the shores of the bluest, clearest, and smoothest sea—like one in Greece or a lake in Switzerland on the most glorious day you can imagine. We are *all* well. Chopin arrived at Perpignan last night . . . the sky is magnificent, we are warm, and if you were only with us our trip would be completely happy. . . . (p. 512)

Having posted her letter, Mme Sand, with her young Polish companion, two excited children, a maid, valises, and trunks all boarded the steamer, *Phénicien,* for the voyage to Barcelona. In the warm afternoon sunlight of a clear November day, the sea was calm and glistening. Their crossing was truly a "delightful excursion," George remarked.

By nightfall the travelers had their first glimpse of Spain. Bathed in the dusky yellow haze of evening, the port buildings of Barcelona came into view over the bow of their boat. Shortly afterwards they glided into the harbor, surrounded by the flickering lights of the city, and enveloped in an exotic aura of adventure.

In Barcelona they spent "several crowded days before embarking for Majorca."[2] They were so intrigued by the city that they devoted their first morning to exploring it and delayed presenting their passports at the French consulate until afternoon. The children were fascinated by the strange sights and sounds that surrounded them. Maurice sketched constantly, as he had done on the earlier part of the trip, while his chubby, wide-eyed, little sister was much too absorbed in all that she saw to have time for her usual mischief. As for their mother and her companion, the two of them reveled in the delicious warmth of the Mediterranean sun. "On the shores of Catalonia in the month of November," George wrote, "we rediscovered the spring-like air which we had just been breathing at Nîmes, but which had deserted us at Perpignan* . . . . At Barcelona a fresh sea breeze tempered the heat of the sun,

---

* In her letter to Mme Marliani from Perpignan, George had described the weather there as "glorious" and "warm."

and swept every cloud away from the wide horizon which was framed by distant mountain peaks, here black and bare, there white with snow" (p. 7).

The peaceful landscape was deceptive, however, for Spain was actually in the throes of a civil war which simmered and exploded spasmodically throughout the country at that time. Fernando VII had died in 1833, leaving two young daughters but no male issue. According to Salic law it was forbidden for a woman to rule Spain. Therefore Fernando's brother, Don Carlos, supported by the Church and conservative elements of the government, claimed the throne for himself. He had not reckoned, however, with the strength and determination of his resolute sister-in-law, the widowed Queen María-Cristina. With the backing of the Liberals, including Mendizábal, she established herself as regent and set about to preserve the throne for her three-year-old daughter, Isabel. A struggle soon broke out as the Spaniards' sympathies became divided between these two "sovereigns," and violence quickly spread throughout the peninsula. The long series of bloody conflicts which followed were to be known as the Carlist war.

It was into this state of political turmoil that the newly ar-rived travelers set foot in Barcelona that November of 1838. "You are aware," George wrote, "that in 1838 the discon-tented part of the populace formed guerrilla bands and over-ran the whole region, barring roads, invading towns and vil-lages, holding even the humblest dwelling-places to ransom, occupying villas as close as half a league from the town, and sallying unexpectedly from the shelter of every rock to assault the traveler with: 'Your money or your life!' " (p. 7). Despite these dangers, the venturesome Parisians decided to get a taste of the Catalonian landscape and set out on an excursion into the embattled environs of Barcelona. What they saw was depressing and disconcerting. "We made one expedition into the countryside," George related, "and met only some detach-ments of Queen Cristina's partisans on their way down to Barcelona. . . . Both men and horses were so thin, the former with such gaunt and yellow countenances, the latter with such hanging heads and hollow sides, that the very sight of them made one feel hungry. The fortifications cast about the smallest hamlet saddened us even more . . . no dweller in these fertile fields believed himself secure. And in many places these wretched little defenses bore recent traces of attack" (p. 7).

In contrast to the countryside, the city showed little evidence of the war's ravages. The atmosphere there was one of peacefulness, almost frivolity. "Once through the formidable and massive fortifications of Barcelona," George claimed, ". . . we found nothing further to suggest that the city was at war . . . the gay youth of Barcelona sunned itself on the *rambla,* a long avenue laid out with trees and houses like our boulevards—the women, beautiful, graceful, and coquettish, preoccupied by the fold of their mantillas and the play of their fans; the men by their cigars, as they strolled along, chatting, laughing, ogling the ladies, discussing the Italian opera, and seeming not to care in the least what might be happening beyond the city walls" (p. 8).

Centuries of intimacy with violence and death had tended to make the Spaniards all but oblivious to their existence. Even within the confines of Barcelona itself George soon discovered sobering reminders that they were indeed an accepted part of Spanish life, condoned and even sanctioned by the Spanish Church. In grim testimony to this fact stood the House of the Inquisition, which she and Chopin visited on one of their tours of the city. The chilling gloom of its "dungeons which had been enclosed in solid blocks of masonry fourteen feet thick" (p. 86), spoke silently of cruelty, fanaticism, and bigotry, aspects of the Spanish character which were to arouse George's indignation over and over again in the months and years to follow.

A more pleasant diversion for the travelers occurred on Sunday when they were invited by M. Gauthier d'Arc, the French consul, to come aboard the warship *Méléagre,* which lay at anchor in Barcelona's harbor. The day proved to be splendid in all respects except for one minor tragedy which occurred when Solange accidentally dropped Maurice's prized puppets in the water as she boarded the bark that was to take them back to shore.

With George's penchant for the theater and Chopin's love of music, the two could not resist an evening at the opera. Unfortunately, the music was a great disappointment and the couple left having paid more attention to the architectural details of the house than to the artistic aspects of the performance.

Seeing Barcelona at night for the first time, the travelers were surprised to discover its atmosphere altogether different from what they had experienced by day. The tranquillity and gaiety of the city suddenly vanished, and sinister rumblings of the war could be heard out of the calm black distance:

> Once night had come, when the opera had ended and the guitars fallen silent and the city was given over to the perambulations of nightwatchmen, the only sounds to be heard, above a monotonous surging of the sea, were the sentries' ominous challenges and certain still more ominous shots. These shots were fired at irregular intervals, now singly, now in rapid volleys, from various places near and far, sometimes independently, sometimes in reply, but always continuing until the first rays of the morning. Then everything returned to silence for an hour or two, and the well-to-do doubtless slept soundly, while the harbor woke up and the sea folk began to stir. If, in the daylight hours of rambling and gossiping, you ventured to ask what these strange and alarming night noises had meant, you were told with a smile that they were nobody's concern, and that it would be unwise to enquire into them. (p. 8)

At the end of a week, trunks and valises were again packed up as the little band of tourists prepared to embark on the final leg of their journey to Majorca. At five o'clock in the afternoon of November 7, a small packet boat, *El Mallorquín*, bearing the figure of a Majorcan peasant in traditional costume on its prow, steamed out of the harbor of Barcelona. In addition to its crew and cargo, it carried the following passengers bound for Palma:

FIRST CLASS: Mad. Dudevant, *married*
                Mr. Mauricio, *her son, a minor*
                Madamoiselle Solange, *her daughter, a minor*
                Mr. Federico Chopin, *artist*
SECOND CLASS: Mad. Amelia, *domestic*[3]

At first the little steamer seemed so small to Mme Sand that she was afraid it might not weather the strong north winds which were known to sweep across that corner of the Mediterranean. But her fears were hardly necessary since the weather was warm and peaceful the evening they set sail; so warm, in fact, they could feel the heat increasing hour by hour. The sea was dark and placid, "illuminated only by an extraordinary phosphorescence in the wake of the ship. Everyone was sleeping on board except the helmsman, who, in order to avoid the risk of falling asleep himself, sang all night long, but with a voice so soft and so subdued that one would have supposed he was afraid of waking up the crew or was half asleep himself." George was entranced. "We never stopped listening to him for a moment," she wrote. "His singing was so strange. It had a rhythmic and melodic character different from anything we had ever heard. He seemed to let his voice wander haphazardly like the smoke from a ship's funnel, wafted along and carried away by the breeze. It was more of a dreamy soliloquy than a song, a sort of vocal meandering, nonchalant and unpremeditated, simply flowing along with the movement of the boat and the faint murmur of its eddy. It seemed like a vague improvisation, yet one limited to a few hauntingly repetitious phrases."[4]

As *El Mallorquín* bobbed gently over the rippling waters of the warm Mediterranean, Chopin too succumbed to the hypnotic melancholy of the helmsman's song. Spellbound, in the swaying shadows next to George, he listened as the two drifted silently through the clear, semitropical night, lost in the languid beauty of the undulating melody.*

---

* It has been claimed that the helmsman's song can be found in the passage marked *sostenuto* from the middle of Chopin's twelfth Nocturne, Opus 37, no. 2.

By daybreak their romantic reveries had dissolved. On the horizon to the east, silhouetted by the morning sun, rose the rugged crags of Majorca's coastline. Like a beautiful rough-hewn jewel which nature had cast away in this remote section of the sea, the island emerged dramatically out of the water, thrusting up its jagged brown cliffs daubed with streaks and splashes of vivid green foliage. As the fiery orange of sunrise gave way to the mellow gold of midmorning, *El Mallorquín* rounded the little island of Dragonera and suddenly before the passengers loomed the massive spectacle of Mount Galatzo. Suspended high above them was the picturesque village of Andraitx, while ahead, the serrated shoreline darted capriciously in and out of the sea, leaving a magnificent trail of boulder-strewn slopes and rocky ledges cascading down into the glistening water below. Here and there a cool, shaded cove, half-hidden from the outside world, curled up calmly in the sandy arms of the steep coastal hills.

By the latter part of the morning the little packet boat veered sharply to portside and entered the Bay of Palma. For the northern travelers the view was breathtaking. Above the sparkling sands of the beaches rose tiers of almond trees and pine groves, while from the crests of the forested slopes, ancient stone watch towers peered out protectively over the open waters of the bay. Mute and motionless on their heights, these august relics of earlier barbarian invasions solemnly surveyed the peaceful passage of the newcomers who now approached their island.

As the ship neared the city, the white façade of a cottage or a villa gleamed brightly through the dark green of the hillsides and, at last, in the sunny distance the travelers could distinguish the city of Palma itself, dominated by the majestic outlines of La Seo, its imposing thirteenth-century cathedral. In the foreground was the turreted Lonja with its graceful gothic stonework, and nearby stood the large Moorish palace of the Almudaina. Rising high above the terraced vineyards on the hills to the left soared the round fortress tower of Bellver Castle, the stolid sentinel of Palma's harbor.

Slowly and cautiously *El Mallorquín* picked its way among the ships at anchor. Sliding forward among schooners, brigantines, and other vessels, it eventually pulled up to its own mooring and the passengers prepared to disembark. With mounting excitement they stepped off the boat at 11:30 on the morning of November 8, 1838. Under the brilliant noonday sun, Palma in mid-autumn seemed just like Paris at the beginning of June.

ଔ CHAPTER TEN ଔ

A S SOON AS they left *El Mallorquín,* George and Frédéric, with the maid and two children, set out to look for a place to stay in Palma. Throughout the long, hot afternoon they wandered up and down the narrow streets and crooked stairs that wound between the yellow, weathered walls of century-old houses. In the early eighteen-hundreds Palma still retained much of the medieval flavor that had largely vanished from most of the continental cities of Europe. The bridges over its moats, the mullioned windows of its houses, and the picturesque colonnades along its streets still lent an authentic air of antiquity to the city. Mystery seemed to lurk behind the dark framed doors laden with massive spikes and twisted iron grillwork.

Abundant in atmosphere, Palma was unfortunately lacking in accommodations, and its medieval charm began to wane with each hour of searching. "We found," George complained with growing irritation, "that the Spaniards who had recommended Majorca to us as the most hospitable and well-supplied island in the world had, like ourselves, been laboring under a great delusion. Who would have guessed that, in a country so close to civilized Europe, we should be unable to find a single inn?"[1]

The scarcity of accommodations was partly due to the fact that Majorca in 1838 had become crowded with immigrants from the war-torn mainland. The islanders did not receive the refugees with any great enthusiasm and the persistent influx of these strangers did little to broaden or enrich their insular perspectives. On the contrary the Majorcans tended to withdraw more and more into themselves and became increasingly chary of all outsiders. They had, in fact, become so suspicious of foreigners, George grumbled, that "one has to carry letters of introduction and recommendation to twenty of the more important local personages, who have been given several months' warning, unless one can face the prospect of sleeping in the open air" (p. 32).

At last, with nightfall, the weary tourists located two small rooms for rent above the workshop of a barrelmaker on the Calle de la Marina in a "disreputable quarter of the town (p. 32). It was not exactly the romantic haven they had pictured, but at least they had a roof over their heads. The rooms were sparsely furnished and the few necessities which they possessed seemed rather crude to the fastidious new inhabitants, fresh from the comforts of Paris. Their day might have ended a little more happily if the landlord had provided them with a decent meal that evening. But the heavy oils and hot spices of the Majorcan diet did not set well on their Parisian palates. In less than twelve hours on the island, George was beginning to realize that in this Mediterranean paradise she had rushed off to so eagerly, "a stranger is lucky if he can find a trestle-bed with a mattress, little more downy and resilient than a slate, a straw-bottomed chair, and a menu dominated by sweet pepper and garlic" (p. 32). In fact, she exploded, "If you want to allow yourself the exorbitant luxury of a chamber pot, it's necessary to write Barcelona."[2] The experiences of their first day left Mme Sand a little disenchanted with Majorca, and by the end of their first week there, she was firmly convinced, "It's a country at least three centuries behind the times" (p. 516).

Resigned to the multitude of inconveniences which greeted them, the travelers soon learned that "unless we professed to be delighted by this reception, we should either earn black looks as impertinent blunderers or, with better luck, pitying stares as idiots. Woe betide the traveler in Spain who is not pleased with everything he encounters! Make the slightest grimace on finding vermin in a bed, or scorpions in the soup, and you draw upon yourself universal scorn and indignation."[3]

Early on their first morning in the Calle de la Marina, the

sleeping guests were awakened by the loud din of hammers coming from the cooper's shop below them. The racket persisted right up until evening, when it finally died away only to start up again the following morning. Under such circumstances it was difficult to relax and impossible to concentrate. While George might be able to accomplish something at night, she would certainly not be able to sleep during the day. And, with all that commotion downstairs, the thought of trying to finish his Preludes there was completely out of the question for Chopin.

Even more insufferable in some respects than the cramped quarters, the primitive furnishings, and the incessant clang of hammers was the maddening buzz of mosquitoes in the Calle de la Marina. Swarming through the tiny rooms of their apartment day and night, the little insects infuriated George more than anything else she had had to endure in Majorca up to that point. As irritating as they were, there was undoubtedly some exaggeration in her claim that "without the mosquitoes we would be completely happy. But," she complained, "all of us have our faces and hands as speckled as a trout and we scratch ourselves like—Oh, enough!"[4] she spluttered, too aggravated to look for words adequate to express her disgust. Within a very few days it was clear to all that the visitors from Paris would have to search for other lodgings.

For a week they scoured Palma, only to find that "not a single habitable flat was available in the entire city." A typical flat there, they discovered, "consists of roof, floor, and bare walls, without doors or windows. In most middle-class houses windowpanes are not used; and anyone wishing to provide himself with this comfort, essential in winter, must first get the frames made. Each tenant, therefore, when he moves (which happens very seldom) takes the windows, the locks, and even the hinges of the door away with him. His successor must begin by replacing these, unless he has a taste for living in the open, which is quite a common one in Palma."[5]

Exasperated, the couple decided to look for a house instead of an apartment. But here, too, they met with frustration.

Nothing in all of Palma was "for rent, for loan, or for sale." The city, George concluded after days of fruitless searching, "is designed to hold only a certain number of inhabitants. As the population increases, they huddle a little closer together. Hardly any new houses are built" (p. 34). As for poor newcomers like themselves, she could find only one solution: "When one arrives, one begins by buying some land, after which one builds and then gets furniture. Next one obtains permission from the government to reside in one place or another, and finally, at the end of five or six years, one begins to open one's suitcase and change one's shirt while waiting to obtain permission from customs to bring in some shoes and pocket handkerchiefs."[6]

Since the couple had letters of introduction to a number of prominent families in the city, they called on several of them, hoping for some advice or assistance. Wherever they went, their reception was always cordial. "This house and all its contents are at your disposal," they heard repeatedly, only to find that the phrase was merely a social formality. "One cannot look at a picture, finger a piece of material, or lift up a chair," George observed, "without being told most charmingly: '*Es(tá) a la disposición de Usted*'. But beware of accepting so much as a pin: that would be a flagrant impropriety."[7]

These basic elements of Majorcan etiquette George learned painfully one day through the humiliating experience of borrowing a carriage. "Having brought a letter of unimpeachably noble introduction to a young marquis," she wrote, "I thought that I could accept his carriage (so charmingly had the offer been made) and go for a drive! But next day a note from him made it quite plain that I had violated the proprieties, and I hastened to send his turnout back unused . . . I was guilty of a breach of good manners, and I am sure, my spirit will never recover from the shame" (p. 34).

There were some families in Palma, however, who treated the strangers more graciously. Despite the fact that the foreign couple was already becoming the subject of considerable gossip among the islanders, the sister and brother-in-law of their Majorcan friend Francisco Frontera behaved most warmly toward them. The French consul, Flury, proved to be an "excellent fellow who puts himself out no end for us,"[8] they reported, and the banker Canut and his lovely wife were especially kind to them.

George's habit of smoking shocked the Majorcan populace even more than it had the Parisians but Sra Choussat de Canut recalled that she "never smoked in my house, although she thought nothing of lighting a cigarette in front of us when she was in her own, or out in open country."[9] The señora's recollections of George that winter are amazingly similar to the Charpentier portrait of her which was exhibited for the first time the following year in the Salon de Paris. She remembered George as a "lovely person, having an expressive countenance, enlivened by very beautiful black eyes. Over her forehead her splendid hair formed two large tresses which swept down and back and were secured by a very pretty little silver dagger. Her clothing was severe in style and almost always black or dark-colored. From her neck hung a cross of beautiful diamonds suspended from a velvet ribbon; and on her arm she wore a bracelet with an enormous number of little ornaments which were doubtless all souvenirs."[10]

At the same time that Sra Choussat was able to appreciate Mme Sand, she also understood the Majorcan temperament and the reasons it tended to be unsympathetic, even hostile to the Parisian visitors. The Majorcans, she explained, simply could not imagine what a thirty-four-year-old woman, accompanied by a twenty-eight-year-old musician, two children, and a maid had come to do on their island. "On inquiring one discovered that this was a woman who wrote books! How awful! She signed herself with a man's name: George Sand! Furthermore her little daughter wore a velvet suit like that of a boy! . . . It was even asserted that Don Burges Zafortesa owned a copy of one of her works which all his friends wanted to read. It was *Lélia.* They found it romantic and incomprehensible and the admirable author was condemned by a bunch of ignoramuses" (p. 54).

Since the islanders in general were not disposed to help the newcomers settle down in their midst, the French consul, Flury, finally located them an attractive whitewashed villa in a delightful setting a few miles northwest of Palma. Surrounded by terraced vineyards and olive groves, it was situated near the village of Establiments on a hillside overlooking a fertile plain in "one of the most prosperous districts"[11] of the island. "For the first time in the memory of man," George gasped in amazement, "a furnished house has been found for rent in Majorca."[12]

The name of the villa was *Son Vent* which, in the Majorcan dialect, means House of the Wind. The name was not without significance although George and Chopin scarcely suspected this at the time they rented it. From the beginning certain undesirable features of the house were apparent, but to the new tenants it still seemed a genuine bargain compared to the cost of houses in Paris or its environs. After some haggling with Señor Gómez, the shrewd Palma businessman who owned it, the rent was fixed at fifty francs a month*—"a very moderate price by French standards but," as George fully realized, "high enough by theirs."[13]

Anxious to leave their stifling, noisy quarters in the city, the travelers decided to move immediately, accepting the house as they found it. A week on the island had already taught them that they might wait forever if they expected Sr. Gómez to make even the most minimal alterations. Such was the tempo of life in Majorca. There the typical inhabitant "always finds some good reason why he should not hurry," George observed. "Life is so long! Only the French, that is to say the extravagant and hysterical, want things done at once" (p. 35). Patience (*"mucha calma"*) was to prove not only a virtue in Majorca but a necessity.

At about the same time that George contracted for *Son Vent* she also made arrangements to rent several rooms in an abandoned monastery at Valldemosa, a village located still farther

---

* George later exaggerated the sum to 100 francs when she wrote *Winter in Majorca*.

north of Palma. The three years earlier Mendizábal, in his anticlerical campaign, had driven the Carthusian monks from
their ancient charterhouse, forced them to give up their monastic way of life, and even forbade them to wear their religious habits. Taking over their property, the government
tried to lease out portions of the monastery to the islanders
for living quarters. But the majority of the Majorcans felt a
certain sense of sacrilege in occupying the confiscated charterhouse, and many had an almost superstitious fear of the
deserted buildings. As a result they stood crumbling and virtually uninhabited in the fall of 1838. The decaying old struc-
tures, however, had a romantic appeal for Mme Sand, who
felt that in this wild and isolated retreat she would find the
tranquillity and inspiration appropriate for her new novel,
Spiridion.

Delighted with both of her real estate ventures, George
wrote enthusiastically to Mme Marliani:

14 November, 1838

Dearest,
    I am writing you on the run; I am leaving the city and moving
to the country; I have a beautiful furnished house with a garden
and a magnificent setting for fifty francs a month. Moreover two
leagues from there I have a cell, that is to say, three rooms and a
garden full of lemon trees for thirty-five francs *a year* in the
enormous monastery of Valldemosa! . . . The poetry, the solitude of this place! Everything that is most exquisite this side of
heaven is here. What a country! We are ecstatic."[14]

Relieved at the thought that they would soon be comfortably settled, the couple now began to enjoy the beauty of the
island for the first time. In her letter to Mme Marliani, George
extolled the loveliness of the countryside.

Valldemosa,* in telling us of the facilities and comforts of his
country, *deceived* us terribly. But the scenery, Nature herself, the
trees, the sky, the sea, the monumental landscape surpass all my

---

*Their mutual friend, the singer Francisco Frontera, who came from Valldemosa.

dreams: this is the promised land, and as we have succeeded in getting quite nicely settled, we are enchanted. We are all in good health. Yesterday Chopin walked three leagues on foot with Maurice and us over sharp, rocky ground. The two of them are a little under the weather today. Solange and I are well on the way to getting atrociously fat though we don't look too pathetic just yet. Altogether our trip couldn't have been happier or more pleasant, and as I had estimated with Manoël, I have spent less than fifteen hundred francs between now and the time I left Paris. (p. 522)

Chopin was equally enchanted if not more so by the island. "Here I am in Palma," he wrote Fontana on November 15,

in the midst of palm trees, cedars, cacti, olive trees, oranges, lemons, aloes, figs, pomegranates, etc., that is to say, surrounded by every kind of tree that the Jardin des Plantes has in its greenhouses. The sky is a turquoise color and the sea lapis lazuli; the mountains are emerald and the air is heavenly. There is sunshine all day long and everyone dresses in summer clothes since it is warm. At night you can hear singing and the sound of guitars for hours at a time. There are enormous balconies, streaming with vines and ancient ramparts dating from the time of the Arabs. The city and everything here in general has an African flavor. In short, life is wonderful . . . I will probably be living in a marvelous cloister in the most beautiful spot on earth: I will have the sea, mountains, palm trees, an old cemetery, a Teutonic church, the ruins of a mosque, and olive trees a thousand years old. Ah, my friend, I am just beginning to live. I have all the most beautiful things in the world here beside me. I feel better. . . . Don't talk much about me to people I know. I will write more soon. Tell them I'll be home by the end of the winter.[15]

The same day that Chopin wrote Fontana, he and George packed themselves and their little entourage into two sturdy carts and wended their way out of the hubbub of Palma to their new home in the country.

ᏋᏒᎩ CHAPTER ELEVEN ᏵᎦᎩ

THE LITTLE VILLA of *Son Vent* was "like all Majorcan country houses," George wrote, "with camp-beds or wooden ones painted green, often consisting simply of two trestles supporting a couple of boards and a thin mattress; straw-bottomed chairs; rough wooden tables; bare but immaculately whitewashed walls and, as a crowning luxury, glazed windows in almost every room. The so-called drawing room contained four dreadful fire screens, like those found in our poorest village inns, which Señor Gómez, our landlord, had been simple-minded enough to get carefully framed, as though they were valuable engravings, to form mural decorations for his country seat. The villa was palatial, well ventilated (too much so), well laid out, and most agreeably situated."[1]

In the silent countryside around Establiments, George and Frédéric at last felt safely removed from the bustle of Paris. In their peaceful corner of the Mediterranean they had a reassuring sense of privacy. Their separate departures from Paris had been accomplished so discreetly that it seemed they now had no cause to fear scandal. However, the very quietness of their disappearance, far from averting suspicion, had actually added a tantalizing aroma of mystery to their absence. In the various circles of their friends curiosity quickly set pens to scribbling and tongues to wagging:

(FRANZ LISZT TO MAJOR ADOLPHE PICTET IN GENEVA)
Florence, 8 November, 1838

. . . George has gone to the Balearic Islands according to what I hear from Paris. Do you have any news from her directly?[2]

Grzymała, Fontana, and the few others who knew the full details of the situation gave out no information, while those who gleaned only scraps and fragments of the affair exchanged and embellished them with gleeful relish. As might be expected, the countess d'Agoult whetted her pen on the subject with typical feline ferocity. *"The trip to the Balearics amuses me,"* she wrote Mme Marliani. "From what I know of the two of them they should be at each other's throats after a month of living together. Their personalities are as different as night and day. But what does that matter? It's all too delicious for words" (p. 261).

While George and Frédéric were oblivious to the commotion their absence was causing on the continent, they soon found other reasons to be annoyed with their friends and colleagues back home. They had not been in Majorca long before George's publisher, Buloz began to pester her about her novel, *Spiridion,* and the other works she had promised him. "I am waiting impatiently, my dear George," he prodded her on November 12, "for the end of *Spiridion;* remember that the first three parts have already appeared and an interruption now would be fatal for us. . . . You would also make me very happy if you would send the other *Lettres d'un Voyageur;* you are visiting a country entirely new to you and it should inspire you with some fine works. I have spoken about your play* to the Théâtre Français: you will be welcomed there; they are delighted to be able to perform something of yours. So send the play to me as soon as you can."[3]

Although Mme Sand had only a few pages to finish in her novel, the task was difficult, for *Spiridion* was a ponderous manifesto of her personal beliefs, a tome in which she attempted to recreate the mystical experiences of her convent years. In it she contrasted religious asceticism with worldly pleasure and leavened the mixture with extracts from the teachings of her two old philosophical mentors, the abbé La-

*The play was *Cosima.* Buloz had recently been made royal Commissioner of the Comédie Française.

mennais and Pierre Leroux.* As a backdrop for the story she utilized the monasteries of Barcelona and Majorca.

Explaining her delay in completing the work, George wrote Mme Buloz; "It is not the easiest thing in the world to sum up one's own religious credo, and I assure you that *while traveling* it is absolutely impossible."[4]

Indeed there was very little time in Mme Sand's day which was not already taken up with household duties and the tutoring of her children. "I am dishing out food instead of literature" (p. 529), she complained half in jest. "I do almost all the cooking. . . . Fortunately the chambermaid I brought from Paris is very devoted and is resigned to doing the heavy chores. But she isn't strong and I have to help her. Furthermore, everything costs so much and it is difficult to keep up one's nourishment when your stomach can't stand rancid oil or pork grease. Mine is beginning to, but Chopin gets sick whenever we don't prepare his food ourselves" (p. 515).

In order to complete *Spiridion,* George had to resume her habit of working at night. "Once, early in December," she wrote, "I stayed out on a terrace until five o'clock in the morning and kept deliciously warm."[5] The task was not entirely unpleasant and she often enjoyed sitting there in the tepid night air, surrounded by the shadowy beauty of the myrtles and the fragrant aroma of lemon blossoms. "In Majorca," she reported, "the silence is deeper than anywhere else, though the asses and mules who spend the night at pasture interrupt it now and then by shaking their bells. . . . So does the music of the *bolero* bursting out in the loneliest places and on the darkest nights. No peasant ever relinquishes his guitar, however late or early the hour. From my terrace I could hear the sea too, but so distant and so faint. . ." (p. 44).

All these captivating little distractions, combined with the "charm of the scented and moonlit landscape," more than compensated George for her nightly labors. Indefatigable, she

---

* In fact, parts of the text may even have been written by Leroux himself, according to Maurois.

was eventually able to get the remaining installments of her book off to Buloz around the twentieth of November, sending them by way of the consul in Barcelona, who was to forward them on to Paris.

While Mme Sand was struggling with the final part of her novel, Chopin was grappling with the last of his Preludes. The piano which Pleyel had promised to send was still somewhere *en route*. Annoyed at the delay, he wrote the manufacturer on November 21: "My piano hasn't arrived yet. How have you sent it? By way of Marseille or by Perpignan? I dream of music but don't produce any—because there aren't any pianos here. In that respect this is a barbaric country."[6] Finally he rented a local piano from some Majorcans. It was a second-rate instrument, in poor condition, and "it irritates him more than it comforts him," George commented. But "in spite of all," she claimed, "he works."[7]

In less than three weeks after they arrived at *Son Vent,* the rainy season set in. Up until then nature at least, if not the Majorcans, had been kind to them. Then suddenly the balmy bliss of their spring-like weather was washed away in a flash. "One early morning," George related,

> after the long drawn-out wailing of the wind had sung us lulla-bies all night, the rain began beating on our windows, and we were awakened at last by the noise of the torrent which had begun to push its way through the stones of its dry bed. Next morning, its voice was louder; and on the third day, it was roll-ing along the boulders that obstructed its path. All the blossom had fallen from the trees, and streams of rainwater were cours-ing through the ill-protected rooms of our house.[8]

Señor Gómez's drafty villa, so aptly christened the House of the Wind, was not constructed to withstand this monsoon-like onslaught, and shortly afterwards became almost uninhabit-able with the winter winds and downpours bombarding it from all sides. While the temperature did not actually drop very low, the moisture retained by the lime in the thin, plas-tered walls (which "swelled up like a sponge") produced a biting chill. "The damp settled like a cloak of ice over our shoulders and reduced me to paralysis," George remembered painfully, "Never have I suffered so much from the cold" (p. 46). Not all of the rooms had glass in the windows and, to make matters worse, there was no fireplace in the entire house, which grew damper and windier day by day. "The lack of precaution taken by Majorcans against these twin scourges of wind and rain is incomprehensible," George noted with astonishment. The reason, she discovered, still more astonished, was that "they insisted it never rained in Majorca" (p. 45).

Without a fireplace the inhabitants of *Son Vent* were forced to adopt the Majorcan custom of heating their house with a charcoal brazier. Improperly regulated, such braziers tended to billow forth volumes of smoke. Unfortunately the Parisians had had no experience in the management of these devices and were soon gasping from their noxious fumes. Desperately they searched for a stove with a chimney, but to no avail— "Chimneys are totally unknown in Majorca,"[9] George found, to her distress.

As the days passed, the rain-soaked, smoke-filled rooms of *Son Vent* became more and more intolerable. Chopin, who had already been sick once since their arrival on the island, now began to suffer again from the dank, unhealthy atmosphere. "We could not get used to the suffocating smell of the charcoal braziers," George wrote, "and our invalid grew seriously ill and began to cough."[10] At last they located a stove with a metal chimney to carry off some of the stifling smoke—none too soon as far as Chopin was concerned. On December 3 he wrote Fontana in Paris, "I have been sick as a dog these last two weeks: I caught cold in spite of the eighteen degrees (centigrade) of heat, the roses, oranges, palms and fig trees." His own diagnosis was "acute bronchitis" and, with the peevishness of an invalid, he railed against his doctor-friend, Matuszyński, for not having warned him how to cope with it. "He could have predicted this would happen to me."[11]

What upset him most about his illness was the fact that it kept him from working now that he had a piano of sorts at his disposal. Recurrent attacks of fever and the chronic, hacking cough were wearing him down to the point where "it is wreaking havoc with the *Preludes*," he informed Fontana. "God only knows when you will receive them" (p. 274).

Because of the persistence of his cough, Chopin finally consulted several of the local physicians. "Three doctors—the most prominent ones on the island—have examined me," he reported, "one sniffed at what I had coughed, the second tapped where I had coughed and the third felt and listened as I coughed. The first said I was going to die, the second that I was in the process of dying and the third that I was already dead—yet up to now I feel the same as ever." But following this rather flippant account, he hastened to add in all seriousness: "Don't tell anyone I have been sick or they will start jabbering about it" (p. 274).

Fortunately Chopin still had enough strength left to resist the recommendations of his doctors, though not without some struggle. "It was all I could do," he asserted, "to escape being bled, blistered, and plastered" (p. 275). As for George, who now had to shoulder the burden of being nursemaid in addition to cook, housekeeper, budget planner, schoolmistress, and novelist, she quickly lost all confidence in the Majorcan medical profession. One doctor's assistant was so filthy, she claimed, that Chopin wouldn't even allow him to take his pulse. Furthermore, she discovered, it was impossible to obtain anything other than the most primitive remedies in the Palma pharmacies. "May heaven help us," she prayed, "for there are neither doctors nor medicine here."[12]

Soon it was evident that Chopin could not possibly endure the sooty, mildewed environment of *Son Vent* for another eight weeks or more of the rainy season, and the beleaguered household began to prepare for an evacuation. George's plan was to move into the cells she had rented in the monastery at Valldemosa, which she hoped to have ready by the first week in December. To furnish them she bargained with a Spanish political refugee and his wife, living in the charterhouse, and for a thousand francs acquired most of what she needed. This consisted of a number of crude items, "charming enough in this country," she admitted, "but which not even a peasant at home would want" (p. 531).

By the third of the month the move seemed imminent and George wrote Grzymała, "In three days we will be living in our beautiful charterhouse in the most magnificent setting. We have bought some furniture and so, here we are, property-owners in Majorca! . . . I still am not able to get any work done yet. We are not settled so far and have to struggle along without beasts of burden, servants, water, fire, or even any means of mailing manuscripts" (p. 529). The same day Chopin, somewhat revived by the prospect of leaving *Son Vent,* wrote Fontana enthusiastically, "In a few days I shall be living in the most beautiful spot on earth, surrounded by sea, mountains, and everything you can imagine. I am moving into an enormous old cloister which has been abandoned. It seems that Mend[izábal] chased the monks out of it just for my benefit. It is near Palma and nothing could be more gorgeous. It has arcades and the most poetic cemetery—in a word, everything will be perfect for me there." [13]

But the anticipated move did not take place as scheduled since George was not able to finish her preparations at the monastery in time. To make things worse she now feared that Chopin was really not in any condition to be moved at all, "especially with the transport available and in such weather." [14] Then suddenly events took an unexpected turn which left her with no choice in the matter. "One morning," she explained, "when we were greatly alarmed by the continuance of the rains and by the troubles directly and indirectly caused by them, a letter reached us from the boorish Gómez, announcing, in Spanish style, that we were harboring a personage, who was harboring a disease, which was bringing infection into his hearth, and constituted a threat to the lives of his family; consequently he requested us to clear out of his palace with the least possible delay" (p. 46). George was furious, but no matter how cold, drenched, bedraggled, and desperate she may have been, her spirit remained undampened: "Sr.

Gómez's edict caused me little regret," she snorted, "since I feared that if we stayed there much longer we should be drowned in our beds" (p. 47).

Where, though, were they to go? "The news of our consumption had spread rapidly," she learned, "and we could no longer hope to find any sort of lodging, even if we paid in gold and stayed for only a single night. We were well aware that whoever might offer to take us in would not be himself immune to prejudice, and that by accepting the favor we should involve him in the burden of censure which weighed upon us" (p. 47).

While it is true that the Majorcans' reaction to the strangers in their midst was one of callous indifference or outright hostility for the most part, it is only fair in defense of the islanders to explain their situation. In the mid-eighteenth century an edict had been promulgated by Fernando VI stating that any doctor who failed to report a case of consumption would be fined 200 ducats and suspended from practice for a year. For a second offence the fine was doubled and the physician condemned to exile for four years. In addition the patient's linens, clothes, furniture, and other objects used by him were ordered to be burned. Any person who waited on the sick patient (such as nurses, domestics, etc.) faced imprisonment for thirty days if they failed to report the illness, and the sentence was increased to four years if they were caught twice in failing to report such a case.

With these harsh penalties, it is somewhat easier to understand why the Majorcans were less than eager to help their unfortunate visitors. Because of his tenants, the law required Sr. Gómez to refurnish much of *Son Vent,* a predicament which did little to elicit George's sympathy. Even years later she could still become incensed whenever she remembered the great scene he had made, threatening "legal action because we had damaged a few earthenware plates, for which he made us pay as though they had been porcelain. He also bullied us into paying for the whitewashing and redecoration of the entire house, to disinfect it after our invalid's catarrh. . . . In his

anxiety to be rid of everything we had touched, he was eager
to sell us all the *Son Vent* household linen . . . charging for his
old linens at the price of new" (p. 47).

With an eviction notice in one hand, an invalid on the other,
two young children underfoot, and torrential rains overhead,
Mme Sand was on the brink of despair. Everywhere she
looked in Palma, doors were closed in her face. Finally M.
Flury, risking ostracism and contagion, took the sick and
stranded travelers into his home on December 10. "But for
the hospitality of the French consul, who worked miracles to
gather us all under his roof," George acknowledged
gratefully, "we should have faced the prospect of camping in
some cave like proper gipsies" (p. 47). Meanwhile, "the deluge
continued," but at least Mme Sand and her brood could endure it now that they were warm and dry for the first time in
weeks. Weary and weatherbeaten, they "rarely left the fireplace which the consul had the good fortune to possess" (p.
49).

For four days they took advantage of M. Flury's comfortable hearth, and during this brief respite George had a chance
to assess her financial status. To her alarm, she discovered that
the purchase of furniture for the cloister, the payment of
"damages" to Sr. Gómez, and the cost of transporting her
flock out of Establiments had depleted her resources more
than she realized. To offset these expenses she was forced to
draw 3,000 francs on her letter of credit to the Banco Canut y
Mugnerot. The price of their little Majorcan "idyll" was
mounting extravagantly!

Tired and disillusioned, George no longer had any enthusiasm for the island. Outside, she watched the gray streaks of
rain spatter against the windowpanes, transforming the Ca'n
Berga palace across the street into a shimmering blur. As the
water trickled slowly across the glass, her whole world seemed
to dissolve into a gloomy nightmare of slithering shadows,
grotesque and frightening. Discouraged to the point of tears,
she sat down at the consul's desk and gave vent to her desperation in an angry letter to Charlotte Marliani. In it she com-

plained of everything. Had Buloz received her manuscript of
Spiridion? If their present misfortunes continued she would
certainly be needing the extra money it would bring. The
manuscript, though, was probably lost at sea, she imagined in
her despondent state of mind—lost, that is, if the mail boat
containing it had ever left Palma in the first place. "The
steamer between Palma and Barcelona," she informed her
friend,

> is primarily concerned with the transport of pigs. Passengers are
> of secondary importance and the mail doesn't count at all. What
> difference does it make to the Majorcans whether they know
> what is going on in the world of politics or fine arts? The pig is
> the major if not the only concern in their lives. The boat is
> scheduled to leave every week; but actually it never goes unless
> the weather is perfectly serene and the sea as smooth as a sheet
> of glass. The slightest puff of wind will make it come back into
> port, even when it is already half-way to Barcelona. Why? . . .
> because the pig has a delicate stomach and might get seasick. If
> one of the little creatures ever dies the whole crew goes into
> mourning and newspapers, passengers, letters, packages, and
> the rest can go to the devil. . . . All in all, our trip here, is, in
> many respects, an appalling fiasco.[15]

Throughout these miserable days, according to George,
Chopin behaved like "an angel." But he, too, was as discouraged as she. Since they had left Establiments he no longer had
any piano at all and could do nothing with his compositions,
even on those days when his strength would permit. This enforced idleness only left his mind all the more free to brood
and fret. When word finally came concerning the piano he
had ordered from Pleyel, it did little to raise his spirits. "On
the first of December," he heard, "the piano was loaded on to
a merchant ship in Marseille. . . . I suppose," he predicted
glumly, "it will spend the winter in port, where the boat will
remain at anchor (for nobody budges here when it rains). . . .
Meanwhile my manuscripts sleep while I can't.[16]
In spite of their hardships, both George and Chopin were
determined to stay on in Majorca and make the most of the

situation until spring. "We wouldn't be able to leave," George calculated, "without exposing ourselves to the bad weather and without creating new expenses hand over fist. Besides," she added, "it cost me so much strength and energy to get here. If Providence is not too hard on us, we can assume that the worst is over and that we are going to enjoy the fruits of our labor. Spring will be delicious."[17] Chopin also looked forward to the coming of spring, though with less optimism than George. "I keep coughing," he groaned, "all covered with poultices, I am waiting for the spring or," he intimated somberly, "something else."[18]

At last the preparations for the monastery were completed and the move to Valldemosa scheduled for the fifteenth of December. "Fortunately my ambulance is running well,"[19] George quipped. The prospects of a new and more congenial environment had brightened the outlook of all concerned. "Tomorrow," Chopin told Fontana, "I am going to that marvelous monastery at Valldemosa to write in the cell of an old monk who may have had more fire in his soul than I have, but who smothered it, smothered and extinguished it because it was wasted on him."[20] And to Mme Marliani, George wrote, "Tomorrow we leave for the charterhouse at Valldemosa, the most poetic home on earth. There we will spend the winter, which has hardly begun but which will soon be over."[21]

&⅗ CHAPTER TWELVE ⅖ঙ

I T WAS A cloudless mid-December morning," George recalled, "during one of those beaming spells of autumn sunshine which soon became more and more uncommon, and we set out for Valldemosa to take possession of our Carthusian cell. After crossing the fertile plain of Establiments, we reached an indeterminate terrain, here covered with trees, there dry and stony, there again moist and fresh—everywhere shifting its character with an abruptness that I have never seen paralleled elsewhere. . . . Neither Switzerland nor the Tyrol had shown this aspect of free primeval creation which was so delightful in Majorca."[1]

So George reminisced several years later about the picturesque nine-mile journey from Palma to the semi-deserted monastery which was to be their home for the next fifty-eight days. But Chopin, sick and miserable, had none of his exuberant companion's enthusiasm. For him the trip was scarcely a delight. Buried under a mound of poultices, he bumped along for three interminable hours in one of the two wooden carts they had hired for the move. "The roads here," he complained, "are dredged out of creekbeds and paved by landslides. One day you can't get through at all and the next, only a mule can make it. And what contraptions you have to ride in here??!!"[2]

Perhaps time had softened the harshness of reality for George since her memoirs record the event as if it were a poetic pilgrimage with nature blooming under "the kisses of a burning sky," and smiling "beneath the gusts of warm winds that brush over her as they roam the seas."[3] Nearing their destination, she wrote, "the narrow vale of Valldemosa

opened before us like a spring garden" (p. 98). As they approached the village the rugged pair of *birlochos* rattled up a
cobblestone road and passed between two walls bearing the
coat-of-arms of Aragon. These heraldic insignia had been
carved in commemoration of the monastery's founding in
1399 by Don Martín d'Aragón. Further ahead, leading to the
charterhouse itself, was a stairway bordered by more stone
walls, overgrown with ivy and brambles, but majestically lined
with columns of tall cypress trees.

The ascent was full of magnificent views. Captivated,
George watched the scenery unfold "at each step, growing
lovelier and lovelier the higher one climbs. I have seen nothing more inviting," she exclaimed, "yet at the same time more
melancholy, than these steep slopes where the varied tints of
holm-oak, carob-trees, pine, olive, poplar, and cypress blend
in thick arbors, unfathomable depths of greenery, and the tor-
rent plunges headlong through groves of lavish exuberance
and incomparable grace" (p. 98).

From time to time, they stopped to look out across the valley. "I shall never forget," George recalled, "a bend of the pass
where a backward glance reveals one of those charming Arab
cottages . . . perched on a hill, half-hidden among its jointed
prickly pears, and dominated by a tall palm tree which leans
over the chasm, its silhouette black against the heavens" (p.
98).

Further up on the slopes of the *Cartuja* the monks, "with
vast labor," had "converted the higher part of the valley into
an extensive garden by terrace-walls." On beyond the monastery, a pass emerged into another broad valley and, in
George's description, "widens as it slopes gently down on the
other side of the hill toward the steep coastal cliffs, at whose
feet the sea pounds and corrodes. . . . It is a sublime picture
. . . one of those overwhelming views that leave nothing to be
desired, nothing to the imagination. Whatever poet and
painter might dream, Nature has here created . . . Art could
never add anything to it" (p. 98).

In order to continue their journey, the travelers had to

abandon the two carts at the foot of the stairway and proceed by foot up to the lovely shaded square in front of the monastery. Over the gateway at its entrance a bas-relief of Saint Bruno projected out above an inscription which read *Jesus Nazarenus Cartucia Maioricar.*

Once inside the charterhouse, George and Frédéric found themselves in a fantastic maze of architectural history. To the original fourteenth-century buildings a conglomeration of newer courtyards, corridors, and chapels had been added, dating from the fifteenth through the eighteenth centuries. Wandering under their arched vaults, the new inhabitants could still detect the stale, sweet odor of incense. Although three years had elapsed since Mendizábal's eviction of the monastic colony, little had changed in the *Cartuja*—the prior's chair, surrounded by withered flowers and half-burned candles, still remained near the altar. Religious paintings hung askew on the walls while dented chalices and broken candle snuffers lay tarnishing in the dust.

Past the Gothic church which stood near the entrance was the abandoned cemetery, now weed-infested but still dominated by a slender white cross. Under a heavy stone arch beside it crouched a squat little well with a rusty iron wheel that creaked and groaned in the autumn breeze. Behind this, three pointed cypress trees swayed gently in the wind like huge metronomes, marking the passage of time against the pale gray of the distant mountains. The walls and window ledges of the cloisters which enclosed the cemetery were overgrown with moss and ivy as were the graves of the nameless Carthusian brothers resting there. Only the weathered orange tiles of the neighboring rooftops brightened the calm solemnity of this ghostly scene.

Across the cemetery, where even the chatter of George's children became absorbed in the damp silence, stood another cloister with a broad corridor five hundred feet in length. Along the walls of this drafty passage the whitewash of previous centuries peeled and flaked into a chalky powder underfoot. From the stone floor the staccato of footsteps echoed with a chilling sharpness down the long hall and faded slowly into the pulsating stillness. In the shadows along one side of the dim corridor twelve large doors lurked in the dark recesses of the wall. Each led through an abandoned cell into a row of ill-kempt gardens overlooking the ravine at the foot of the charterhouse. One of these austere monastic enclaves, consisting of three barren rooms, was to lodge the five newcomers for the succeeding two months.

Passing through their cells to the terrace on the other side, Mme Sand looked down into the valley below as the rays of the late afternoon sun filtered through the cloud-filled sky and slashed across the treetops in sparkling yellow streaks. "What lovely plays of light we were able to study," she wrote. The mountain ridges were bathed in a liquid glow of gold and purple while "the clusters of dates on our palm trees seemed clusters of rubies, and a long line of shadow, cutting obliquely across the valley divided it into two zones, one flooded with summer lights, the other blue-tinged and cold as a winter landscape" (p. 100).

Carried away by the luxury with which nature had endowed this corner of the island, the little band of newcomers set down their luggage and began to take stock of their musty quarters. They consisted of "three large, gracefully arched rooms, ventilated at the base by rosettes—no two alike and of a very graceful design—cut through the yard-thick wall to the outside air" (p. 118). The three rooms, situated side by side in a row, had once constituted a single monk's cell and their walls still bore printed fragments of latin prayers pasted there by an earlier occupant. When inhabited by the Carthusian brothers, the middle room had been intended for reading, prayer, and contemplation, and a large combined prayer desk and grandfather chair, from six to eight feet tall still remained firmly attached to the wall. Next to this room was another which had served as the monk's bedroom. Through the doorway leading into it an old bed could still be seen standing against the opposite wall, "in a very low recess . . . with stone slabs piled above it in sepulchral style." The third room had originally been a combination "workshop, dining room, and store room." A fireplace had been built into it at one time, but in typical Majorcan fashion, "the architect had not been skillful enough to design a chimney that drew" (pp. 118, 119). As a result, George and her maid were forced to cook outdoors as the monks had done, using two small charcoal stoves protected by a porch at the entrance to the garden. A third stove inside proved to be the only source of heat for the rooms and exposed the unlucky travelers once more to the same foul-smelling smoke that had tormented them so recently in *Son Vent.*

Beyond the small porch which sheltered their "kitchen" was a lovely garden occupying the same space as the three rooms of the cell and overlooking "an orange grove that spread from one end to the other of the mountain tier immediately below." Beneath this stretched a series of more distant terraces filled with grape arbors, almond trees, and palms, "down to the bottom of the valley which . . . seemed one huge garden" (p. 119).

In the small plot that served as George and Frédéric's garden were four square flower beds irrigated by a network of stone conduits and separated by neatly laid-out brick paths. Here pomegranate, lemon, and orange trees as well as "fragrant arbors" shaded the narrow walkways, making the cultivated little enclosure like "an elegant drawing room full of flowers and greenery" (p. 119).

The furniture George had bought was "magnificent," she claimed with a certain degree of sarcasm. What they owned, according to her account, included several "trestle-beds with which nobody could have quarreled; clean, new mattresses, though not very soft and more expensive than in Paris; and those fine large coverlets, made of quilted and padded chintz purchaseable for a fair enough price from the Palma Jews." Sra Choussat de Canut "kindly lent us several pounds of feathers . . . and with these we made our invalid a couple of pillows . . . the height of luxury in a country where geese are regarded as beings from another world. . . ." In addition, "we had several tables, numerous straw-bottomed chairs like those seen in French peasants' cottages; also a voluptuous deal sofa and cushions for it of wool-stuffed ticking. The uneven, crumbling floor of the cell was covered with those long-strawed Valencian mats which resemble sun-yellowed turf, and with those splendid long-haired sheepskins, of admirable quality and whiteness . . ." (p. 141). As the cell contained no cupboards or chests, the new inhabitants had to use the trunks they had brought for storage and, considering the general tone of their rustic quarters, George felt they could easily "pass for elegant pieces of furniture. A big, multi-colored tartan shawl, used as a foot rug on our journey," her *Winter in Majorca* records, "now became a magnificent curtain to screen the alcove, and my son enlivened the stove with one of those delightful clay vases from the town of Felanitx, shaped and decorated in pure Moorish style." Their most prized piece of furniture they wheedled out of the sacristan, who had "been persuaded," so George claimed, "to move into our cell a large splendid Gothic chair of carved oak, which was being eaten away by worms and rats in a disused Carthusian chapel. Its frame served us as a book-case while, after dark, by the gleam of lamplight, its pierced fretwork and tapering spires cast on the wall a rich, lacy shadow with magnificent pinnacles, and completely restored the ancient monastic character of the cell" (p. 142).

Admittedly cramped and crude, their new lodgings nevertheless charmed Mme Sand, whose fertile imagination grew all but delirious in an atmosphere so heavily saturated with history, romance, and the supernatural. "I do hope," she wrote in an exuberant moment, "we shall have some ghosts."[4]

The *Cartuja,* however, did not inspire Chopin with such amusing fancies. The setting was indeed dramatic and beautiful, but at the same time grim and bleak. In the eerie loneliness of their remote hideaway he began to feel a morbid uneasiness. Shortly after his arrival he wrote Fontana,

> You can imagine me, between the cliffs and the sea, in a cell of a huge deserted Carthusian monastery with doors larger than any

carriage entrance in Paris. My hair is disheveled, I am without my white gloves, and look as pale as always. My cell, which is shaped like a big coffin, has an enormous dusty vaulted ceiling and a small window opening onto orange trees, palms, and cypresses in the garden. Opposite the window under a Moorish filagreed rose window stands my trestle bed. Beside the bed is a horrible old square so-called desk that is almost impossible to write on, and on top of this there is a leaden candlestick with (what they consider a great luxury here) a candle. . . . On the same desk there are volumes of Bach, my own scribbled manuscripts, and some other papers which don't belong to me. Silence . . you can shout at the top of your voice . . . still silence. In brief, I am writing you from a very weird place.[5]

Even George had to agree that the forsaken old charterhouse had a somewhat unsettling effect on her, too, and ventured to "challenge the calmest and coolest brain to preserve perfect sanity here over a long period."[6] Sudden and unexpected noises were forever shattering the stillness of the cavernous old structure, and with it the equilibrium of its occupants. "When the wind slams a door," she wrote a friend in Paris, "it sounds like a cannon blast throughout the whole building."[7] While she never, in fact, saw the ghosts she had looked forward to with so much relish it was not because she didn't search for them. Often at midnight she would take her children walking through the cemetery in a mood of "mingled distress and pleasure." Maurice and Solange, however, appeared quite insensitive to the atmosphere, and "would run gladly in the moonlight under broken arches that seemed to be summoning witches to their Sabbath merry-making."[8] One night, though, when they encountered an old servant of the Carthusians prowling the cloisters, drunk and half-crazed, "uttering threats and fearful curses," these macabre nocturnal strolls abruptly ceased.

As it turned out, this poor, demented creature proved to be only one of several bizarre inmates of the sprawling old monastery. Another, less frightening but equally unwelcome, was María Antonia, whom George described as "what you might call a woman of confidence" (p. 101). She lived next door to them and soon insinuated herself into their household under the guise of a solicitous friend, all the while stealthily making off with whatever she could lay her hands on. Her program of infiltration was simple but clever. In exchange for putting up George's maid from Paris and allowing them the use of a few battered kitchen utensils, she made herself at home in their quarters and helped herself to their clothes and provisions. "I have never seen a pious mouth with a greater relish for delicacies," George cried, "or fingers nimbler at snatching morsels from the bottom of boiling stews without getting scalded, or a more capacious throat for slyly ingurgitating her beloved host's sugar and coffee while continuing to hum a hymn or a *bolero*" (p. 102).

The other two residents of the delapidated structure that winter were the sacristan and the apothecary. Although they were both eccentrics of rather dubious character, neither was as meddlesome or as avaricious as María Antonia. "The sacristan was a hefty young fellow who had once perhaps acted as acolyte for the Carthusians and since taken charge of the monastery keys. He had a disgraceful record: being guilty in fact and in law of having seduced and got with child a young lady who had spent a few months there with her parents. He pleaded in excuse that the only virgins whom the state had commissioned him to protect were the ones in the monastery paintings." To George's dismay, both the sacristan and his sister were great "cronies of María Antonia, who, if she did not happen to feel hungry, would often invite them to eat our dinner for her" (p. 103).

The apothecary, on the other hand, was something of a recluse and seldom, if ever, bothered his neighbors. For the most part he remained in his own quarters lined with jars of Catalan porcelain and Majorcan glass which contained a variety of medieval remedies of obscure origin. Among these, George swore, were "drugs with curious names and long forgotten virtues such as 'the Nail Parings of the Great Beast.' "[9] A former monk at Valldemosa, the devout old man would regularly "shut himself up in his cell, resume his once-white habit, and chant the offices in solitary state. . . . If we had not visited him several times to buy his juleps," George declared, "we should never have suspected that a Carthusian was still about."[10]

Apart from these few souls, she and Chopin found themselves alone in that vast, windswept charterhouse perched in crumbling grandeur on the rocky slopes of Valldemosa.

THE SINISTER GLOOM that stalked the empty corridors of the charterhouse at night seemed to vanish with the morning mists as they rose out of the valley below the semi-deserted building. The spirits from previous centuries that haunted its chapel and roamed its graveyard receded swiftly into the past at daybreak. While the rambling old *Cartuja* lost none of its poetic charm after sunrise, life within its doors nevertheless assumed a more prosaic tenor during the daylight hours. Each morning George and her little household abandoned their narrow trestle beds to set about the daily chores necessary for survival in their secluded mountain refuge.

To live they had to eat, but the Majorcan diet, which consisted mainly of pork, pepper, and oil, was unpalatable to Chopin. He simply could not tolerate it and even George herself found it highly disagreeable. "I am sure," she insisted, "that more than two thousands different dishes are prepared from the pig in Majorca, and at least two hundred kinds of black pudding, so liberally seasoned with garlic, black and red pepper, and corrosive spices of every sort that you hazard your life with every bite."[1] Heavy, greasy, and ubiquitous, pork was second in popularity only to pepper, which George complained was "the very essence of Majorcan existence. They eat it, drink it, plant it, breathe it, talk about it, and dream of it."[2] Unable to stomach "the incendiary methods of the native kitchen," Mme Sand and her family resorted to a diet of "lean meat, fish, and vegetables" to which they added "as an occasional indulgence" the juices of a sour orange freshly picked from their garden.

Astonishingly enough even these simple items proved almost impossible to acquire. The reason, George claimed, was their failure to attend mass on Sundays. Because of this the villagers regarded them as heathens and took it upon themselves "to avenge the glory of God in a most un-Christian manner," by banding together in a refusal to sell "their fish, eggs, or vegetables except at prohibitive cost. At the slightest objection a peasant would reply with the air of a Spanish grandee: 'You don't want any? Then you shan't have any!' and, replacing the onions or potatoes in his sack, would stalk augustly away. . . . The punishment thus inflicted on us for bargaining," she discovered, "was to go hungry. . . . On wet days no carrier was willing to venture out at any price; and since it rained on and off for two months, we frequently nibbled bread as hard as ship's biscuit and dined like true Carthusians."[3] Finally, to ensure a reliable source of sustenance, they purchased a goat and a sheep which they milked themselves. The poor animals were not very productive but the thin liquid they yielded made "a quite wholesome and pleasant infusion when mixed with milk of almonds" (p. 151).

Overseeing the kitchen could easily have become a full-time occupation if George had not had so many other tasks that demanded her attention at the same time. "Everyday," she wrote, "I spend six or seven hours working with my children."[4] "I have plunged with Maurice into Thucydides and Co.: with Solange, into indirect objects and the agreement of the participle" (p. 537).

At the end of the day when the youngsters had gone to bed, she settled down to her manuscripts. "I spend half the night doing my own work" (p. 534), she wrote, and with typical perseverance she now began to accomplish many of the things she intended to do when they first arrived on the island. The revealing portrait she had inadvertantly drawn of herself in the first edition of *Lélia* eventually became an embarrassment to the author, who had grown less impulsive and more philosophic over the years. As early as 1836 she had begun to revise several of the more notorious passages in the novel, and during her stay in Majorca, she completed her revision which appeared in print for the first time in 1839. This altered version of the book tempered some of the more sensational features that had shocked the public six years before. In the new *Lélia* chastity is no longer something which love is meant to conquer; it exists as an ideal above and beyond love. Apparently the combination of George's exhaustion and Chopin's illness had brought the novelist to realize that love could still flourish even in the face of enforced chastity—a condition once so abhorent to her.

In addition to refurbishing *Lélia,* George was still attempting to put the finishing touches on *Spiridion*. Finally, after endless delays, she wrote Mme Marliani on the twenty-eighth of December: "I am sending you the last part of *Spiridion*. . . . Please see that it gets to Buloz immediately" (p. 536). As it turned out, her publisher was not at all happy with the high-flown sentiments expressed in Mme Sand's pretentious new work. "For God's sake . . . not so much mysticism,"[5] he wrote back after having read it. Undaunted, George explained to countess Marliani, "I must tell you that anything the least bit profound in scope terrifies . . . Buloz."[6] In reality Mme Sand herself was not too pleased with the ending of her novel, "but what can you do," she protested, "when you are being rushed to death by a blasted magazine?" (p. 561).

Despite her irritation, she could not afford to be too independent since she was badly in need of money just then. Before their return to France she realized that she would have to ask Buloz for an advance of 3,000 francs in order to repay her loan from the bank of Canut y Mugnerot. Even with this, her financial situation still remained so desperate that she directed her half-brother, Hippolyte, to sell Côte-Noire, a portion of her estate at Nohant. "It is absolutely necessary to give up some of my rents," she informed him. "It is a matter of survival, and I assure you that I must be made of iron to endure what I am doing (p. 557). Had it not truly been a matter of survival, nothing could have induced George to sacrifice a part of Nohant. But she and her little clan would soon be reduced to the barest necessities if money were not quickly available.

Whenever the weather permitted George loved to escape from the monastery, leave her chores and worries behind, and take her children for a walk over the rugged countryside around Valldemosa. Chopin, however, seldom accompanied them on these excursions, preferring instead to remain in the charterhouse and devote himself to his compositions. All the unexpected expenses of their trip had put him in a position where he had to work now despite his illness and lack of a decent piano. Back in Paris, Léo was becoming impatient over the 1,000 francs he owed him, but until the Preludes were finished there was no way to repay the banker. "What a Jew that Léo is!" he fumed in a letter to Fontana. "I can't possibly send you the Preludes; they aren't done yet. My health is better and I will hurry up. As for the Jew, he will be receiving a short, explicit letter from me which he can swallow right down to his heels (or wherever you like), the scoundrel!"[7]

Struggling against the weakness and depression brought on by the damp gloom of the Majorcan winter, Chopin sat day after day in front of the wretched little piano they had brought from *Son Vent* while he worked and re-worked each of the unfinished Preludes. "With what poetry his music filled that sanctuary," George recalled, "even in the midst of his most painful sufferings."[8] Often he found himself alone when the others went for a walk or rode into Palma for household supplies. Sitting by himself in the dimness of his starkly furnished cell he could hear the wind howling down the corridor outside his door and the rain splashing on the tiles overhead. From the roof the water trickled down the gutter into the stone conduits of the garden and overflowed in small rivulets on to the soggy soil beneath his window. The acrid smell of smoke from the stove irritated his throat while the incense George bought in the monastery pharmacy to combat the stench of burned charcoal only aggravated his cough all the more. As his strength waned, his spirits flagged. He became so morose that he could scarcely concentrate on his work.

Small things irritated him out of all proportion to their significance and he grew so moody and unpredictable in his behavior that he seemed almost irrational at times.

George noted all this and brooded over it. "The mournful cry of the famished eagle from the Majorcan crags, the sharp whistling of the winter wind and the bleak desolation of the snow-clad yews," she observed, "depressed him much longer and more acutely than he could ever be cheered by the perfume of the orange trees, the graceful beauty of the vines, or the moorish songs of the laborer" (p. 442).*

Yet, under these adverse circumstances Chopin eventually succeeded in completing the last of his Preludes. "They are masterpieces" (p. 442), George asserted, and her musical judgment, though often fallible, has generally been supported in regard to these compositions. "Several," she wrote, "bring to mind visions of departed monks with the sound of funeral dirges hovering over them. Others are soft and melancholy. . . . Still others have a mournful sadness that charms the ear as it breaks the heart. There is one," she remembered,

> which he composed one dismal rainy evening and which plunges the soul into the depths of despair. Maurice and I had left him in fine shape that morning to go to Palma to buy some essential items for our little outpost. The rains had come and the creeks had overflowed. It took us six hours to go three leagues, and we came back in the midst of a flood. We arrived back in the middle of the night, having lost our shoes and been abandoned by our driver to face the most incredible dangers alone. Knowing our invalid would be worried, we tried to hurry. He had, in fact, been quite upset and had become almost transfixed in a sort of quiet despair, sobbing as he played his marvelous prelude. When he saw us enter, he jumped up with a loud cry and spoke with a strange voice in a distraught manner. "Ah, I knew for sure you were dead!" After he had recovered his spirits and saw the state we were in he became sick at the thought of all the perils we had been through. Later he told me that in waiting for us he had seen all that had occurred in a

---

*The reference to "snow-clad yews" (if George Sand's memory is correct) would suggest that the winter of 1838–1839 must have been unusually severe in Majorca.

dream, and mistaking the dream for reality he tried to calm himself by playing the piano, which lulled him into a state where he was convinced that he himself was dead. He saw himself drowned in a lake with drops of icy water falling heavily and rhythmically on his chest. When I made him listen to the noise of the water falling in the same rhythm on the roof he denied having heard it. He even got mad at what I described as "imitative harmony." He objected, vehemently and rightly so, to the childishness of such auditory imitations. His genius was full of the mysterious harmonies of Nature, translated sublimely in his musical phrases without the slavish repetition of external sounds. His composition that evening was indeed full of raindrops echoing on the resonant tiles of the Charterhouse but transformed by his imagination and his music into tears from heaven falling on his heart. (p. 439)*

Around the twenty-first of December the Pleyel piano finally arrived in Palma. Each day Chopin hoped to move it up to Valldemosa, but there were interminable delays. For over a week the piano sat untouched in the port because the customs officials were demanding a "gold mine" for it. The amount, in the neighborhood of 700 francs, was, according to George, almost the price of the instrument. "We would have liked to send it back," she said, "but that's not permissible; to leave it in port pending a new appraisal in not allowed; to have it moved outside the city in order to avoid at least the port duty, which is something aside from the customs duty, is against the law; to leave it in the city in order to avoid the exit duty which is different from the entry duty is not possible; to toss it into the sea costs still more if we are even allowed to do that."[9]

Since Chopin was too ill to go to Palma to extract the piano from the obstinate officials, the burden fell on George. With the incessant rains, one could never predict when, if ever, the

* If there is a certain fanciful ring to George's account of this so-called "Raindrop" prelude, it should be remembered that even Chopin came to admit "she does not always tell the truth—but," he pointed out philosophically, "that is the privilege of a novelist." The exact identity of the prelude in question has never been determined. Candidates for the honor have included: no. 6 in B Minor, no. 8 in F-sharp Minor, no. 15 in D-flat Major, no. 17 in A-flat Major, no. 19 in E-flat Major and no. 20 in C Minor.

roads would be passable. But, knowing how much the piano meant to her companion, Mme Sand shuttled back and forth between Palma and the charterhouse in all sorts of weather to retrieve the valuable instrument, which, as expenses mounted, was growing more and more precious every day.

At last, sometime after the fifteenth of January, Chopin received the piano and wrote Pleyel on the twenty-second: "I am sending you my *Preludes.* I finished them on your little piano which arrived in the best possible condition despite the sea, the bad weather, and the Palma customs."[10] In the same letter he added, "I should let you know that there are still other manuscripts at your disposal: 1. The Ballade [in F Major, Opus 38] . . . 2. Two Polonaises [in A major and C Minor, Opus 40] . . . 3. A third Scherzo [in C Minor, Opus 39]" (p. 292).* From all of these he hoped to be able to make enough to pay for the rest of the trip.

The effort of finishing these compositions had exhausted Chopin, who now seldom ventured outside his cell at all. This was just as well, since the Majorcans' hostility toward the couple in the *Cartuja* was increasing to the point where George claimed some of the islanders even threw stones at them when they appeared in public. Except for their next door neighbor, María Antonia and her friends (who exuded such a "smell of rancid oil and garlic" that it "literally caught at one's throat")[11] she and Chopin had virtually no contact with anyone in the village.

The truth was, George did not really care for the Majorcans any more than they did for her. She looked down on them, peasant and aristocrat alike, with a contempt which she made little attempt to disguise. "A people's character," she pointed out,

> stands revealed by their domestic customs and furnishings, as clearly as by their features and language. . . . I visited a fair

---

*In addition Chopin also composed the so-called "Palman" Mazurka in E Minor, Opus 41, no. 2 and probably worked on parts of the Sonata in B-flat Minor, Opus 35 and the two Nocturnes of Opus 37.

number of houses. The contents of all were so remarkably alike that I could deduce from them a character common to the inhabitants. . . . Everything cried out in witness against carelessness and indolence; there was never a book to be seen, never a piece of handiwork. The men did not read, the women did not even sew. A smell of garlic from the kitchen was the only indication of domestic activity; and the only signs of private recreation were cigar butts littering the floor. (p. 54)

In a typical upper class home, she noted, "The master of the house will be found on his feet, smoking amid a deep silence, the mistress will be occupying a huge chair and flirting her fan without a thought in her head. No children are ever to be seen: they live with the servants in the kitchen, or the attic, or somewhere else; the parents do not bother about them. A chaplain wanders idly around the house. The twenty or thirty menservants take their siesta, while a hirsute chambermaid opens the door at the visitor's fifteenth ring of the bell" (p. 55). In short, George found the Majorcan upper classes to be "the enemy of activity, of innovation, traditionalist to the core,"[12] a vegetative society, totally opposed to any notion of progress.

As for the Majorcan peasant, her opinion of him was equally low. He might be "a gentle, kind creature with peaceful habits and a tranquil, patient nature," she admitted. But, while he had "no love of evil," neither did he seem to have any "knowledge of good" as far as she could see.

He goes to confession, prays, and thinks incessantly of how to earn an entry to paradise, yet is ignorant of the true obligations of humankind. You can no more hate him than you could an ox or a sheep, for he is close to the savage, whose soul is lulled in animal innocence. He recites his prayer like the superstitious savage; but he would eat his fellow man without a qualm, were that the custom of his country, and were he unable to satisfy himself fully with pork. He cheats, extorts, lies, abuses, and plunders without the least scruple, where foreigners are concerned, not regarding these as fellow men. Though he would never rob his neighbor of so much as an olive he believes that in God's scheme of things the only use for human beings from overseas is to bring the Majorcans nice little profits.[13]

So generous and considerate with her own Berrichon peasantry around Nohant, Mme Sand not only scorned the poor
Majorcan peasants, she scarcely even condescended to pay
them any attention at all. Such arrogant indifferences seemed
in their eyes an even more cutting insult than her invective.
When she failed to put in an appearance at the local feast of
St. Anthony which took place virtually on her doorstep, the
villagers were exceedingly miffed. After all, St. Anthony was
the patron saint of Majorca. "You can't imagine how offended
these good people were that G. Sand had not deigned to attend their celebration that morning," another visitor to the
island commented. "The curate, especially, was highly mortified over it. *'Por cierto,'* he said to me, *'que esta señora francesa
tiene que ser una muger [sic] muy particular*—certainly this french
lady must be a very strange woman. Can you imagine? She
doesn't speak to a living soul, never leaves the Charterhouse,
and never makes an appearance in church, not even on Sundays, piling up God knows how many mortal sins on her
soul." [14]

"Almost to the end of our stay," George wrote, "we remained unaware of how profoundly our way of life shocked
them." [15] Nothing could have indicated more clearly how little
she came to understand the people they lived among that winter.

A further source of alienation between the islanders and the
couple in the *Cartuja* was, of course, Chopin's illness. As the
weeks passed and his cough grew worse, the fearful population shunned the travelers to the point where they were practically cut off from all living contact. "We were alone in Majorca," George realized in the end,

> no less isolated than if we had been living in a desert. . . . Our
> invalid's health continued to deteriorate, the wind sobbed in the
> ravine, the rain beat on our window panes, the voice of the
> thunder penetrated our thick walls, and its gloomy note min-
> gled with the children's laughter and games . . . we felt our-
> selves prisoners far from enlightened help or effectual sympa-
> thy. We could almost see Death hovering over our heads waiting

to seize the sufferer, whom we were single handedly battling to keep alive. No human being within reach but would willingly have hastened him toward the grave, so as to remove the alleged danger of his proximity. (p. 148)

Even with the return of warmer weather and the advent of some sunshine, Chopin's strength failed to revive; if anything, his condition became worse. He grew visibly weaker and hopelessly despondent. "His spirit was flayed alive," George wrote, "the fold of a rose leaf or the shadow of a fly could devastate him."[16] Later in her memoirs she accused him of being "a detestable invalid" (p. 443), and maintained that his disposition became capricious, irritable, and demanding as a result of his suffering. In 1839, however, she was still sufficiently in love to see him only as "an angel of sweetness and goodness."[17]

As the days crept by, Chopin slipped steadily downhill until he began to look like a specter, pale, gaunt, and lifeless. Seeing him so near death, George became frightened. Her fear soon turned to panic, but she could not make up her mind what to do. "Our invalid did not seem fit to stand the crossing," she noted, "but he seemed equally unfit to endure another week in Majorca."[18]

Then, abruptly in early February she decided out of desperation to leave the island immediately. "Our stay at the monastery of Valldemosa was torture for him and a torment for me," she explained. "It is the most beautiful spot I have ever lived in and one of the most magnificent I have ever seen. And yet I hardly enjoyed it at all."[19]

On the eleventh of the month she hired two rough wooden carts and loaded her family and belongings into them. In the harsh winter sunlight of that February morning, the cheerless little band jolted down the ramp leading away from the charterhouse for the last time. Slowly the monastery receded into the background. Little by little the tops of the cypresses faded out of sight. Finally, not even the outline of the cross on the steeple was visible. Within three hours the sick and disillusioned travelers were back in Palma ready to begin the long voyage home to France.

৫%X CHAPTER FOURTEEN ¥৩

I LEFT THE CHARTERHOUSE," George wrote, "with a mixture of joy and sadness. I could easily have spent two or three years there alone with my children. . . . The sky was becoming magnificent, and the island an enchanted spot. Our romantic quarters charmed us. Maurice was growing visibly stronger, and so far as we were concerned we simply laughed off our hardships . . . the invalid himself would have been absolutely fine if he could only have gotten well. . . . And the charterhouse was so beautiful under its festoons of ivy; the blossoming valley so splendid, the air so pure on our mountain, and the sea so blue on the horizon!"[1]

It was only years later, however, that Mme Sand could afford the luxury of rhapsodizing so nostalgically about the Majorcan spring and the happiness it might have held for her.

At noon on February 11, 1839, when the two *birlochos* rattled up to the outskirts of Palma, George was, in fact, quite sated "with weariness and isolation." The warm midday sun and the long, strenuous journey had depleted what little strength remained in her sick companion, and Chopin was now feverish and coughing while she herself was bruised and sore from three hours of ceaseless jogging over the rough mountain roads. Despite her exhaustion, George could find no time to relax. Much still remained to be done prior to their departure. Not only did she have to book their passage on the boat to Barcelona, she also had to arrange for the disposition of the recently-arrived Pleyel piano. This entailed the unpleasant task of returning to the customs office in order to pay the re-entry duties for bringing the instrument back to Palma. Then came the task of trying to sell it.

Because of Chopin's illness, no buyer could be found. The Majorcans' overwhelming fear of contagion made them regard the instrument as contaminated. Mme Choussat de Canut, to whom George had gone for help, tried to persuade a friend, Mme Gradoli, to take the piano. However she did not succeed; Mme Gradoli firmly refused on the grounds that she dared not expose her three young daughters to infection. At last, Mme Choussat herself paid 1,200 francs for it and sold her own piano to the timorous Mme Gradoli.

As for the passage back to the mainland, George discovered that *El Mallorquín,* the boat on which they had come over the previous autumn, was scheduled to depart in two days. Of course, she realized that the erratic nature of the Majorcans left the actual departure date subject to change at any moment. This caused her considerable worry, for Chopin had begun to fail even more swiftly than before. He had not borne the trip to Palma well, and his last bit of endurance was ebbing visibly minute by minute. Tired and tense, she waited nervously for *El Mallorquín;* by then she knew that if Chopin did not leave the island soon there would be no hope for him.

Suddenly, on the evening of the twelfth, Frédéric, who had been coughing up blood from time to time, began to hemorrhage alarmingly. Sitting up in bed, he rasped and choked in such a terrifying manner that he almost collapsed in prostration and George in panic. After that neither could sleep; fear and anxiety plagued them throughout the rest of the night.

Fortunately, the next afternoon the boat sailed as scheduled. Huddled together in their tiny cabin George and Chopin listened gratefully to the noisy bustle overhead as the gangplank was taken up. Soon a muffled rumbling of chains followed as the anchor was weighed, and by three o'clock *El Mallorquín* began to glide out of the harbor. The rhythm of the water splashing on its bow increased gradually as the boat moved slowly into the open part of the bay, rocking restlessly from side to side.

Relieved by their departure, George and Frédéric found little else to comfort them in the crude accommodations to which they had been assigned. The weather was hot, their cabin stuffy, and its dilapidated furnishings filthy. Everywhere the nauseating odor from the ship's cargo of pigs hung in the sickening, stale air.

"On our return journey to Barcelona," George wrote, "it was stiflingly hot, yet we were unable to set foot on deck. Even had we braved the danger of having our legs lopped off by some bad-tempered hog, the captain would never, I am sure, have allowed us to annoy them by our presence."[2]

In these circumstances it is not surprising that Chopin grew still worse on the voyage. Having been given the oldest and most uncomfortable bed on shipboard, he got little if any sleep, which George blamed on the captain. Since he "had already decided to burn the bed in which the invalid slept," she observed, "he naturally wanted it to be the worst one" (p. 26).

On the morning of the fourteenth, as the ship pulled into Barcelona, Chopin was "spitting up one bowl full of blood after another and dragging along like a wraith."[3] George, at this point, was boiling with rage and could scarcely stand the sight of another Spaniard. In such haste "to be done forever with this inhuman race," she did not have the patience to wait for the formalities of their landing. Instead, she "scribbled a note to the French naval commander stationed there, M. Belvès, and sent it to him by a dinghy. Almost at once he came in his barge to fetch us to his ship, the *Méléagre*. When we boarded this fine brig, as clean and elegantly kept as a drawing room; and found ourselves surrounded by intelligent, pleasant faces . . . we felt as if we had been round the world, and come back to civilization after a long stay among the savages of Polynesia."[4]

Within twenty-four hours the ship's doctor had stopped Chopin's hemorrhaging and he was able to be moved ashore into a hotel. "From then on he began to improve steadily."[5]

During the following week while he rested, George sat for long hours at his bedside, smouldering with anger and resentment. Spain and everything Spanish were now anathema to her. "God grant I may leave here soon and never set foot in Spain again," she wrote Mme Marliani on their second day in Barcelona (p. 568). "It would take ten volumes to give you an idea of the cowardice, deceitfulness, selfishness, crudeness, and maliciousness of this stupid, thieving, and bigoted race" (p. 569). The more she thought, the angrier she grew. "Spain is an odious nation! . . . There is no such thing as friendship, trust, honor, devotion, or sociability here. Oh! the wretches! how I hate and despise them!" (p. 586).

By February 18, four days after they had landed, Frédéric was feeling well enough to go to a small seaside resort, Arenys de Mar, where he and George spent several days. On their return to Barcelona they set sail in *Le Phénecien* for Marseille, where they landed thirty-six hours later after a pleasant voyage across the Gulf of Lions.

Although George was safely back on French soil once more, she still could not extinguish her bitter memories of Spain. Like a raging conflagration they swept through her mind and consumed her thoughts. "Oh how I hate Spain!" she cried. "I have left it like the ancients . . . placing a curse on it with every ritual I could invoke. I have shaken the dust from my feet and have made a vow never to speak to a Spaniard again in my life" (p. 577).

After having dashed off this hasty tirade to Mme Marliani, George suddenly recalled with a touch of chagrin that her friend's husband, Manoël, came from Spain. Extricating herself, she insisted with flagrant abandon, "Manoël is not Spanish, my dear. His goodness and warmth, his spirit of justice, his generous and sympathetic instincts all categorically deny any such presumption. He is Italian in regard to his intellect; as for his heart, he is from the planet of the Ideal and insofar as education and manners go, he is French" (p. 577).

Satisfied with this bit of sophistry, George promptly resumed her assault on the Spanish: "One month more and we would have died in Spain, Chopin and I; he of melancholy and disgust and I of anger and indignation" (p. 577). The return to France had fortunately spared them this fate. Their chambermaid, Mme Amélie, however, did not come through the ordeal quite so luckily. As a result of her exposure to the detestable Spaniards it seems she had sunk into the grossest depravity and turned overnight into "a wicked creature who could pervert the very devil himself" (p. 580). Clearly George had no choice but to dismiss her.

Without any help, Mme Sand now found herself even more burdened with responsibilities than before. Her immediate concern, of course, was Chopin, whom she promptly took to be examined by a Dr. Cauvières at the recommendation of the Marlianis. "Your good doctor," she wrote her friends in Paris, "received him like a son and will undoubtedly cure him. I haven't yet been able to talk with him in private," she said, "but I can tell by his manner that he is not worried and has no doubt about the success of his treatment" (p. 578). Only a few days later she was feeling even more optimistic, having been assured by Dr. Cauvières that Chopin showed "no evidence of harm from his illness, no cavity, nothing seriously wrong" (p. 588).

During the quiet weeks that followed, the patient rested and gradually regained his strength. "My health is improving day by day," he wrote Grzymała, "the vesicants, the diet, the pills, the baths, and above all the indefatigable attentions of my angel are putting me back on my feet again—even if they are a little shaky. . . . I have gotten terribly pale and thin, but now I am eating well."[6]

At no time before was Chopin ever so fully aware just how much his survival in Majorca and his recovery in Marseille owed to his "angel," George. She "nursed me all alone," he acknowledged gratefully, "I have seen her make my bed, straighten up my room, prepare hot drinks for me, and deprive herself of everything just for my sake. . . . Besides all this she still manages to write" (p. 310).

Indeed, George never ceased writing. "My angel is finishing her new novel: *Gabriel,*" Chopin told Grzymała in April. "She's going to spend the whole of today writing in bed. You know, you would love her still more if you knew her as I have come to. . . . I understand now what it means to take care of someone" (p. 325).

For George, Chopin was becoming more and more like a second son. "I care for him like a child and he loves me like his mother,"[7] she wrote that February of 1839. In her letters to Grzymała she even began calling the latter "husband" facetiously while referring to Frédéric as their "little boy." This change in her relationship with Chopin, far from disturbing George, actually seemed to please her. She had always preferred the role of mother to that of mistress and, in many respects, nothing could have been better for Chopin himself than the maternal attitude which she now adopted toward him. "She was like those sturdily healthy mothers that seem to transfer magnetically some of their strength to children,"[8] Liszt once commented with unusual accuracy.

Indicative of Chopin's remarkable improvement in Marseille was the fact that he now resumed pestering Fontana and Grzymała with long harangues against his publishers and badgering them with incessant requests for personal favors. "My dear Julian," he wrote the patient Fontana in March of 1839, "you must certainly have heard all about my health and my manuscripts from Grzymała. I forwarded you my preludes from Palma two months ago and asked you to recopy them for Probst. According to my instructions you should have given Léo the 1,000 francs which Probst was to have sent you and used the 1,500 francs from Pleyel for the preludes to pay Nouguès and an installment on my rent to the landlord. . . . I have asked Grzymała to send me at least 500 francs immediately, but don't let that prevent you from sending me the rest as soon as possible."[9]

Hardly had Fontana laid down this letter than others followed with instructions to "pay the concierge those 50 francs. . . . As for the glove-maker and the little tailor, they can wait, the imbeciles! What has become of my papers? Leave my letters in the desk and take my notes home with you or give them to Jasio [Matuszyński]. There are also some letters in the drawer of the little table in the vestibule. Be sure they are locked up. Seal the letter to Schlesinger (and shut him up in it too if you like) with wax" (p. 309). Fearful that something might be left undone, he would scold his poor colleague, "Now don't go to sleep on the job. Love me and write. Forgive me for burdening you with commissions but I believe that you are happy to do what I ask you" (p. 320).

What Frédéric did not request of Fontana, he asked of Grzymała, an equally faithful and long-suffering friend. In fact, so great was Grzymała's devotion that even Chopin found it a bit astonishing: "You know," he wrote him that same March, "your good will amazes me. I am really very grateful in my heart, even if I don't always show it outwardly. You are so kind to have agreed to take in my furniture. Be good enough also," he continued, leading up to the inevitable request, "to pay for the moving. I wouldn't dare to ask you except that I know it won't cost much" (p. 322).

Chopin, as usual, was hard-pressed for money and furious at his publishers whom he blamed for his predicament. Pleyel, he ranted in one of his diatribes, "has dragged me into all sorts of trouble" (p. 322), while Probst "would cheat me even more," and Schlesinger "has tricked me all along" (p. 307). In short, he spluttered, the whole lot of them was nothing more than a bunch of "trashy Germans, Jews, rascals, pigs, swindlers, etc. etc." (p. 329).

Strangely enough now that George and Chopin were settled in Marseille, they began to long for the beautiful calm of their isolated life in Majorca. "I am plagued here just as in Paris," George complained. "From morning until night the idle, curious, and literary beggars lay siege to my door, some by letter, some in person. I have to keep myself on the defensive. I remain inflexible; I neither reply to them nor receive them. I pretend I am sick." Just as she was persecuted by all the "literary rabble" of the city, all the "musical rabble" turned out to hound Chopin. "If this keeps up," George declared, "we will send out announcements that we are both dead so that we can be mourned and left in peace."[10]

Only once did Chopin come out of his self-imposed seclusion to make a public appearance in Marseille. The occasion was a memorial service for his old friend, the celebrated tenor Adolphe Nourrit who committed suicide by throwing himself from a window in Naples that March. He died instantly, "smashed on the pavement into a thousand pieces" (p. 600), George related graphically to Mme Marliani. Chopin was stunned. "What he did was a great shock to us,"[11] he reported to Grzymała. "A requiem mass [at Notre Dame du Mont] was celebrated here and at his family's request I played during the Elevation" (p. 329).

It was a pathetic occasion. "They gave Nourrit a very skimpy funeral service," George mentioned in one of her letters, the reason being that the bishop disapproved of Nourrit's suicide. "I don't know whether the singers did it on purpose or not," she said,

> but I have never heard such off-key singing. Chopin made a great effort to play the organ at the Elevation. What an organ! . . . However our little one made it sound as good as possible. He used the least shrill stops and played [Schubert's] *Die Gestirne,* not with the exalted and glorious tone that Nourrit gave it, but with a soft, plaintive sound like a distant echo from another world. Only two or three of us there, at most, were really deeply moved by it—our eyes filled with tears. The rest of the congregation, which had come in droves, curious to the point of paying 50 centimes a seat (an unheard-of price in Marseille), were terribly disappointed since they expected Chopin to raise the roof and break at least two or three stops on the organ.[12]

Much of the crowd had paid not only to hear Chopin but also to catch a glimpse of his famous companion. George, however, concealed herself in the organ loft, from where she could peer down, unseen, through the balustrade at the black-draped coffin and the forlorn figures of Nourrit's widow and children.

Outside of this tragic episode, the remaining weeks which George and Frédéric spent in Marseille passed uneventfully. They did not enjoy the city and had it not been for the sake of

Chopin's health, they would have left much sooner. "Marseille is ugly," Chopin wrote Grzymała, "it is an old city but not an ancient one. It bores us a little."[13] George did not care for the city either, but "such as it is I find it charming after Spain,"[14] she admitted.

By May Chopin had recuperated enough to make a short excursion to Genoa which provided a pleasant contrast to the tedium of Marseille. "We saw some magnificent paintings," George wrote, "beautiful scenery, palaces, and gardens piled gracefully one on top of the other in a most unique manner. . . . Chopin was in good health there and got a lot of exercise." Coming back, however, was a different story. "Bad weather held us at sea for twice the time the trip usually takes," she reported. "We spent over forty hours rolling and tossing, the likes of which I haven't seen in a long time. . . . Chopin was terribly tired and the children, although less affected, suffered also. I myself was sick" (p. 653). As everyone was exhausted from the voyage, they stopped briefly in Marseille to rest at Dr. Cauvières' before departing for Nohant on May 22.

The trip to Majorca had certainly not been the romantic escapade that George had expected. For months she had had to nurse an ill, often irritable—and at times nearly moribund—lover. Over this period she had grown accustomed to thinking of him as an invalid, a helpless charge, practically a child. Any element of physical passion which had sparked their relationship at the outset was now virtually extinguished. Chopin had proved so fragile, his grip on life so tenuous, and his grasp of reality so ephemeral that he often gave George a sense of other-worldliness. Seeing him in that light, she realized how much he needed her devotion, her protection, and her maternal solicitude. In providing him with these, she derived a certain spiritual satisfaction which—at least for the time being—compensated for the sensual starvation it entailed.

Despite the strain of her many new responsibilities, George still remained happy with her ethereal young companion, though he often perplexed her. "This Chopin is an angel," she confided to Charlotte Marliani shortly before they left Marseille, "his goodness, his tenderness, and patience sometimes disturb me. I am afraid he has been too delicately constituted; he is too exquisite, too perfect to survive long in our coarse, crude, earthly life. When he was sick unto death in Majorca, he composed music imbued with the very fragrance of Paradise. But I am so used to seeing him lost in the clouds that it doesn't seem to me as if life or death means anything to him. He himself really doesn't know on what planet he is living, and has no awareness of life as we conceive and experience it" (p. 646).

ᏋᏋᐊ CHAPTER FIFTEEN ᐊᏋᏋ

T O REACH ARLES, where Mme Sand's carriage was waiting, Chopin, George, and the children took a boat from Port de Bouc, a small town just west of Marseille. "Our trip on a dirty, narrow, slow ferry in the wilting heat, locked in between two arid river banks, was hardly very pleasant,"[1] George remarked. At Arles they stopped briefly to view the antiquities, after which Chopin complained of fatigue and George of swollen feet. Having been away from home for seven months, they had lost their enthusiasm for sightseeing.

On Friday morning, May 25, they were happy to climb into their own carriage and head on toward Nohant. Bouncing uncomfortably over the "badly paved" streets of Arles, the four passengers were soon riding through the open countryside with the hills and fields of Provence stretching out before them. On all sides the subtle green hues of spring contrasted sharply with the warm orange-brown of the rocky soil.

At a gentle pace the horses trotted along the tree-lined roads, winding under luxuriant arches of foliage, meandering along river beds bordered by terraced vineyards, and passing through leveled fields, freshly furrowed with the spring planting. This was the country that Caesar had conquered, Hannibal had traversed, and the Moors had invaded. Charles Martel defended it, the Popes sought refuge in it, and the Renaissance found it a fertile garden in which to flourish. This was the Provence that was to inspire Cezanne and Van Gogh years later. But the travel-worn tourists took scant notice of their surroundings and made little comment as their carriage rolled past the exquisite landscape so full of history. To George, Provence was all "barren and dusty" (p. 664). "Why travel unless you must?" she sighed wearily.[2] There was little of the vagabond left in her any more.

On the first of June, after a monotonous week of jolting over country roads, the impatient travelers finally caught sight of the rooftops of La Châtre. A few miles beyond they would soon be pulling up in front of the rustic little church at Nohant. Crouched at its entrance was a narrow semi-enclosed porch with a steeply sloping roof that almost gave it the appearance of a lean-to, while practically within the shadow of its sturdy square steeple stood the gate to George Sand's house. As their carriage drove past the long, high walls separating the chateau from the village square, the fragrance of lindens, spruce, and pines filtered through its open windows. Turning into the drive, Chopin caught his first glimpse of the lovely country retreat which Mme Sand loved so much and had described so often. There it sat, a large three-story structure, simple to the point of severity with its brusque rectangular lines resting proudly beneath the graceful old trees that shaded it.

The atmosphere of serenity which this scene presented at first was quickly dispelled in the excitement that followed. Surrounded by servants who had rushed out to greet their long-absent mistress, George and her companion alighted from the carriage. Passing through the wide double doors of the great house, they were led under a bend of the front staircase into a dark flagstone foyer lit by a heavy black lantern suspended from the ironwork of the bannister. Recessed high above this, a small round window admitted a thin shaft of sunlight that shot diagonally downwards, slicing the gloomy hall in two with its bright yellow rays. Halfway up the wall in a niche along the stairs, an ancient laurel-wreathed bust stared placidly down at the noisy party which had just arrived.

After the chaotic babble of greetings and introductions, Mme Sand escorted her new guest up the stairs past the curious eyes of the domestics to the quarters he was to inhabit for the summer months ahead. There he would rest and recover from the ordeals of the past winter.

As soon as they were settled, George, who was still worried about Chopin's health, wasted little time in contacting her good friend, Gustave Papet, a young physician in whom she had great confidence. Papet came immediately, examined the convalescent houseguest thoroughly and delighted his hostess by announcing that he could find nothing whatsoever wrong with his lungs. All that was the matter, the twenty-seven-year-old doctor assured her, was "a minor but chronic inflammation of the larynx which he couldn't promise to cure but in which he saw no cause for alarm."[3] The verdict was comforting: a little rest in the country would quickly rehabilitate him.

The warm days that followed soon found Chopin completely absorbed in the peaceful routine of country life. After seven days of confinement in a close, hot carriage, he discovered the tranquil spaciousness of Nohant a refreshing contrast. "We have arrived at last," he wrote Grzymała on June 2, "after a week of traveling. We all feel perfectly fine. What a beautiful countryside; larks, nightingales—the only bird missing is you."[4] In the mornings he rose late, breakfasted in his room, and was at leisure throughout the day to do as he pleased. Tired but happy, he soon became animated and cheerful once more.

In the undisturbed atmosphere of Nohant, Chopin found he was able to concentrate on his music and write with a facility he seldom achieved in Paris. Although these delightful summer days were productive, Chopin's output was hardly prolific. In composition, as in everything else, he remained fastidious to a fault and would dwell for weeks upon a single passage. Inspiration came quickly, but sudden improvisations were followed by ceaseless revisions. "His musical composition," George noted

> was spontaneous and miraculous. It would come to him unexpectedly and without effort. It simply burst forth out of his piano, sublime and complete. . . . But then began the most heart-breaking labor I have ever seen, consisting of a succession of struggles, uncertainties, and impatience to recapture certain details of the theme he had heard. What he had conceived as a

whole, he analyzed too much in trying to write it down, and his dismay in not being able to capture it exactly again threw him into a kind of despair. He would shut himself up in his room for whole days at a time, weeping, pacing back and forth, smashing his pens, repeating or changing one measure a hundred times, writing and erasing it as many times, and starting all over again the next day with the most minute and desperate perseverance. He sometimes spent six weeks on one page, only to finish by writing it exactly as he had sketched it at the first draft.[5]

The result of these efforts was the production of three movements of a new sonata (B-flat Minor, Op. 35),* three new mazurkas (Op. 41),† a second impromptu (F-sharp Major, Op. 36), and a new nocturne (G Major, Op. 37). All in all the young musician was quite pleased. "They seem pretty to me," he wrote Fontana, "just as their youngest children seem beautiful to parents who are growing old."[6] George, too, was delighted. "He has already written some ravishing things since he has been here,"[7] she boasted of her guest that June.

In addition to composing, Chopin found time to embark on a revision of the works of Bach, one of his favorite composers, and to give piano lessons to Solange. Although she was only ten, George's irrepressible little daughter was already coquettish enough to charm her mother's lover, and the two grew increasingly fond of each other. As a means of humoring his new pupil, Chopin would send to Paris for four-hand music and together they often played duets with a great gusto that amused the entire household.

George's habits that summer were similar to Chopin's in that she also rose late in the mornings. The reason in her case was that she sat up half the nights working on *Cosima,* her new drama which the Théâtre Français was to produce that fall. For hours she labored over her desk scratching out page upon page in her sharp upright script. As morning broke, the oil in her lamp would be exhausted as was George herself. With the

*The third of the four movements, the famous Funeral March, had already been written.
†Nos. 1, 3, and 4. (No. 2 was written in Majorca.)

first rays of dawn she would lay down her pen, blow out the lamp, and succumb to the fatigue of her long night's effort. When she finally revived later in the day as the sunlight warmed her tiny bedroom, she would get up, eat breakfast, and set about tutoring her children.

At five o'clock in the afternoon all activity ceased at Nohant. A bell was rung and the inhabitants of the house assembled for dinner, which, in Chopin's case usually consisted of his perennial "pills and excellent milk."[8] Whenever possible, the family ate outdoors and the hours of relaxation that followed were pleasant but for the most part uneventful. "Our life at Nohant is the same as always, monotonous, quiet, and agreeable . . ." George wrote in June. "We eat outside; friends come to see us, first one, then the other; we smoke, we chat, and in the evening when they have gone, Chopin plays to me at twilight, after which he goes to bed like a child at the same time as Maurice and Solange."[9] These restful interludes were a delight to George; Nohant was her "nest" and she was comfortable in it once more.

At the beginning Chopin shared her happiness, but as the summer progressed he began to find their quiet life a bit tedious. While he had loved the country as a child, it seemed less and less attractive to him as he got older. Mme Sand was quick to observe his restlessness and tried to provide more variety in their daily routine. Sometimes she took the family off to the neighboring countryside for a picnic. In the woods of Vavray near her house was a "charming spot" where she loved to go. There they would sit "on the moss-covered ground, shaded by ancient oak trees" with a "sweeping view of the distant and melancholy horizons of the Black Valley."[10] These excursions, however, did not really interest Chopin very much. He would walk around a bit, pick a few flowers, and then lounge under a tree, ready to go back to the house as soon as possible.

In the evenings George took to inviting more of her local Berry friends to dinner. Often her half-brother, Hippolyte, would come. With his rough and noisy personality, his garrulous manner, and hearty love of the wine bottle, he seemed completely alien to Chopin's delicate nature. But, surprisingly enough, the two men found a certain enjoyment in each other's company. Hippolyte's wife, Émilie, however, did little to stimulate the scene at Nohant. She was as quiet as her husband was loud, sweet enough, but rather lazy. She was, in fact, addicted to her bed as much as her husband was to his wine, and it was just as difficult to find her fully awake as it was to find Hippolyte fully sober. George was never especially fond of Émilie, but she had to admit that the poor girl was not always bad company, "particularly when she is sleeping." [11]

From time to time evenings at Nohant were enlivened by "charades, pantomimes, and theatrical productions." Since childhood Chopin had had a marvelous gift of mimicry and could be hilarious when he launched into an impromptu characterization of some well-known individual or type. "Sneaking in front of a mirror, he would ruffle up his hair and necktie and suddenly appear transformed into a phlegmatic or sentimental ridiculous Englishman, an impertinant old man, or a greedy Jew." [12] With a minimum of encouragement he would enter heartily into such antics which he found far more entertaining than playing billiards, the other favorite pastime of George's rural guests.

Although Chopin continued to miss city life it was agreed by all that he should remain in the country through the rest of the summer for the sake of his health. Since he could not go to Paris, the next best thing was to bring a bit of Paris to Nohant. Both he and George attempted to persuade their friends to visit. In early July Chopin wrote Grzymała, insisting that he come. Despite the fact that it was a tiring two day journey by coach, he coaxed and wheedled his friend into it. His invitation was half a plea, half a command: "Take the express coach to Chateauroux," he instructed, "you will get there by noon the next day. From there you will have a two and a half hour trip by diligence to La Châtre, but you will get off in front of [George's] garden which is along the route. . . . How much good it would do us if you could come and see us.

What's more, Mme d'Agoult's bed awaits you, if that would give you any pleasure in addition to two hearts that look for you like a kite waiting for the wind."[13]

When he had finished his letter Chopin showed it to George. Taking it aside she added an urgent postscript. "You really must come, my dear friend, we need to see you. Your little boy's health is still only so-so. I feel he needs a little less calm, less solitude, and less of the sameness that life at Nohant offers. . . . He will never admit to me that he is bored, but I think I can sense it. He has not been accustomed to such an austere way of life. . . . Come and see us."[14]

Grzymała responded to the plea and paid a brief visit to Nohant that summer as did two of George's close friends, Marie Dorval and Emmanuel Arago. Their arrivals proved to be pleasant interruptions in the placid humdrum of provincial life and "revived Chopin's health a little" (p. 737).

Although only a few people from Paris came to Nohant that summer, there were many who talked about it a great deal. "I am not surprised at all the stories that are circulating about me," Chopin wrote. "You must remember that I was well aware of exposing myself to such things. Anyhow it will pass."[15] Even in Warsaw there was such curiosity and talk that Nicholas Chopin finally wrote his son, "We are very happy that you are being looked after, as you mention, but we are quite anxious to know something of this intimacy."[16] All he was to learn of Mme Sand, however, was that she was *"Pani domu,"* the lady of the house.

The most vicious source of gossip came from Italy where Marie d'Agoult showered the couple at Nohant with her sarcasm and ridicule. That two such different individuals as George and Frédéric should be attracted to each other puzzled many people, but for Mme d'Agoult the explanation was simple: "The easiest person in the world to understand is our poor Piffoël," she asserted, intimating that George remained attached to Chopin simply for the sake of satisfying physiologic urges. "She mistakes pebbles for diamonds and frogs for swans. I'd rather you not talk to me about her," she told Mme

Marliani, "except to tell me whether she is dead or alive. When I lived at her house I did all I could *not to know* certain details of her life . . . the only thing that really worries me and I would tell her so if she were here, is the deterioration of her talent. . . . It is evident that the period of emotional intensity (so magnificently revealed in *Lélia* and the *Lettres d'un Voyageur*) is over. Today she needs to study, reflect, and distill her ideas."[17]

Liszt too commented that "the last productions of Dr. Piffoëls (*les Aldini* [*sic*], *Spiridion,* and *Les Sept Cordes de la Lyre*) have left me with a painful impression. *Lélia* and the *Lettres d'un Voyageur* were certainly by a different hand. She has evidently suffered from laziness, exhaustion, and decadence since then."[18]

Prompted by Lamennais, Charlotte Marliani informed George of all that Mme d'Agoult had written about her. She even showed her some of the letters in Marie's own handwriting. As a result George decided to have nothing more to do with either her or Liszt. Mme d'Agoult, however, unaware of Mme Marliani's breach of confidence, was perplexed by George's lack of communication. "Without any reproach meant," she wrote George in June of 1839, "it has been more than a year now that you have not given us any indication that you are still alive." Then in a friendly tone she invited George to visit her in Lucques. "One of my friends has rented me a *casino* where I intend to prepare a room for Piffoëls: the macaroni plate will always be out . . . I will try to resume my role, a little bit forgotten, of Princess Mirabella, and extend to you in Lucques some of the hospitality of the hostess of Nohant" (p. 342).

George was suspicious, however, and feared that Mme d'Agoult's renewed friendliness bore the "imprint of hypocrisy." While she was trying to decide what course to take, another letter from the countess arrived in August and read:

Perhaps you will be surprised at my persistence in writing you since your absolute silence for almost eighteen months, the silence which you appear to have *imposed* on Carlota [Marliani] in regard to me, and above all your own *failure to reply* to my last letter in which I asked you to come spend the summer with us make it clear enough that our relationship has become an inconvenience for you. But that relationship, having been for me something serious, certain words having been exchanged between us which *for me* still have an inalterable significance, it is impossible for me, even if only out of self respect, to allow our ties to become broken without knowing why. In my opinion they are bonds which ought to last a lifetime. I cannot accept the fact that you should have any complaint against me because in such a case you would not lose any time in telling me of it. . . . I have combed the recesses of my conscience and cannot find the least shadow of any wrong there. Franz has also asked himself why it is that your intimate association with a man whom he believes he has the right to call his friend [Chopin], has promptly resulted in a cessation of all communication between us? . . . Frequent warnings and the discouraging experience of so many broken affections in your past doesn't seem to me, at this point, to be a sufficient reason for such sad conclusions, i.e., that you are incapable of any enduring feelings, that a whim outweighs a proven affection for you, that there is no such word in your vocabulary as *obligation,* that you expose the most profound depths of your soul haphazardly to any breeze that comes along, and that there is no shelter in your heart where those who have been dear to you can take refuge from the abuse of the latest comer. I still hope . . . *I sincerely desire* an explanation worthy of you. . . . If you persist in your silence I will know that you have *wanted* this rupture. The same fickleness which has led you to betray a sacred friendship will probably help you to forget it.[19]

Having had her say, Marie sealed the letter and sent it to George in care of Mme Marliani since she was not sure of her friend's whereabouts just then. Sensing that the letter could only add tinder to the fire, the countess returned it to Marie, explaining that it would have exactly the opposite effect on George from the one she intended. Mme d'Agoult, however, ignored this advice and promptly readdressed the letter directly to Mme Sand herself.

George hesitated for some time before answering. But finally in the fall, after consulting with the abbé Lamennais and Mme Marliani, she sent a reply.

I do not know exactly what Madame Marliani has told you recently, Marie. I have not complained of you to anybody *but her* whom you love and excuse. You, on the other hand, complain of me to many people who hate me and vilify me. If I live in a world of gossip I am not the one who creates it, and I will try to imitate you as little as possible in that respect. I don't know what this appeal is that you are making to our past. I really don't understand. You know how wholeheartedly, how enthusiastically even, I threw myself into our friendship which seemed so charming. But infatuation is one of the things that you laugh at in me and I can hardly consider that charitable when you go around at the same time destroying what I had of it for you. Your understanding of friendship is different from mine. . . . You don't have the least illusions about it or the least indulgence in regard to it. . . . You have nothing but sweet words, tender caresses, even a profusion of sympathetic tears for those whom you love but then when you speak of them and above all when you write about them, you are caustic and contemptuous. You laugh at them, degrade them, humiliate them, and even *slander* them, all with a light touch and a charming gracefulness. Those whom you treat this way are in for a rude awakening and a rather disagreeable surprise. They should be allowed to reflect and to remain silent in their astonishment for a while. . . . You inflict upon them the sort of abuse which, among friends who have hurt each other, betrays only sorrow and regret, but which, in other circumstances, reveals a spitefulness and hatred. Yes, *hatred*, my poor Marie! Don't try to deceive yourself any longer. You bear a mortal hatred toward me. (pp. 798–800)

A smoldering volcano of repressed emotions had erupted and, as its fiery glow subsided, all that remained when the smoke had cleared was a stark and desolate mountain of pride scattered with the ashes of a friendship.

Feeling somewhat more collected after this catharsis, George added toward the end of her letter

You have done all that you could to substitute heart for intelligence in dealing with me, but intelligence has regained the upper hand. Beware of having too much of it, my poor friend . . . an excess of clearsightedness leads to isolation and loneliness. . . . Get hold of yourself, Marie. Such sorry behavior is unworthy of you. I know you well, and recognize in your intelligence a desire and a need to play the grand role. But a certain little feminine uneasiness always rebels against this. You would like to behave chivalrously like a man, but cannot renounce the role of a beautiful and witty woman forever immolating and crushing others. . . . This is the first and last sermon you will receive from me. Please forgive it, as I forgive you the lectures you have read me—behind my back. (pp. 801–3)

By September all thoughts were turned toward Paris. It had been nearly a year since the couple at Nohant had last seen the city, and Chopin was especially anxious to return. "Paris is good for his morale," George realized. "Nervous natures like his need a refined civilization" (p. 750). Even Mme Sand herself was beginning to look forward to their return. Financially it would be beneficial to both of them. George could live in Paris for half the sum it cost her to maintain her family, servants, and guests at Nohant. Besides, she anticipated some additional revenue from the production of her new play, *Cosima*, that winter and felt she should be present for the rehearsals to ensure its success. Chopin could deal much more effectively with his publishers on a face-to-face basis rather than by correspondance, and on resuming his lessons in Paris he could add 100 francs a day to his income.

Where, though, was the couple to live on their return to the city? During their long absence both George and Chopin had given up their quarters in Paris and now had to delegate friends to search out new accommodations for them. Neither felt they could afford anything extravagant. Chopin sent instructions to Grzymała and with them George enclosed a letter for Arago. "Raise the price if absolutely necessary, but as little as possible," she told him. "It is not essential that all the rooms be large and elegant. The children's rooms, for example, can be small, provided they have fireplaces and the rooms for the grown-ups must be on the south. This is especially important for the little boy [Chopin] and for my rheumatism also. I don't need a large or elaborate drawing-room since I never have to entertain more than a dozen people at a time. The most important thing is that the lay-out should be good" (p. 755). By this George meant that her bedroom should be well separated from those of the children and she sketched a small plan indicating explicitly the type of arrangement she wanted. Although her relationship with Chopin had undergone considerable change in the past few months, it was apparently still intimate enough to demand absolute privacy of the boudoir at least on certain occasions.

To make sure that Mme Sand found exactly the kind of apartment she was looking for, Chopin wrote Fontana for further help. "Above all it should be *quiet*," he specified, "with no blacksmith in the neighborhood, no ladies on the street, etc., etc. You know precisely what I mean. The stairs should be convenient and the apartment should have a good sunny exposure. . . . Once more, now," he emphasized, "the third bedroom with its adjoining study should be separated from the other two and, if possible, the study or the third bedroom should have a private entrance. . . . There are a lot of such apartments in the Faubourg St. Germain and the Faubourg St. Honoré."[20]

As for Chopin's quarters, (which, for propriety's sake, were to be separate from Mme Sand's) George explained to Grzymała, "He must have somewhere to put up his manservant and room to turn around in himself." To this she added facetiously, "He will always have the means to pay his rent, even if it means giving up a little of his drinking, gambling, women, and smoking."[21]

Within a short while a satisfactory apartment consisting of two rooms and a foyer was found for Chopin at No. 5 rue Tronchet. Finicky as usual, he sent detailed instructions to Fontana as to how it should be prepared for him. "Choose a wallpaper," Chopin wrote

like the one I used to have in my old quarters, dove-gray, but slick and shiny. Have both rooms papered with a dark green border, not too wide. For the vestibule, choose something else but make it suitable also. If there are other wallpapers which are prettier and more fashionable that you like and think I would too, then order them. I prefer something simple, unpretentious, and very neat rather than something common and flashy. I like

a pearl color because it's not loud or vulgar. Thank you for
finding a room for my servant—that's a great help. As for the
furniture, everything will be fine since you are looking after it.
. . . You will have to send the bed and my desk to the cabinet
maker for repairs. You ought to take the papers out of the desk
and lock them up somewhere. Think about finding me a servant. A good honest Pole if possible. . . . Don't give him more
than eighty francs in wages and have him take care of his own
meals. . . . The mattress of my bed should be fixed—if it
doesn't cost too much. . . . Have the chairs beaten etc. . . .[22]

Later, on the third of October, he wrote again, urging Fontana to speed things along. "In five, six, or—at the latest—
seven days I shall be in Paris. Even if everything is not ready,
see that I at least find the rooms papered and a bed available.
Take pity on me and see that this is done. I am leaving earlier
than I planned since George has to be in Paris because of her
play" (p. 365).

Somehow in the rush Chopin had overlooked one of the
most important items of all—his wardrobe. "I forgot to ask
you to order me a hat from my M. *Dupont* in your street," he
wrote Fontana jotting down still more instructions for his
overburdened factotum. "Tell him to make it according to the
fashion this year but not too extreme since I have no idea
what sort of things you are wearing these days. One more
thing, when you go past *Dautremont's*, my tailor on the boulevard, go in and have him make me a pair of gray trousers
right away. Choose something dark for winter without stripes,
something smooth and well-fitting. An Englishman like you
should know what I need. . . . Also order me a black velvet
waistcoat with a discrete little pattern, in short, something elegant and very simple at the same time. . . . I will repay you"
(p. 365).

Only a few days before they were to leave, word came that
Fontana had found two small pavilions for George at No. 16
rue Pigalle. They were extremely private, located off the street
in a sort of mews behind an enclosed garden and the interior
arrangement conformed exactly to Mme Sand's stipulations.

"You are invaluable!" Chopin congratulated his friend. "Take the two apartments on the rue Pigalle without looking any further. Try to bargain a little for them. . . . If that doesn't work, then *take everything* for 2,500 francs but don't lose them. They are the best there is and seem perfect to us" (p. 369).

At last, all arrangements were completed and at five o'clock on the morning of October 10, George, Chopin, and the children bade the servants farewell and boarded the carriage for Paris. In the gray autumn dawn they drove through the gates of Nohant onto the dusty road leading into the village square. From there they struck out toward Chateauroux and the north. That night they stopped at Orléans and resumed their journey the next morning. By evening of the second day they had reached Paris. As the little houses in the rue Pigalle were not yet ready, George and her children moved in with Mme Marliani while Chopin went directly to his new rooms on the rue Tronchet. There his valet, Tineau, had been waiting for him since morning with his new gray trousers, waistcoat, and hat, all neatly laid out for him.

eÞx CHAPTER SIXTEEN ×ÞÐ

PARIS IN OCTOBER of 1839 still possessed the same exhilarating mystique which Chopin had experienced there on his first arrival in September of 1831. An absence of eleven months had only served to increase his passionate fascination with the magnificent metropolis, sprawled along the curving banks of the Seine. Paris had become Chopin's mistress long before he had known Mme Sand, and for years to come his affections were to be divided between the two. Both adored him just as each, in turn, was worshipped by him, and both were essential to his existence. In his weakened condition, the young musician could no longer survive the stimulus of the one without the sustenance of the other.

It was about this time that Heinrich Heine had proclaimed Paris to be inundated with music, and it was exactly this aspect of the city that Chopin found to be one of her most delightful charms. He enjoyed being caught up in this flood of music and was especially pleased at the waves of enthusiasm which his own recent compositions created in it. Pleyel had finally published his Preludes that September and they were selling well not only in Paris but throughout Europe. In Germany his long-time admirer, Robert Schumann wrote: "I regard the Preludes as outstanding. . . . They are sketches, introductions to studies, or, if you will, ruins, wild, multicolored feathers plucked from an eagle. But, like a pearl, each piece bears the stamp, 'Frédéric Chopin has composed it.' In each pause we recognize his pulsating breath. He is and remains the most daring and most splendid poetic spirit of the times."[1]

Needless to say, this addition to his fame only increased the number of pupils who flocked to his doorstep once more. Princesses and countesses along with other titled and untitled, talented and untalented young ladies from the Parisian elite now tripped across the threshold of the rue Tronchet apartment just as they had formerly climbed the stairs of his old quarters in the Chausée d'Antin. Each day four to five of them, elegantly attired with their music rolls under their arms, swept past the gray curtains of the vestibule into the salon of his apartment. Seated at the beautiful Pleyel grand they played while Chopin stood nearby at the little upright, ready to interrupt and illustrate the proper phrasing as necessary. For a full hour he would listen to them, watching their heads bob to the music as they bent intently over the keyboard, their hair drawn tightly back into a stylish bun while ringlets of curls fell quivering over their ears. Patiently he heard them out, leaning sometimes against the large armoire between the windows or resting quietly on the red upholstery of the sofa. Still pale and feeble from the preceding winter, he often dabbed away the perspiration from his forehead with some cooling eau de cologne or sipped gum-water with sugar and opium to relieve the painful irritation of his hacking cough.

By four o'clock most afternoons Chopin had finished his lessons. At the same time George Sand was just beginning to wake up. On the desk in her study, adjacent to the darkened bedroom, stood eight to ten pages of fresh manuscript which she had written out the previous night. Just what those pages contained she was not always quite sure. "I forget so completely what I have written," she claimed, "I have such an aversion to re-reading myself."[2]

Once awake, George had little time to lounge about, for Chopin would soon be arriving for dinner. Often other guests were expected also. In the obscurity of her bedroom, which was painted brown to absorb the daylight while she slept, she rose from the two mattresses stacked on the floor in the style of a Turkish bed, dressed hurriedly, and emerged to supervise the preparations for dinner. The new quarters in the rue Pigalle pleased her immensely despite "having riled, raged,

pestered, and sworn at the upholsterers, locksmiths, etc. etc."
during the aggravating process of moving in. "What a long,
horrible, intolerable affair it is to get settled here,"[3] she
moaned exhaustedly. But the effort had proved worthwhile.
Her apartments, as Balzac described them, were located "over
the coach house and stables, at one end of a garden, in a residence, facing on the street." To reach them one had to climb
up a long steep stairway known in those days as a "miller's
staircase." "She has a dining room with carved oak furniture,"
Balzac continued. "Her antechamber is a café-au-lait color and
the drawing room in which she receives is filled with superb
Chinese vases containing flowers. There is also a jardiniere
always full of flowers. The furniture is upholstered in green
and there is a side table covered with knicknacks. On the walls
are pictures by Delacroix and that portrait of her by Calamatta. . . . The piano is magnificent, a square upright in rose-
wood. Chopin is constantly there."[4]

The guests who climbed those steps of an evening could
never be certain whom they would find milling around the
Chinese vases in the green drawing room. The crowd was seldom large but often covered a spectrum of society not likely to
be assembled under any other roof. The diversity of Mme
Sand's guests was always impressive and often startling.
August members of the Polish aristocracy, speaking a cultivated but broken French, mingled with rustic provincials
from Berry whose quaint idioms amused their more sophisticated Parisian countrymen. Side by side, in uncomfortable
proximity, was a colorful assortment of noisy bohemians and
unkempt socialists whose table manners and bathing habits
tended to reflect their obvious preoccupation with transcendental matters rather than mundane niceties. Elizabeth Barrett
Browning, who later witnessed such a soirée, found George
surrounded by "crowds of ill-bred men who adore her *á gen-
oux bas* betwixt a puff of smoke and ejection of saliva. . . . I
did not mind much the Greek in Greek costume who tutoyed
her, and kissed her, I believe, so Robert said: or the other
vulgar man of the theater who went down on his knees and

called her "sublime.' '*Caprice d'amitié*,' said she, with her quiet, gentle scorn."⁵ One of Mrs. Browning's less indulgent friends simply dismissed the whole lot as mere "rubbish."

Alien to such raucous spectacles, Chopin nevertheless endured them out of affection for his hostess. There were times, no doubt, when he must have felt more inclined to hold his nose than his tongue. But instead, whenever the noise and cigar smoke became too oppressive, he would retreat quietly into a corner for a civilized *tête-à-tête* with the Princess Czartoryska or the sensitive and impeccably mannered Delacroix.

On the evening of October 29 that fall, Chopin was relieved to forego the usual gathering in the rue Pigalle. Louis-Philippe had summoned him to play for the court at St. Cloud. The invitation came about as a result of Chopin's introduction to the famous pianist, Ignaz Moscheles, at the home of the latter's cousin, Auguste Léo. Subsequently, the two musicians visited one another and on one occasion count Perthuis, the king's aide-de-camp, heard them playing a duet. Impressed, the count related the incident to the royal family and was promptly delegated to invite both men to court.

At nine o'clock on the designated evening, count Perthuis' carriage drove up the rue Tronchet in a pouring rain. At the entrance to No. 5 the carriage stopped and Chopin dashed from the doorway into the vehicle where the count, his wife, and Moscheles were waiting for him. Some time later, after the carriage had arrived at St. Cloud, the little party was escorted into "the warm and brilliantly lighted palace. We passed through some splendid apartments," Moscheles related, "to the *salon carré* where only the royal family was assembled; the Queen at a round table with an elegant work basket before her. . . . Next to her were Mme Adélaïde [the king's sister], the Duchess of Orleans, and the ladies of the court. They one and all treated us kindly as if we were old acquaintances. . . . The queen asked if the instrument—a Pleyel—was placed as we liked it; was the lighting what we wanted? if the chairs were the right height, etc.; and was as anxious for our comfort as a Citizen Queen might well be."⁶

The concert proved to be "a spectacular success," according to Moscheles.

> First of all, Chopin played a "melange of Nocturnes and Etudes" and was extolled and admired as an old court favorite. I followed with some old and new "Studies" and was honored with similar applause. We then sat down together at the instrument, he again playing the bass, a thing he always insists on. The small audience now listened intently to my "E-flat Major Sonata" which was interrupted by such exclamations as "divin!, delicieux!." After the Andante the Queen whispered to one of her suite: "Ne serait-il pas indiscret de leur redemander?" which was tantamount to a command; so we played it again with increased *abandon* and in the finale gave ourselves up to a "musical delirium."
>
> Chopin's enthusiasm throughout the whole performance of the piece must, I think, have kindled that of his hearers who overwhelmed us with compliments equally divided. Chopin played another solo as charmingly as before and met with the same reception. I then improvised on some of Mozart's sweetest airs and finally dashed away at the "Zauberflöte" Overture. Better than all the words of praise which flow so glibly from the lips of princes was the King's close attention during the entire evening. Chopin and I revelled like brothers in the triumph achieved by the individual talent of each; there was no tinge of jealousy on either side. At last, after being allowed to enjoy some refreshments, we left the palace at 11:30, this time under only a shower of compliments, for the rain had ceased and we had a clear night. (p. 59)

Moscheles's glowing account of their success was essentially substantiated by the review which appeared two days later in the *Revue et Gazette Musicale*. Toward the end of the week the king sent Chopin a lovely Sèvres vase and Moscheles a traveling bag.

Later in the fall, as the weather grew colder, Chopin found the constant shuttling between the rue Tronchet and the rue Pigalle more and more of a strain. In addition, the rue Tronchet apartment had turned out to be quite damp and chilly despite its southern exposure. Because of these unfavorable circumstances his cough grew worse and his strength began to

fail. George could not help but notice the change that was taking place and was disturbed by it. Each day, she wrote, he
came to "tell me, with a haggard face and a weak voice that he
was feeling marvellous."[7] As much as she was concerned
about her friend's health, she also worried about the inconvenience that a recurrence of his illness would pose for her in
their current situation. "I saw myself forced either to give up
my role of nursemaid," she reflected, "or to spend my life running back and forth in the most impossible manner" (p. 456).
The thought undoubtedly occurred to her at this point to let
Chopin move into one of the pavilions in the rue Pigalle.
However, for the sake of appearances this would not have
been a very satisfactory solution, especially as far as Chopin
was concerned. For the time being, therefore, it was decided
to leave things as they were with Chopin living and teaching in
the rue Tronchet apartment while he took his meals regularly
at Mme Sand's. As inconvenient as this arrangement was, it
lasted for the next two years until the fall of 1841.

Often, on a cold winter evening, as George watched Chopin
drive away "shivering in his fiacre" (p. 456), she wished the
two of them could go back to the country again. She longed
for the open air and quiet life of Nohant. In Paris, she complained, "I grow fat in body and thin in spirit.[8] "There's no
getting around it," she sighed, "when you are born a country
bumpkin, you can never really adjust to the hubbub of the
city. It even seems to me that the mud at home is beautiful
mud while here it makes me sick" (p. 801). As the winter
progressed she grew more disgruntled, and late in February
she wrote her brother, "I don't know anything more depressing, gloomier, or filthier than Paris this time of year; I hate
it."[9]

But the city did have certain advantages and one of these
was the fact that her son, Maurice, could study with Delacroix
as long as they remained. She had always been aware of the
boy's artistic nature and when he was only seven she had written a friend: "I believe he has little ability for things that
require calculation or reflection but a great deal for those

which attract the eyes and imagination. It seems he is a born artist; we shall see."[10] On the trip to Majorca he had sketched incessantly and produced a number of charming scenes of the island. These, George felt, showed definite promise and Delacroix indulged her maternal ambitions by accepting Maurice on a regular basis in his atelier.

Another facet of Paris which George found rewarding that winter was the opportunity to get acquainted with the large colony of Polish emigrés who lived there. Chopin had introduced her to them prior to their Mediterranean excursion, but it was only after their return that she had the chance to know them well. Among this group of exiles the poet, Mickiewicz, particularly intrigued her. In December 1839 the *Revue des Deux Mondes* published the article which she had written in Marseille with Chopin's help, entitled *Essay on the Fantastic Drama: Goethe, Byron, and Mickiewicz*. The philosophy of the Polish poet appealed to George, and his vision of Poland's role in history captivated her liberal sentiments. Poland, Mickiewicz claimed, was the Christ of nations which was being crucified for the salvation of humanity in order to grant freedom to all oppressed peoples of the world. This doctrine fitted in with the teachings of her old friend and mentor, Pierre Leroux, who declared that Poland represented truth incarnate and had become the propagator of Christianity, equality, and fraternity in their age. Roused by these statements, George avidly immersed herself in the problems and aspirations of the Polish colony. In fact, so great was her appetite for anything and everything Polish, Balzac could not resist snickering that she had become "stuffed with Poles."

As much as this new interest absorbed her, George did not neglect her writing. She could hardly afford to. With her finances exhausted after the Majorcan fiasco she was badly in need of a quick source of income. Because of this she had taken to writing plays on the theory that she could earn more money with less effort in the theater. Already she had completed *Cosima* which was scheduled for production in the spring of 1840 and had begun another drama, *Les Mississippiens,* which she also hoped to stage soon.

Unfortunately, *Cosima,* which was influenced by Leroux's socialistic theories, proved to be a complete artistic and financial disaster. It opened on the night of April 29, 1840 with Marie Dorval in the lead. So noisy was the hostile reception of the drama that not even a long-time veteran of the stage like Mme Dorval could maintain her equilibrium. The other actors were also affected and the performance was barely able to limp to its sorry finish. Only one person emerged from the theater that evening with a feeling of exultation: Marie d'Agoult. Sitting with Liszt in a box she had listened with obvious enjoyment to the loud jeers and hisses from the crowd and took great delight in the discomfort they were causing her old friend. Despite the blatant failure of *Cosima,* Buloz insisted on dragging it through six additional nights after which George convinced him to close it.

Although the countess always behaved in a civil—if somewhat icy—manner to George when they were in public, she continued to write and talk scathingly about her in private. Commenting on a dinner party at which George had been present that February, Marie described her as a "bit sulky." At the table she claimed George "made Grzymała, who was all lit up by the champagne, feel her knee (literally), saying 'Come on now Grzymała, let's see, what's my knee like'. *Grzymała:* 'It's made of pink skin'. *George:* 'Oh, stop it! you're tickling me. I'll scratch if you aren't careful!' " With chilly disdain, Mme d'Agoult concluded, "I can hardly bear to see *those people* any more." [11] But the less she saw of George the more she gossiped about her. She loved to resurrect the scandal which had surrounded Mme Sand's relationship with Marie Dorval. So great was her rancor toward George that she did not even attempt to shade her remarks with the delicate veil of innuendo. George, she openly asserted, was responsible for having seduced Dorval.

Not content with stabbing at George alone the countess

sniped at Chopin also, calling him "an oyster powdered with sugar" (p. 321). In spite of this she was quite piqued that he no longer visited her. "I think the Chopin household is going to break up soon," she announced in March of 1840. "Their mutual friends claim he is sick with jealousy, consumed by passion and is a torment to himself as well as to others. She [George] has had enough of it all and only fears that he might drop dead on the spot if she leaves him!" (p. 412).

Liszt, who had also lost his affection for the Sand-Chopin menage, made little effort to suppress his mistress's vitriolic remarks. Indeed he encouraged them but cautioned Marie to use discretion in order to make the most out of the whole affair. "Your behavior toward George pleases me very much," he told the countess. "You must be patient and show moderation. You can because you are strong . . . I don't think the time to break with George has come yet. . . . Insofar as possible try to ignore certain things and excuse others. Up to now everything is perfect. . . . When you *do* break, it should be with a clear and decided advantage on your side" (p. 349).

In January of that winter Marie was obviously delighted to be able to inform Liszt, "Chopin is supposed to have gone to a friend (Probst, I assume) to ask for a loan of 150 francs. What's more, he is said to have insisted that the price of one of his pieces be raised, to which the exasperated friend replied, 'Listen, for the sake of delicacy I didn't want to say anything, but you are forcing me to. I have a letter from Breitkopf telling me not to buy anything more from you except at cut-rate prices because your compositions don't sell in Germany anymore'" (p. 367). Unfortunately the countess was quite right about Chopin's financial problems. The preceding month he had, indeed, written his publishers, Breitkopf and Haertel in Leipzig, refusing to sell any further works at the prices they offered.

Whether his popularity in Germany was really on the wane or whether Breitkopf and Haertel were simply trying to take advantage of the composer, the fact remained that Chopin, as usual, was low on funds. Because of the failure of George's play, she too was in financial straits. Under such circumstances the two decided not to return to Nohant for the summer as they had planned. One of the drawbacks of living in the country, George complained, was that "before I can get out of bed there are apt to be twelve persons installed in the house."[12] Even without a steady stream of guests the cost of running a large household in the country was considerable. At Nohant George estimated that her monthly expenditures were about 750 francs more than in Paris. Clearly, it was much more economical to remain in the city.

CHAPTER SEVENTEEN

THE SUMMER OF 1840 passed quietly. George took Maurice and Solange to riding school and spent long hours galloping through the Bois de Boulogne with them. She missed the country terribly and would have preferred the open fields and tree-lined river banks of Berry, but the prim paths and elegant allées of the Bois had to suffice. Solange, who was just learning to ride, had absolutely "no qualms," her mother observed, "and trots off in every direction all alone on a huge horse." As for Maurice, he was being taught to ride without stirrups, which he did not find very pleasant. "It's rather hard on his posterior,"[1] George chuckled. On warm sunny days Chopin followed them in his carriage. In spite of Mme Sand's attentive care through the winter he still remained delicate and weighed only 97 pounds.

Solange enjoyed these excursions in the park, but for all her intrepid behavior on horseback, she was nothing like the tomboy her mother had been at the same age. On the contrary, she loved to act "the little princess" and possessed a certain flirtatious manner which was highly feminine. Nearly twelve that summer, she was still slightly plump-cheeked and a little rotund but was already beginning to develop into a beautiful young girl. Fully aware of this, she liked to practice her seductive charms on the men around her, a fact which amused Chopin and annoyed her mother. "Solange . . . wastes so much time primping," George complained to her brother that year. "She has become such a little coquette. I hope you will tease her about it when you see her in order to cure her of it."[2]

Beneath the casual nature of this complaint, there was actually a great deal of tension building up between mother and daughter. Solange had always been a determined girl with a strong will of her own and was not easily "cured" of her capricious habits. When she was only two years old George had already discovered that she could be quite "monstruous and very obstreperous." But, she assumed optimistically that "there is still time enough to change her for the better."[3] Nine years later, however, she began to realize that time was not working in her favor. By the summer of 1840 Solange was, if anything, more headstrong than before and her mother was finding it increasingly difficult to cope with the child. The tutors she hired invariably gave up in the face of the young girl's stubbornness and laziness, and as fall approached, Mme Sand's patience was all but exhausted. "Solange," she wrote Maurice, who was visiting his father in Guillery, "has been well behaved for two or three days; but yesterday she had a terrible temper tantrum. . . . I am very much afraid that I am going to be forced to put her in boarding school if she doesn't make up her mind to work. She is costing me a fortune in tutors who can't do a thing with her.[4]

By the end of September matters were still worse. "God, but she is lazy" (p. 150), George fumed. Finally, on the thirteenth of October, at wit's end, Mme Sand entered her daughter in the Pension Héreau, a "very well-maintained" boarding school near the Parc Monceau. "Solange has simply become so independent," she announced to Chopin, "that I can never hope to regain control over her (which I never really had). She has no conception of discipline and only with someone else, in a place where she is subject to absolute regimentation, will I ever hope to see her rebellious nature squelched and brought under control" (p. 154).

Unfortunately M. and Mme Héreau did not measure up to this formidable task and, in George's opinion, even spoiled the child further. After six months in boarding school Solange remained as "intolerable in character" as ever. Consequently by mid-April of 1841 her mother had her transferred to the

Pension Bascans where she felt she would be "just as well off materially, but better controlled morally" (p. 274).

In all these skirmishes between mother and daughter, Chopin often found himself in a rather awkward position. When it came to family matters George would brook no interference. By now she had come to accept Chopin as an established member of her household, but she resolutely intended to remain mistress of it herself. Frédéric had entered her life as a lover, and lived in her house as a "guest," and was to develop in her affections as a "second son," but under no circumstances would she ever allow him to entertain the notion that he might be "head" of her family. The poor man, however, could not remain entirely detached, and having grown fond of Solange he instinctively tended to place himself as a buffer between the girl and her mother.

Fortunately these family squabbles did not develop into any major crises during the summer of 1840, and life in the rue Pigalle ran on much as it had the previous winter. Many friends remained in Paris or came to the city for visits so that the regular evening gatherings in the little pavilions continued to include such guests as Balzac, Delacroix, Lamennais, Leroux, and the Marliani's. Occasionally George and Chopin went to the opera or visited the museums. That summer there was an exhibition of Michelangelo's work and another by Ingre's pupils. The latter, George told Maurice, was "pitiful in every respect" (p. 124). But Chopin, who was a great admirer of Ingres, did not share his mistress' taste in art, as in many other things.

In August George spent a few days in Cambrai where her friend, Pauline Viardot, went to give some recitals. She hoped at first that Chopin would come along, but after a few days of excruciating boredom, she was glad he didn't. "We are lodged like princes," she wrote, "but what hosts, what conversations, what dinners! . . . I hope we will leave very soon" (p. 95). They did, and George refrained from complaining any further about having to remain in Paris for the rest of the summer. "If I hadn't been in the company of the greatest singer and most delightful woman in the world," she told her brother after her return to Paris, "I would have died of suffocation at Cambrai from the atrocious food they serve and the stench of the local inhabitant's teeth" (p. 114).

Later in August George signed a contract for a complete new edition of her works which was to bring her around 12,000 francs a year. With this sort of income she would be able to escape Paris in the summer from now on and live at Nohant as she had always wanted. In the meantime, however, both she and Frédéric planned to remain in the city for the coming winter.

Chopin continued to teach regularly and compose sporadically while George plunged into a new novel on working class life, her *Compagnon du Tour de France.* At the same time she also began to jot down her caustic impressions of their winter in Majorca. At least once a week she managed to stop by and visit Charlotte Marliani who prided herself on the literary salon she maintained during the winter months. There Mme Sand would sit, busily hemming away at pocket handkerchiefs while she silently absorbed the lively discussions that whirled about her. Still keenly interested in all things Polish, she went several times with Chopin to hear Mickiewicz give a course on Slavonic literature at the Collège de France that December. By now the famous couple had become so lionized that their entrance into the lecture hall was often greeted with bursts of applause.

Such displays of public adulation were accepted by Mme Sand with perfect equanimity, but for the timid Chopin they were painful. As usual he preferred to seclude himself in the privacy of his own studio or the drawing rooms of close friends. It was rather surprising, therefore, that in the spring of 1841 he began to contemplate giving a public concert again. George was very excited: "A great, absolutely the greatest piece of news!" she exclaimed to her good friend Pauline Viardot that April, little Chip-Chip is going to give a Grrrrrand Concert. His friends have plagued him so much that he has finally been persuaded. . . . He had hardly uttered the fatal *yes* when everything was miraculously taken care of. Three quarters of the tickets were snatched up before it had even been announced. Then he woke up as if from a dream; and you can't imagine a more comical sight than our meticulous and irresolute Chip-Chip trapped in a situation where he can't change his mind. . . . This Chopinesque nightmare will take place in Pleyel's rooms on the 26th. He doesn't want any posters, he doesn't want any programs, and he doesn't want many people. He doesn't even want anyone to talk about it. He is afraid of so many things that I suggested he play without candles and without an audience on a dumb keyboard. (p. 282)

All Paris welcomed Chopin's return to the concert stage after his long absence. All, that is, except the rancorous Mme d'Agoult, who feared the impact this might have on Liszt's reputation. "A malicious little clique is trying to resuscitate Chopin who is going to play at Pleyel's,"[5] she wrote a friend on April 21. The "malicious little clique" to which she referred was none other than Mme Sand. She is "furious with me," the countess declared, and insisted that it was only because George was mortified by Liszt's successes that she "forced Chopin to give a private concert, just for friends."[6]

On the evening of April 26, 1841 the concert took place as scheduled despite Chopin's qualms and the countess' jibes. For the program Chopin chose his F Major Ballade, the C-sharp Minor Scherzo, the four Mazurkas, Opus 41, and the A Major Polonaise, among other works. According to the custom of the period, he was assisted by two other musicians: a singer, Mme Cinti-Damoreau, and a violinist, H. W. Ernst.

The reviews were ecstatic: *La France Musicale* raved about both his compositions and his pianistic ability. It compared him to Schubert:

The one has done for the piano what the other has done for the voice. . . . Chopin is a pianist of conviction. He composes and plays for himself; everyone listens to him with interest, charm, and an infinite pleasure. . . . How he expresses with perfection all the tenderest and most elevated emotions. Chopin is the pianist of feeling *par excellence*. . . . Nothing can equal his works so full of originality, of distinction and of grace. Chopin is a pianist apart who should not and cannot be compared to anyone.[7]

Le Ménestrel was also effusive, but the review which attracted Chopin's attention most was the one written by Franz Liszt for the *Revue et Gazette Musicale*. While the Hungarian pianist was full of praise for his Polish colleague, there was a calculated condescension in his article which focused as much upon the luster of the audience as upon the quality of the performance. Mme d'Agoult who, no doubt, had a hand in it, thought the review a splendid barb. "Liszt wrote a magnificent article on the . . . concert." she recounted gleefully. "I think it must have really irritated them."[8] It certainly annoyed Chopin. On the surface, Liszt had treated him quite royally, but in the manner, he felt, of an emperor dealing with a vassal king. The affront was obvious to Chopin, but to the average reader it was perhaps difficult to detect the subtle arrogance in Liszt's suave and scintillating phrases. The account read:

Last Monday, at eight o'clock in the evening, the salons of M. Pleyel were splendidly illuminated: at the foot of a stairway carpeted and perfumed with flowers, a steady stream of carriages brought the most elegant ladies, the most fashionable young men, the most renowned artists, the wealthiest financiers, the most illustrious lords, all of the most elite society, representing an aristocracy of birth, fortune, talent and beauty.

A grand piano stood open on the platform; a crowd was gathered about it; everyone hoped to get the nearest seats; long in advance the crowd was settled and attentive, for no one wanted to miss even one sound, one note, one nuance or musical thought of the person who was about to come and seat himself there. And they had good reason to be so avidly attentive, so devoutly moved. For he whom they awaited, whom they were so anxious to see, to hear, to admire, and to applaud was not only a capable virtuoso, a pianist expert in the technique of his arts, an artist of great renown, he was all that and more: he was Chopin . . .

Similar to those flowers whose fragrant calyces open only at night, he requires an atmosphere of peace and composure in order to pour out freely the melodic treasures which repose within him. Music is his tongue; the divine language in which he expresses a range of emotion that only the few can understand . . . this exquisite celebrity from on high, this perfect aristocrat, has remained untainted by any attack. All criticism has been completely silenced around him as if posterity were already present. In the brilliant audience congregated about the poet, who for too long had remained silent, there was no one reticent or restrained; all voices rose in his praise.[9]

As for his compositions, Liszt declined to go into any detailed analysis. Suffice it to say, Chopin "was *himself*," he claimed, "as much indeed in the style as in the conception of his works. To his original ideas he has given an original form. The wild and harsh qualities which he has derived from his native land have found expression in the bold dissonances and strange harmonies while the delicacy and grace of his own personality are revealed in a thousand forms and embellishments of an inimitable fantasy. . . . Addressing himself more to an exclusive society than to the public at large, he was able to reveal himself without fear as he really is, an elegaic poet, profound, pure, and idealistic" (p. 246).

Just as one can damn with faint praise, so one can also deride with flagrant flattery. "The best thing in this sort of situation," Liszt told Marie d'Agoult earlier that year, "is to smile as you twist the knife more deeply."[10] And in so doing, the two of them were able to achieve a certain petty triumph over George and Chopin, their erstwhile friends, long-time rivals, and current enemies.

One consolation for all the effort Chopin's concert had cost him was the financial reward it brought with it. "Chopin has placed himself in a position to loaf away the whole summer," George joked, "simply by giving a concert where, in two hours and with two flicks of the wrist, he has put six thousand and several hundred francs in his pocket."[11]

In Warsaw news of the concert filtered back to his family. For some reason Chopin had not written them and they felt slighted by his neglect. Later, when he did write, he mentioned the recent strain in his relationship with Liszt, to which his father replied, "It would be a pity if there has been some coolness in your friendship."[12] Valuing his father's opinion, Chopin suppressed the temptation to retaliate and continued to behave toward Liszt with restraint and discretion. At times the effort seems to have taxed him to the utmost. Liszt recalled having seen him "pale and blanch to such a point that his complexion turned greenish and cadaverous. But in his most violent emotions," he acknowledged, "he retained self-control and then he was usually reluctant to talk about what he resented." All the same, "hurts struck deep in his soul, they fermented there in undefined pain and inward suffering to such a degree that long after their causes had vanished from memory he still felt their secret sting."[13]

Through the month of May, Chopin's pique gradually abated and by the middle of June he and George, along with Maurice and Chopin's manservant, left the petty vexations and irritating rivalries of Paris behind. In a carriage bound for Nohant they looked forward to a summer of peaceful relaxation.

W E HAVE BEEN at Nohant for a month and are 'enjoying' the most *abominable* weather."[1] George wrote a friend in Algeria during July of 1841. By mid-fall there had been little change: "It's pouring here and the ground is muddy,"[2] Chopin commented glumly. Except for an occasional clear day the entire summer tended to be cool and rainy that year. At one point there was even a small "earthquake" which uprooted trees and left the stolid Berry folk rather shaken up.

Chopin—"who always wanted to go to Nohant and then could never tolerate it"[3]—became extremely depressed during those dark, drizzling days. From his second floor room he looked out at the gray clouds hovering over the bleak, wet fields and brooded gloomily about his future. "It is crutches or wooden legs that await me if I keep heading into old age at this rate," he wrote Fontana. "Just recently I dreamed that I died in a hospital and it is so deeply engraved in my mind that it seems it was only yesterday."[4]

Feeling isolated and lonely in the country, he longed for the little luxuries of the city and began pestering his friends for them. "I am sending you 100 francs for all sorts of purchases," he told Fontana. "First of all, keep what you need for the *Charivari*.* . . ." Then, he continued, "buy me some scented soap, two pairs of suede gloves,

. . . a bottle of *patchouli* and a bottle of *Bouquet de Chantilly* at Houbigant Chardin's in the Faub[ourg] Saint-Honoré. In the galleries of the Palais Royal, almost in the middle of the side by

* A humerous journal whose satires on the Parisian scene amused Chopin.

the theater there is a large shop of *galanteries* (as we call them). It has two windows with all sorts of boxes, trinkets, and knick-knacks, which are dazzling, elegant, and expensive. Ask them for a little ivory hand to scratch one's head with. You must have seen such things many times. . . . It seems to me I saw one in that store. Go and find out. If they have the little gadget, send it to me. . . . At the top of my armoire you will find a flat tin bottle covered with flannel to be filled with warm water and placed on the stomach; you will also find there an inflatable pillow which I bought for traveling. Put Kastner['s *Treatise on Counterpoint*] in with the lot and send them all to me after having them well packed. . . . Please be quick![5]

Within a few days even more requests followed:

Please buy me a copy of Witwicki's poem [*A Pilgrim's Evening*]. I don't have it. Then go to the Palais Royal in the arcade on the theater side—number 37, I think, and buy me a plain unbleached smock for 14 francs. . . . If it isn't number 37, it must be 47 or 57, at one of those tailors' shops. There are dozens of them. . . . One of them sells these smocks: I bought one last week, neatly sewn with two breast pockets and pearl buttons etc. . . . (p. 56)

As in Majorca the one item which concerned him most was a good piano. He preferred one from Pleyel, but as he told Fontana, "if Pleyel won't give you any satisfaction and you think Erard will make a better deal then switch. . . . Why stick with Pleyel when the other is willing to be more accommodating?" (p. 60).

Partly because of the weather and partly because of difficulties with the movers, the piano did not arrive until August 9. But, while waiting for it, Chopin was by no means deprived of an instrument since George still had the one she bought for Liszt only four summers before. By coincidence the new piano reached Nohant just one day before the arrival of the singer, Pauline Viardot, and her husband, Louis. This double treat not only broke the quiet monotony of country life but also heralded the onset of a brief period of sunshine. "The weather has been very good for several days," Chopin reported happily. "As for my music, however," he added, "it is awful. Mme Viardot was here for two weeks and we spent less time on music than on other things" (p. 69).

The welcomed appearance of the Viardots at Nohant was one of the few bright moments in a rather troubled summer, clouded by petty dissensions. For one thing, George's domestic staff could not get along with the Polish servant Chopin had brought with him. Mme Sand had not objected to his presence at first although she usually did not like her guests to bring servants from the city. Invariably they stirred up trouble among her own help, leaving them disgruntled with their lot in the provinces. She was soon sorry she had made an exception in Chopin's case since the trouble she anticipated was not long in coming. By early August matters had come to a head and on the tenth Chopin reluctantly conceded to his hostess' wishes. "Without doubt I will dismiss my old manservant tomorrow," he wrote Fontana. "He has gone crazy here. He is a good man and knows his job well but he dawdles and irritates everyone" (p. 62).

A much more serious source of trouble that summer was the news from Paris that one of Chopin's pupils, Mlle de Rozières, was having an affair with Antoni Wodziński, the brother of Frédéric's former fiancée, Maria. Reports had it that Mlle de Rozières was chasing young Wodziński all around the countryside and even threatened to follow him clear across Europe if necessary. George, who was all for the assertion of women's rights, applauded the girl's spirit and encouraged her. When a lively correspondance sprang up between the two women Chopin became annoyed, feeling excluded from their intimacy and worried by what they might say about him. He knew that Marie de Rozières must have gleaned the humiliating details of his affair with Maria from Antoni and was not anxious for George to learn any more about that than she already knew. In addition he was sure that the gossipy mademoiselle would tell Antoni all about his relationship with Mme Sand and feared this information would then filter back to his family and friends in Poland. Upset, he accused Mlle de Rozières of meddling in other people's business, distorting the truth, and sewing dissension. "Just between ourselves," he wrote Fontana, "she is an insufferable old pig who has figured out how to slip into my private garden in the most astonishing fashion in order to rip up my rosebeds, grubbing in the dirt for truffles. She is a creature never to be trusted; she is nothing but a regular old maid with the most atrocious lack of discretion!" (p. 68).

Later, when he found out that Antoni was sick in Poland and that Mlle de Rozières was about to rush off to "save his life," Chopin was fit to be tied. "I am convinced that Antoni's illness is not as serious as they say," he informed Fontana. "You wrote to me too late for anything to be done since his little lovebird had already sent the Mistress of the House here a desperately sentimental letter, full of confidences: that she was going off to join him, that she would flaunt all convention. . . . I introduced this scarecrow to Mme Sand," he went on, fuming with indignation, "as a piano teacher for her daughter without knowing the true character of the hussy. She has wasted no time digging her claws in by posing as a victim of love while pretending to be *fully informed about my past,* thanks to the Polish colony which she has met on various occasions. In this way she wormed herself into Mme Sand's confidence (and you wouldn't believe how sly and deceptive she has been in exploiting my relations with Antoni). You can imagine how much all this pleases me, especially since Antoni (you must have noticed) only loves her because she clings to him like a leech and doesn't cost him anything" (p. 73).

George, not being directly affected by the young lady's indiscretions, and viewing the situation with a woman's eyes, saw things in an entirely different light. Writing Mlle de Rozières, she noted, "There is a certain antagonism here against you for which I really can't find any cause. It makes no sense at all and is almost like a disease. . . . Really I don't know how you could have wounded him so deeply. He is very spitful towards you. . . . He considers my friendship for you and the way I have defended your rights to *independence* as crimes. . . . If I

had not been a witness of these sick infatuations which suddenly turn into hostilities over the past three years I should be
baffled."[6]

Because of this situation George took to concealing most of
Mlle de Rozières' letters from Chopin. She knew all too well
what would happen if he were to read them. "We would have
an entire day of silence, moroseness, suffering, and bizarre behavior" (p. 361), she predicted. Once when she tried to set
Chopin's mind to rest by assuring him that Antoni would not
come to Nohant that summer, the result was explosive. "He
hit the ceiling," she told Mlle de Rozières, "saying that if I was
so sure of it, apparently it was because I had told Wodziński
the whole story. [i.e., how Chopin disapproved of Antoni's
seeing Mlle de Rozières] to which I said *yes* and thought he
would go crazy. He wanted to leave, saying that I was making
him look like a fool, that I was stirring up trouble between
him and his best friends, that the cause of it all was my gossip-
ing with you etc." (p. 361).

While George was dying to ask Mlle de Rozières to Nohant
that summer she didn't dare. "I can't invite you into the midst
of a hornet's nest" (p. 362), she told the young girl. But not
being able to have whom she wanted in her own house irked
George tremendously and it began to dawn on her that Chopin, in his quiet, unassertive way, was subtly manipulating her
to his own advantage. Firmly intent on keeping hold of the
domestic reins herself, she changed her mind and wrote back
to Mlle de Rozières, "I shall persist in telling you that you are
invited and that I expect you. I don't want him to think he is
master here" (p. 363).

It was easy enough to say this to someone else, but when it
came to dealing with Chopin himself, George found she simply could not broach matters in such a head-on manner. If she
did he would grow evasive and retreat into a sullen silence
rather than face an open conflict. There were, in fact, times
she had seen him spend "a whole day without saying a word to
anyone. Was he sick? Had someone made him mad? Had I
said anything to upset him? . . . I shall never know" (p. 363)

she concluded. Living with such a highly sensitive person was more than she could bear sometimes. "I have never had any peace with him," she declared that summer, "and I never will" (p. 362).

One person responsible for the unpredictable moodiness of her friend, George suspected, might be Julian Fontana. Surprisingly enough she had hardly ever laid eyes on the man and knew very little about him. He wrote Chopin every week and his letters ("I don't know whether they contain news or mere twaddle," she claimed) "always cause a noticeable change for the worse in his frame of mind. I only know this individual by sight but I think he has gotten burned in life and is forever ready to wish his own misfortunes on others. This character is perhaps more worthy of pity than blame but he causes a lot of harm to the *other one* who has such a delicate skin that even a flea bite can produce a deep wound" (p. 426).

Solange's arrival at Nohant in mid-summer did little to facilitate family harmony. George had sent Maurice to Paris for her with the warning, "Your brother and I love you, but we have no illusions about certain faults which you will have to correct and which you will certainly have to try to rid yourself of: self-centeredness, the need to dominate others, and your silly, insane jealousy . . . Chopin sends you a kiss and is waiting to spoil you but I won't let him do it" (p. 398).

The unusual touchiness which afflicted both George and Frédéric that summer may have been due, in part, to the fact that both were working very hard. At night George poured over endless pages of proof which she had to correct for the new edition of her works. In addition she had become involved with Pierre Leroux and Louis Viardot in founding a new periodical, the *Revue Indépendante,* which was to serve as a vehicle for Leroux's socialistic ideas. Mme Sand was convinced that the impact of her friend's philosophical theories would equal that of Jean Jacques Rousseau and insisted that "people will read Leroux as they do the *Contrat Social*" (p. 546). Full of optimism, she spent long hours laboring for the new journal in which she planned to serialize her latest novel, *Horace,* a work very much influenced by Leroux's doctrines. Buloz had refused to publish the book in the *Revue des Deux Mondes* because of its political overtones, and the abbé Lamennais even accused George of preaching communism in it. Unfortunately, as enthusiastic as she was about the book's message, she could not get herself very excited about writing it. This worried her. "It is impossible," she realized, "to be so completely bored writing without the reader becoming bored also" (p. 400).

In the new novel she succumbed to the irresistible temptation of thrusting a spiteful jab at her old friend, Marie d'Agoult, whom she portrayed as the vicomtesse de Chailly, a hypocritical aristocrat whose "nobility was as artificial as all the rest of her, teeth, bosom, and heart."[7] Through this attack George had at least guaranteed herself one reader who would respond to *Horace* with something other than boredom. If the countess had any misgivings about the author's intentions, Liszt quickly suppressed them. "There is no doubt," he told her mercilessly, "that it was you whom Mme Sand attempted to portray in her description of Madame de Chailly's artificial mind, her artificial beauty, and her artificial aristocracy."[8] By now even Liszt was beginning to lose patience with his beautiful but vindictive mistress.

While George was exhausting herself in these literary and philosophical ventures, Chopin was also busy. However tiresome he may have found the country at times, Nohant ultimately proved to be the only place in which he could really accomplish any work, and it was not unusual to find him hovering over his piano as late as three o'clock in the morning. By the beginning of that autumn he had sketched out or completed most of the works he was to publish for the entire year. Considering how meticulous a composer he was, this added up to a large output for him, consisting of all the material in Opuses 43 through 49 plus several other small works which were to appear later. When a publisher complained about his prices, Chopin reminded him of the vast amount of time and effort he devoted to each of his laboriously polished works.

This, he argued, prevented him from being more prolific and therefore justified the cost of his compositions. "If I wanted to exploit the situation . . ." he wrote, "I could write fifteen second-rate pieces a year which he could buy for 300 francs each and that way I could make *a larger income*. But would that be honest?"[9]

As he finished each composition he would wrap it up carefully and send it off to Fontana with detailed instructions. "In the name of heaven, be careful of my manuscript," he would chide, "don't crumple it or stain or tear it. . . . Recopy it. . . . If the recopying bores you, do it anyway *for the absolution of all your great sins*, because I wouldn't want to trust these fly tracks of mine to some clumsy copyist. . . . Be sure now not to mess up the pages! (p. 88). Chopin realized how much he owed to the incredibly patient Fontana and fully appreciated his loyalty but he was often rather casual in acknowledging it. "You are capable and devoted," he would simply tell his friend, "that's why I pile all these jobs on you" (p. 66).

One of the biggest assignments thrust on Fontana that summer was the task of finding Chopin a new apartment. He had never really been happy in the rue Tronchet and now finally decided to look for something else. "In walking along the streets, where I might like to live, if you see an apartment that would seem to suit me, please let me know" (p. 68). When Fontana wrote back that he had found several, Chopin answered, "Tell me the house number and give me all the details. What are the stairs like? Is the entrance near the stables? Is it exhausting to climb? Are the rooms conveniently arranged? Are the ceilings high? Is there any smoke? Is the light good? etc. I would like to live in the *rue du Mont-Blanc* or the *rue des Mathurins* or even on the boulevard near the Chaussée d'Antin (p. 74).

After considerable deliberation he concluded it was best to remain in the rue Tronchet after all: "I think I'll take the one next to where I am" (p. 76) he wrote Fontana. That was in September. By October he had changed his mind again and wrote back, "You can take the sofa from the sitting room and have the rest sent to Pelletan, *16 rue Pigalle*, I would also be obliged if you would have the bed taken out of my bedroom since I am *definitely* going to live in one of the pavilions in the rue Pigal [*sic*]" (p. 83).

Despite their frequent bickering that summer, George had apparently suggested that Chopin share the smaller of the two pavilions with Maurice while she and Solange continued to occupy the larger one. With a new tenant for the fall, particularly such a fastidious one, Mme Sand had certain changes to make. "If Chopin is to give lessons in the salon," she wrote Eugène Pelletan (who was living in the pavilions for the summer), "he cannot let his chaste young Misses be exposed to the Giorgone nudes there. Would you try, therefore, to relieve us of the burden of having to remove those canvasses in the midst of all the confusion when we get back?"[10]

Except for three days which Chopin spent in Paris toward the end of September, he and George remained at Nohant until early November. As they prepared to return to the city for the winter Chopin once more saddled Fontana with a host of last minute chores. "See that the windows are opened (if it isn't raining) and air the rooms—particularly Mme Sand's quarters. You must have fires lit in the stoves and fireplaces several days in advance . . . I hope this is not a bother to you."[11]

On the second of November the couple arrived back in the rue Pigalle, just one day after George's new journal, the *Revue Indépendante* had made its debut. "Our household is very economical and very calm since we have become neighbors with Chopin, and he himself is much better too," George wrote after they had gotten settled.

Several fine ladies complained that the rue Pigalle was too far from their elegant districts, to which he answered: "Ladies, I give my lessons much better in my own room and on my own piano for twenty francs than I do on the outside for thirty. And besides you would have to send for me in a carriage, so do what you like." Some of them have decided to come here while others are paying the thirty francs and sending their carriages to pick him up and return him. The dear boy doesn't pay enough attention to money for the idea to have occurred to him by himself. I suggested it to him and had a lot of trouble getting him to agree. But I congratulate myself for it because with his feeble health he must earn a lot of money without working too hard.[12]

Fortunately the separation of the two pavilions prevented the sound of her companion's piano lessons from disturbing Mme Sand who, as usual, slept late into the day.

On December second Chopin again played for the Court but according to him he was "not in a good mood" and George commented that he was "not too happy" (p. 522). However, from Warsaw, his sister wrote that she heard he was "in great favor with the Queen and the Court."[13]

On February 21, 1842 he appeared in public for the first time that winter, assisted by his good friends, Pauline Viardot and Auguste Franchomme. In the words of M. Escudier of *La France Musicale,* it was a "festive occasion, full of charming smiles, dainty pink faces and well-shaped tiny white hands; a magnificent fête in which simplicity was combined with grace and elegance, while good taste served as a pedestal for wealth. . . . The public collapsed in ecstasy." The critic himself experienced such transports of joy that Chopin's "simple and original" melodies sounded to him like "the faint voices of fairies sighing under silver bells," and "showers of pearls falling on crystal tables."[14]

In less fanciful phrases, Maurice Bourge, writing for the *Revue et Gazette Musicale,* spoke of Chopin's "exceptional playing," claiming that he possessed "personality to which no one else holds the secret. . . . As we know, Liszt and Thalberg excite by producing an effect of violent delirium. Chopin does the same but in a less vigorous, less fiery manner, precisely because he strikes the most intimate strings of the heart."[15]

Unknown to Chopin, on the same day as his concert, his old music teacher, Adalbert Żywny, who had given him his first formal lessons, died in Warsaw at the age of eighty.

Shortly after the concert, Chopin began to suffer more than usual from the bitter Parisian winter, and during the following months Mme Sand had a semi-invalid on her hands. In fact she had two, for Frédéric's long-time friend, Jan Matuszyński,

also a victim of tuberculosis, fell ill and was taken into the rue
Pigalle household. There he rapidly grew worse and eventually died on April 20. His death was a "slow and cruel agony
which caused Chopin as much suffering as if it had been his
own," George wrote Pauline Viardot. "He was strong, coura-
geous, and devoted, more so than one might have expected
from such a frail being. But when it was over he was shattered."[16] For Chopin, afflicted with the same disease, the loss
of his close friend took on an especially ominous significance.
His own condition had already deteriorated that spring to the
point where he complained, "I must stay in bed all day, my
head and my glands ache so much."[17] During these dis-
heartening weeks Chopin had little strength and less inclina-
tion to see anyone. He seldom even wrote his family who
began to grow alarmed at the "months of silence" that passed.

The pall of death which now hung over the little houses in
the rue Pigalle became so oppressive that George decided to
take Chopin away as quickly as possible. Within a week after
they had buried Matuszyński in the little cemetery in Montmartre, George was packed and ready to leave for the country. The decision was wise and Chopin offered no resistance.
"He is beginning to revive somewhat and is getting ready for
our departure," George wrote Pauline. "I hope that Nohant
will restore him, as far as possible, to health."[18]

As she had been so often in the past Mme Sand was again
proving to be Chopin's ministering angel. But the burden of
caring for her "second son" was not as easy for her as it had
once been. To some of her friends the strain was beginning to
show. Mickiewicz felt she had become a victim of her own generosity. "Chopin," he claimed, "is her evil genius, her moral
vampire . . . who torments her and may well end by killing
her" (p. 610 n.3). Surprisingly enough Mlle de Rozières had
the opposite opinion. Chopin, she suspected, not George,
would ultimately be the one to suffer because Mme Sand, with
all her benevolent instincts, tended to be more solicitous than
sensitive. "He calls her his angel," she observed, "but the angel
has enormous wings which can sometimes crush you."[19]

*édéric François Chopin, age thirty-six
robably copied from the Ary Scheffer
portrait, 1846)*

*George   Sand   (Amantine-Aurore-Lucile
Dupin,   baroness   Dudevant),   age   thirty-
three (by Julien, c.1837)*

*urice Sand, age fourteen, 1837 (by
Luigi Calamatta)*

*Solange Sand, age nineteen, 1847 (by J.-B.
Clésinger)*

Pauline Viardot-Garcia

Eugène Delacroix

Auguste Franchomme

The abbé Félicité de Lamennais

Palma, on Majorca, as seen from the bay (painted in 1842)

The house of Son Vent

The monastery of Valldemosa

PHOTOGRAPH, 1961, COURTESY OF DR. SIDNEY ISENBERG

The Pleyel piano on which Chopin finished his Preludes in Majorca

The walls and gate to Nohant (on the right) with the village church in front

The château of Nohant, front façade and entrance drive

The garden at Nohant, painted by Delacroix

*George Sand's study at Nohant
with the desk at which she wrote*

The dining room at Nohant

The salon at Nohant

One of the galleries at the Palais Royal where Chopin often shopped for such items as ivory head-scratchers and smocks

The Bois de Boulogne, where Chopin and Mme Sand liked to take outings on good days, George on horseback, Chopin in a carriage

*No. 9 Square d'Orléans, where Chopin lived on the first floor
from 1842 until 1849*

The Théâtre Français, where George Sand's play, **Cosima,**
ran for one week in April 1840

*Alphonse de Lamartine, poet and Saint Simonian, head of
the provisional government of France during the revolution of 1848*

*Manifestation of May 15, 1848, felt by many to have been instigated by George Sand's writings.
On the same day Chopin played for Queen Victoria and Prince Albert in London.*

The interior of the Church of the Madeleine, where Chopin's funeral was held on October 30, 1849

The cemetery of Père la Chaise, where Chopin is buried

❦ CHAPTER NINETEEN ❧

THE TALL, SLENDER POPLARS which lined the road in front of Nohant swayed drowsily in the warm May sun. Their leaves, trembling in the breeze, cast cool, quivering shadows over the grassy lawn of the small chateau near the village square. The monotonous rustle of the foliage was interrupted spasmodically by bursts of music coming from the piano on the second floor. At times long, flowing passages of magnificent sound were followed by prolonged periods of silence or the maddening repetition of a single phrase hammered out over and over again. Chopin would write and rewrite the same piece a thousand times before he achieved the exact effect he wanted. From time to time the dogs would bark as a carriage rattled past the front gates or the "mistress of the house" returned from a ride across the neighboring fields. Above the clatter of horses' hoofs her voice could often be heard calling to the dogs or laughing and chatting with some friend who had accompanied her. Apart from these sounds there was little to disturb the peaceful hush of the quiet Berry countryside during the pleasant summer months of 1842. Nohant, as usual, had a marvellous restorative effect upon both George and her companion. Fatigue and depression evaporated in the warm air, while the wounds of winter healed quickly in the languid stillness of this restful setting.

Despite the calming influence of Nohant—or perhaps because of it—Mme Sand found it difficult to work much that summer. Since February she had been serializing her new novel, *Consuelo*, for the *Revue Indépendante* which had survived the winter and was still struggling along in its first year of life.

Even when she shut herself up for four or five days a week, "like a bat in the darkness," George still found that she could barely get her installments off on time.

For Chopin, work came more easily. He had already begun his vigorous Polonaise in A-flat Major and was soon to finish his Ballade in F Minor as well as his Scherzo in E Major. He was visibly improved, both in body and in spirit. At times, though, he suffered from terrible nightmares or "hallucinations" which disturbed George so much that she finally moved her bed into the study next to his bedroom where she could watch over him more easily at night.

Maurice, who continued to study with Delacroix, was also at Nohant that summer, "sweet, industrious, and calm as the calmest sea,"[1] according to his doting mother. Delacroix himself arrived in early June, exhausted from a bad cold and the long journey down from Paris, but still energetic enough to set up a studio in the loft of a stable near the main house. There he resumed his painting as well as his lessons with Maurice. The casual atmosphere of the country agreed with him. "This spot is very pleasant," he wrote, "And the hosts couldn't be more gracious in entertaining me. When we are not all together at dinner, lunch, playing billiards, or out walking, each of us stays in his room, reading or lounging around on a couch. Sometimes, through the window which opens on to the garden, a gust of music wafts up from Chopin at work. All this mingles with the songs of nightingales and the fragrance of roses. Thus far, obviously, I have nothing to complain about." It was not only Chopin's music that pleased Delacroix but the composer himself. "He is a man of rare distinction, the most genuine artist I have ever met," the painter professed. "He is one of the few whom one can admire and respect."[2]

Along with Delacroix, George had expected Balzac to arrive at Nohant for a visit. He never appeared, however, much to Delacroix's relief. Balzac, he complained, "is such a chatterbox; he would have interrupted the peace and quiet I enjoy here so much" (p. 112).

In July Solange returned from boarding school and, as always, her presence proved a disruptive influence around the household. "Pretty and proud," she was nearing her fourteenth birthday and growing more and more independent with each passing year. "She is an unmanageable creature," her mother groaned, "an unusually intelligent girl with a laziness beyond conception. She can do anything and yet doesn't want to do a single thing. Her future is a mystery, a ray of sunlight obscured by the clouds."[3]

Besides Solange, George had other problems that summer, one of the most urgent being to find a new apartment in Paris. The rooms in the little pavilions off the rue Pigalle were small and overcrowded, in addition to which Chopin complained that they were "too cold." At the end of July the couple returned briefly to Paris to look for other quarters. After a short search they signed a lease on August 5 for two apartments in the Square d'Orléans which opened then on to the rue Saint Lazare. Long a haunt for artists such as Kalkbrenner, Alexander Dumas, père, and the actress Mlle Mars, the handsome shuttered building, arranged around a central courtyard, looked out on a lovely tree-shaded lawn with gravelled walks and a small fountain. Shut off from the noise of the street, the new quarters offered all the quiet privacy of the houses in the rue Pigalle along with considerably more room. The situation seemed ideal. With two separate but readily accessible apartments, the appearance of propriety was easily preserved. George took a suite of rooms on the second floor at No. 5 for 3,000 francs a year while Chopin rented a drawing room and bedroom on street level at No. 9 for 600 francs. Between them at No. 7 lived the Marlianis. Happy with their new accommodations, the couple returned to Nohant early in August and remained there for the rest of the summer.

By the beginning of November they were back in Paris and comfortably installed in the Square d'Orléans on either side of their good friends, Manöel and Charlotte Marliani. With three such intimate households so closely situated, the square took on a pleasant communal atmosphere. "We run back and forth during the evening," George wrote, "from one apartment to the other like good provincial neighbors. We have even come to share one cooking pot and all eat together at Mme Marliani's which is more economical and much more enjoyable than letting each one fare for himself" (p. 799).

This new arrangement pleased Chopin immensely, but with his family in Poland he still tried to minimize the closeness of his relationship to Mme Sand. His parents were too perceptive, however, not to grasp the situation, and where their son's health and happiness were concerned, Nicholas and Justyna Chopin were willing to be quite tolerant. "We have learned with pleasure from your last letter," his father wrote him on October 16, 1842, "that the country air has strengthened your health and that you are anticipating a good winter. We also learned that you have moved into a new apartment because your previous one was too cold. Won't you feel lonely, though, if *other persons* don't move too?"[4] Tacitly, without any criticism, the elder Chopins had accepted George's presence in Frédéric's life. They would, in fact, have felt greatly reassured to know that she still lived only a few yards away from their son and continued to look after him with her unfailing maternal solicitude.

As far as finances went, Chopin, for once, had little to worry about. His list of pupils in the Square d'Orléans read like the *Almanach de Gotha,* including such names as Princess de Chimay, Princess Czartoryska, the countesses Esterhazy, Branicka, Potocka, de Kalergis and d'Est. Of course there were others also, distinguished at least by ability if not aristocracy, such as Mlle Fredericke Mueller, Mme Rubio, and Messrs. Georges Mathias and Adolphe Gutmann.

The salon in which Chopin now gave his lessons was a high-ceilinged room with a graceful mantelpiece of white marble which he decorated with an ornate clock, porcelain vases, and elaborate candelabra. In front of the mantel stood a firescreen with extravagantly carved scrollwork, while above it hung a large but simply framed mirror. A plush, undulating, rococo-style sofa and matching chair framed this scene at either end of the fireplace. In front of the large window with its heavy draperies stood the magnificent grand piano from Pleyel's.

George's second floor drawing room, where she did most of her entertaining, was more spacious and contained a large billiard table which she had rented for twenty francs a month. On the mantelpiece stood "the things a smoker requires" and according to those who knew her, George was invariably "the first to light up her cigar."[5] To one side, in a smaller salon opening onto the main one, was the piano she always kept on hand during the years she lived with Chopin, and hardly an evening passed that didn't find him seated at it playing for her or her guests. On the rare occasion when he failed to appear for one reason or another, George would become quite anxious. Calling in the servants she would quiz them as to "what he is doing, whether he is working or sleeping, whether he is in a good or bad mood . . ." (p. 226). Certainly a strong sense of devotion still existed between the couple in the Square d'Orléans, even if they were no longer exactly "in love" as Mlle de Rozières claimed earlier. Perhaps it was just as well that way. After all "love is selfish compared to friendship,"[6] George concluded many years before.

On the more typical evenings when Chopin did visit Mme Sand, he would walk home across the courtyard between ten and eleven o'clock while George would sit down to write until daybreak. Having done relatively little work that summer she now found herself struggling to keep up the installments of her new novel for the *Revue Indépendante*. Despite her contributions, however, the new periodical was not doing well. Louis Viardot, one of its three originators, was increasingly occupied by the "trips, engagements, and performances" of his wife. Most of the editing, arrangements for printing, and other business matters were being left up to Leroux who found these more than he could handle. Even with an adequate staff, he could have done little, for the publication was running out of funds. Its core of subscribers had never been substantial and, as George observed gloomily, "zeal and courage count for nothing without money."[7]

Perhaps the *Revue* was too far ahead of its time. Much of what it published was oriented toward the glorification of the proletarian writer (in 1843 Karl Marx, visiting Paris, was

urged to contact George Sand because of her radical and proletarian sympathies!)[8] and it is hardly surprising that such a
journal should not thrive in the bourgeois society of Louis-
Philippe's France. Certainly the journal's failure was not due
to George Sand's lack of effort. In one of the *Revue's* early
issues she had published an essay on proletarian poets and
began to cultivate many of them personally. Among these
were Charles Poncy, a mason from Toulon, Savinien La-
pointe, a cobbler, and many others including a locksmith, a
baker, a barber, and a weaver. She would receive their manuscripts, criticize them, edit them and, if possible, publish them.
To these aspiring young authors whom she considered the
voices of the masses, she never ceased preaching Leroux's philosophy. "It is the only philosophy that is as clear as day and
which speaks to the heart like the gospel," she avowed enthusiastically. "It . . . recognizes all that is true, good, and beautiful in every moral and scientific system of the past and
present."[9]

The propagation of this doctrine soon buried George in an
avalanche of correspondence. Each month she received about
a hundred letters, most of which she tried to answer in some
fashion or other. This was a time-consuming project, but fortunately Mme Sand was relatively unencumbered with household duties just then and could devote herself wholeheartedly
to it. Solange was back in boarding school and Maurice was
usually off in Delacroix's atelier or at the medical school, attending anatomy lessons for his Beaux-Art's examinations.
Chopin was conveniently lodged in separate quarters and
Mme Marliani had assumed all the responsibilities of the
kitchen. Free from distractions during most of the day George
would begin each morning by attending to her correspondence. "My son brings me all my letters . . . when I
arise," she stated, "and it is he who reads them to me" (p. 16).
Those which were "only written in idleness, curiosity, and vanity" she did not bother to answer. The rest she attended to
personally in her own hand.

With the arrival of spring George and Frédéric returned to

Nohant. Solange remained at the pension Bascans and Maurice went to Guillery to visit his father. Although Mme Sand was forced to respect her son's paternal obligations, his absence always upset her, and this time, to make matters worse while he was away, she suffered from terrible migraine headaches. The weather was wretched: "We light a fire every day," she wrote Mme Marliani in mid-June. "In spite of this sorry spring we are having, I can't say that . . . I really miss Paris. . . . With nothing to do but stare at the clouds passing overhead, the trees bending down in the wind, and the rain beating on the windowpanes I feel very much in the country" (p. 154). Nohant under any conditions was always a solace to her.

A visit from Delacroix brightened her up temporarily but on the whole June and July proved to be dreary months. When the rains let up sufficiently she wrote Maurice, "Chopin and I go on great excursions, he mounted on a donkey, I on my own legs since I feel the need to walk and to breathe" (p. 156).

In August Chopin suddenly made up his mind to go to Paris for two or three days to see his publisher and discuss business. Restless by himself, however, he concluded his affairs quickly and returned to the country sooner than he had intended, bringing Solange home from boarding school with him. Then, because the weather finally took a turn for the better, he decided to remain at Nohant until the end of October. As he told the banker, Léo, in Paris, "Autumn is usually the most beautiful season in Berry—and so I shall be staying on here for some time yet."[10]

By the first of November, though, he was back in the Square d'Orléans. Maurice had accompanied him there while George stayed behind at Nohant in order to attend to certain business matters. Undaunted by her struggles with the *Revue Indépendante,* she now had plans for starting a new journal with friends in nearby La Châtre. Tentatively she thought of calling it *"The Popular Conscience*—or something like that."[11] In addition she was involved in leasing some property to a neighboring family, the Meillants, and felt she must finish these negotiations before returning to Paris.

While Chopin was concerned about leaving George alone in the country, she, in turn, was equally anxious about his being in Paris without her. No sooner had he left than she dispatched a note to Mme Marliani: "Here he comes, my little Chopin. I entrust him to you so take care of him in spite of himself. He does not look after his health well when I am not there. He has a servant who is good but stupid. I am not worried about his dinners because he will be invited out on all sides, and by that time of the day it will be just as well if he has to exert himself a little bit. But in the morning, as he is hurrying for his lessons, I am afraid he will forget to drink a cup of chocolate or bouillon which I force down him in spite of himself when I am there. . . . Nothing could be simpler than for his Polish servant to cook him a simple stew or a chop. But he won't ask him and may even try to prevent him from doing it. . . . Chopin is quite well now: all he needs is to eat and sleep like everyone else. . . . I count on you to warn me if Chopin becomes sick, whether it is serious or not, because I would drop everything to go and take care of him . . ." (p. 253).

A few days later she wrote Mlle de Rozières, explaining why she was delayed in the country and asking her to look in on Chopin from time to time.

> I am staying on for several more days at Nohant . . . because of chores around the house and some business affairs which aren't completely finished. I have forced Chopin to go start his lessons again and leave the country, which would be unhealthy for him in bad weather since it is devilishly cold in our big rooms at Nohant. . . . Check up on my little Chopin frequently, please, and force him to look after himself. . . . Just stroll by on some pretext or other to keep an eye on the aforesaid Chopin. See if he has lunch, is he neglecting himself or not, and inform me if he behaves like a fool in regard to his health. . . . Don't let him know that I have put you on his trail. (p. 254)

As a final measure she instructed her son to watch over him also. "Take my place a little," she wrote Maurice, "He would be as conscientious in looking after you as I would if you were sick" (p. 283).

Although genuinely concerned about Chopin, George, at the same time, was rather relieved to be away from him for a while. He could be so demanding of her time and attention. "I can tell you quite frankly and simply," she wrote a friend that fall, "Chopin's friendship for me has the character of an exclusive and jealous passion. It is a little whimsical and sickly like he is himself, the poor angel." Furthermore she was finally beginning to realize how little the two of them really shared in common. "Chopin," she observed, ". . . doesn't live by the same ideas as I do and doesn't understand mine in the least" (p. 915). In fact their rapport had become so limited that fall, she didn't even bother to tell him anything about the new journal she had stayed behind in Berry to work on.

Not until the end of November did Mme Sand begin to consider leaving Nohant. Chopin was more than anxious for her return. The city was wet, gloomy, and quite lonely for him without "the lady of the house." "So you have finished your assessments, and your stables have left you exhausted," he wrote her one dark, cloudy Sunday afternoon. "For God's sake, collect yourself for your departure and bring us your beautiful Nohant weather." [12]

The truth was, Chopin did not feel at all well then, and George, suspecting that matters were not as they should be, wrote Maurice, "Tell me if he isn't sick. His letters are short and sound sad." [13] At last on the twenty-third of November she wrote again, saying, "I don't want to stay here any longer. The beauty of the countryside is not worth it. I need you and Chopinet more than anything else, and I couldn't stand the worry again of knowing that you both might be sick at the same time" (p. 294).

When George finally arrived back in Paris she found Chopin looking very haggard, and over the following months he became bedridden many times with recurrent attacks of his illness. This, of course, put a great burden on George, who already had problems enough of her own. Disputes had begun to arise over the organization of the new journal at La Châtre. The paper, finally entitled *L'Éclaireur de l'Indre,* was intended by its founders "to decentralize Paris, morally, intellectually, and politically." The provinces, they felt, had been neglected by the Parisian press and had become "the gagged and bound victims of all the abuses of power that the government bureaucrats perpetrate" (p. 307). To set this new publication into operation was a major undertaking and George found that she was being delegated to do "all the secretarial work, the programs, the professions of faith, and the circulars" (p. 304). Because of this she could barely keep up the installments of her new novel, *La Comtesse de Rudolstadt* which was already being serialized in the *Revue Indépendante.*

Despite her efforts for the *Éclaireur de l'Indre,* George seemed to be the constant victim of misunderstanding and opposition. She had disagreements with her associates over who was to be the editor of the new journal, where it was to be published, and what political and philosophical stands it should take. She was first accused of not offering enough help and then of having imposed herself too much on the others. In the end she decided to limit her contributions to a few articles for the first issue and have little or nothing more to do with the whole venture. "Two or three pieces will suffice to attract a few more subscribers for you," she informed her colleagues, "and that is all I am prepared to do. . . . With all your wranglings you have killed the enthusiasm that is necessary if one is to perform a miracle" (p. 536).

By spring Chopin had recovered sufficiently to participate in a concert where he was assigned to play one part of a four-piano arrangement of Beethoven's Seventh Symphony. Then shortly afterwards, on May 3, 1844, his father, Nicholas Chopin, died in Warsaw. He was seventy-three years old. "His age and the fatigue of a long and painful struggle were the causes of our father's last illness," Frédéric's brother-in-law, Antoni Barciński, wrote him. "He spoke of you often, and during the last moments of his earthly journey he urged us to encourage you, in his name, to bear with resignation the blow which was about to fall on us all. . . . I stayed beside him with all the family and it was in distributing his blessings on us and on you, that his gaze wandered to your portrait and bust and he rendered up his soul to God.[14]

This news left Chopin in a state of collapse, and George immediately called some of his old friends in for help. "Our poor Chopin has just learned of his father's death," she explained to one, Franchomme. "He wants to remain by himself today, but for my part I beg you to come see him tomorrow since you are one of the two or three people who can do him good. As for me, I suffer too much from his grief: I don't have the strength to console him."[15]

For the next few days Frédéric remained in bed unable even to rouse himself enough to write his family. Then, just as George had done when Matuszyński died, she began making preparations to take Chopin back to the country. On the twenty-ninth of May she wrote his mother a very warm letter, taking care to conceal the actual state of her son's condition. "Dear Madame," she began,

I do not believe I can offer any other consolation to the excellent mother of my dear Frédéric than to assure her of the courage and resignation of her admirable child. You know how profound his grief is and how overwhelmed his spirit feels. But thank God he is not ill, and we are leaving in a few hours for the country. . . . As for yourself, please don't worry about his physical surroundings. I can never take away his deep and lasting sorrow which is certainly a justifiable one, but I can at least take care of his health and provide him with as much affection and attention as you yourself would do. This is indeed a most agreeable obligation which I have imposed upon myself quite happily and I will never fail in it. I promise you that, Madame, and I hope you trust in my devotion to him. . . . My sympathy, sincere as it is, cannot soften this terrible blow, but I know that by telling you that I will devote my days to his son, and that I regard him as my own, I can give you some tranquillity of spirit as far as matters here are concerned. (p. 559)

Justyna Chopin was comforted by George's letter.

I thank you, Madame, for the touching words you wrote me. They brought some consolation to my poor soul, racked by grief and anxiety. . . . As for my concern over Frédéric, it knew no bounds. After the blow came my only thought was of the dear child, who, alone in a far-off country with his frail health and highly sensitive nature, could not help but be crushed by such fatal news. In that terrible moment, surrounded by my other children, I suffered from not being able to take that beloved son in my arms and help relieve his grief. I was in despair because of him and could find no peace of mind. You understood my situation well, Madame, and it required the heart of a mother to comprehend this and to know how to bring true consolation to mine. And so Frédéric's mother thanks you sincerely and entrusts her dear child to your maternal care. Be, Madame, his guardian angel as you have been my comforting angel.[16]

CHAPTER TWENTY

THE TWO DAY coach trip from Paris to Nohant
was an unusually strenuous one for Mme Sand and
her companion in May of 1844. When they finally
arrived, it took them some time to recover. "Chopin
still doesn't have enough strength to tell us what he wants,"
George wrote Marie de Rozières a full week later. "The poor
child has spent these past eight days in misery. On the way
here he had a flare-up of the inflammation in his lungs and a
toothache which has tortured him mercilessly. It is only this
evening that the pain has subsided and the swelling in his
cheek has gone down. . . . But there is some good in every
misfortune and this physical affliction has forced him to forget
his mental anguish a little."[1]

In his grief Chopin found his thoughts turning back to his
childhood faith as a source of comfort. This alarmed George
who considered such an attitude unhealthy. "The catholic religion," she insisted with typical anticlerical fervor, ". . . can
no longer accomplish anything but evil in the world" (p. 855).
"Catholic dogma surrounds death with atrocious terrors," she
asserted and complained that "instead of dreaming of a better
world for those whose souls are pure, Chopin had only frightening visions."[2]

Work fortunately provided a beneficial escape for the
bereaved musician. Shut up in the dank, drafty rooms of the
old chateau, he labored over the first drafts of his Sonata in B
Minor. In addition, he had to handle his own business affairs
now since he no longer had the faithful Fontana to take care
of such things for him. His friend, a talented but none-too-
successful pianist, had finally despaired of a musical career in

Paris and set out for America in 1841. In his absence Frédéric besieged Albert Grzymała and Auguste Franchomme with his incessant demands, but while both were obliging and patient, neither was disposed to put up with the constant impositions poor Fontana had endured.

Unexpectedly in the midst of this depressing season came welcome news from Warsaw: Chopin's sister, Louise, and her husband, Kalasanty Jędrzejewicz, decided to spend part of the summer in France. It was nearly nine years since Frédéric had seen any of his family and fourteen since he had last seen Louise. While he was still recovering from the shock of this surprise, George picked up her pen and invited the couple to Nohant. "Dear Madame," she wrote her friend's sister,

> I await you here with the greatest impatience. I think Fritz [Chopin] will arrive in Paris before you, but if you should not find him there I will see to it that one of my friends [Mlle de Rozières] gives you the keys to my apartment, which I beg you to use as if it were your own. I shall be very upset if you don't accept. You are going to find my dear boy frail and considerably changed since you last saw him! But don't be too disturbed over his health. It has remained about the same for the past six years during which time I have seen him every day. He has a rather severe bout of coughing every morning and, in winter, two or three worse attacks, but they only last around two or three days. In addition he has an occasional spell of neuralgia . . . I still hope his health will improve with time but I am sure that he will last at least as long as anyone else if his life is well-regulated and cared for. The joy of seeing you, while mixed with deep and painful emotions, may shake him up a little the first day, but will do him much good. . . . Come then and see us, and believe me when I say that I already love you as a sister.[3]

On the fifteenth of July Frédéric dashed off to Paris, full of excitement. There, after an emotional reunion with his two guests, he suddenly turned around and headed back to Nohant on the twenty-fifth. George, who hardly expected him back so soon, scolded him for not staying longer. "It was in spite of me that he left his sister," she protested, "but he claims he didn't want to deprive her of seeing Paris and didn't have the strength to run around anymore" (p. 587).

Through an unfortunate misunderstanding the Jędrzejewiczes delayed their departure for Nohant, waiting for Pauline Viardot to join them. When she failed to appear after ten days they finally left without her and arrived at Mme Sand's on August 9. "Our first days here," Frédéric exclaimed, "were like those in Paris—happiness enough to drive you out of your mind."[4]

In order for her guests to be as close as possible to their brother, the "mistress of the house" moved them into her study which adjoined Chopin's bedroom. Every morning as soon as he was up, Frédéric hurried next door to have chocolate with the Jędrzejewiczes and remained there for hours with Louise while she sat embroidering as they reminisced. During these long tête-à-têtes, Kalasanty Jędrzejewicz often roamed the countryside with Maurice. Sketching scenes of the Berry landscape together, the two men became good friends. In exchange for artistic instruction Kalasanty taught Maurice Polish words and phrases which he loved to spring on Chopin later in the day.

The long summer evenings were frequently hot, humid, and mosquito-ridden, but none of these annoyances could detract from the enjoyment of the two families as they relaxed quietly after dinner and listened to Chopin play. Some nights they would draw their chairs up to the large round table in the middle of Mme Sand's cluttered salon and there, with the doors open on to the garden, George would read aloud from her latest novel, *Le Meunier d'Angibault,* while a warm breeze wafted the fragrant scent of lime leaves and pine needles through the room.

By the end of the month the guests from Warsaw had to leave. Their hostess was genuinely sorry to see them go; their presence had revived Chopin beyond all expectations and the exuberant young musician was still floating on clouds when he returned to Paris with them on the twenty-eighth.

The days that followed there were hectic. "I am continually on the go, running around with my sister," Chopin explained to Grzymała by way of an apology for having neglected him recently. "The mornings fly by and I get nothing done. They will stay in Paris on Monday and Tuesday [September 3] and then I shall leave for Nohant and they will start back home" (p. 167). In the little time that remained Frédéric whisked Louise and Kalasanty all over the city, sightseeing, visiting friends, and calling on celebrities. During the evenings he entertained them with musical soirées in the Square d'Orléans or took them to the opera where they saw Meyerbeer's *Les Huguenots* and Balfe's *Les Quatre Fils Aymon.*

Suddenly the third of September arrived and with great sadness the Jędrzejewiczes boarded the carriage for Warsaw. Among the souvenirs which they carried back with them were two gifts from George Sand: a pencil sketch she had done of their brother, and a rosary she was sending to their mother.

On the following day Frédéric returned to Nohant, tired from more than six weeks of constant excitement and activity. Even though nostalgic traces of Louise's presence filled the large country house with pleasant memories, Nohant still seemed lonely now in her absence. "My dearest Louise," George wrote later that month, "we live only in the thought of you since you left us. It was hard for Frédéric to part from you, as you can well imagine, but physically he has survived the strain quite well. All in all, your good and blessed revolve to come see him has borne fruit. It has taken all the bitterness from his spirit and given him back his strength and courage. . . . I assure you that you are the best doctor he has ever had" (p. 171).

As fall approached Chopin grew anxious for Paris, but since George was tied up with domestic problems just then he decided to remain in the country with her a while longer. "I plan to stay here several more weeks," he wrote Louise at the end of October. "The leaves have turned yellow but they have not all fallen and for the past week the weather has been wonderful. The mistress of the house is taking advantage of this to have some landscaping and other changes made in the court-yard. . . . A large lawn and banks of flowers are to be laid out there" (p. 175).

George was also planning some renovations inside the house and with so much to be done she kept putting off her return to the city. Restless, Chopin finally wrote Mlle de Rozières on November 13, "As you wanted me to forewarn you of my arrival I hasten to let you know that I shall have the pleasure of greeting you in Paris on Sunday (at half-past noon, I think). . . . Be so kind as to have a fire lit in my rooms" (p. 178).

His return to Paris was soon followed by the season's first blizzards. "It is snowing so heavily that I am very glad you are not on the road," he wrote George on the second of December as he watched a flurry of glistening white flakes settle over the courtyard in the Square d'Orléans. "It has been snowing since yesterday morning. . . . Your little garden is all covered with balls of snow just like sugar, swansdown, cream cheese, or Solange's hands and Maurice's teeth." "It's fantastic!" he cried, "everyone declares that winter is arriving far too suddenly" (p. 181–82).

Ignoring the gray skies and the sharp chill, Chopin bustled around the city preparing for his mistress' return. Looking "yellow, withered, cold, and swathed in three layers of flannel" (p. 182), he still managed to run all the errands she requested of him, even down to shopping for her winter wardrobe. "Your dress," he wrote concerning the latter, "is of black *levantine,* all of the finest quality. *I chose it myself* according to your orders . . . I think you will like it. . . . It costs 9 francs a yard, so you see it is the best there is" (p. 181).

Around mid-December George finally got back to Paris and was greatly relieved to find Frédéric shuffling about cheerfully in the midst of all the snow and ice. After six years he still remained a source of great concern to her. Worrying over him—his health, his state of mind, his finances, and his professional problems—had grown to be second nature with her. "It has become almost a necessity for me to wait on him and to care for him,"[5] she told Mme Marliani.

Unhappily Maurice Sand did not share his mother's attachment to the young musician. Twenty-one years old the previous June, he resembled his mother in appearance, having dark hair, an olive complexion, rather full cheeks, and a slightly receding chin. His expression was somewhat pouting and his disposition sullen and arrogant. He was not an individual of great resolution and, in general, he gave the impression of being a more or less colorless creature. This was no doubt the result of having been spoiled since birth by a doting mother, from whom he was finally beginning to develop some independence. For many years he had looked upon Chopin as a rival for his mother's affections, but only now, as a young adult, did he begin to express his feelings openly. Superficially the two men remained civil but there was less and less warmth in their relationship and Maurice's behavior toward Chopin became noticeably abrupt at times. "Politeness is not his strongest point,"[6] the latter commented to his sister that fall.

While Maurice often irritated Chopin, Solange, who turned sixteen in 1844, never failed to delight him. He was flattered by her adulation and enjoyed having her lounge around his room, reading a book, nibbling candy, or listening to him play. She liked to do this not only because she was rather indolent by nature ("the queen of sloths"[7] her mother christened her) but also because there was hardly anyone else in the house that would put up with her. George had never made any real attempt to conceal her preference for Maurice and continually scolded his younger sister for having "too violent a character." The poor girl's father, living miles away, almost always made a practice of ignoring her, while in Maurice's case there was the usual sibling rivalry. Solange, being by far the more spirited of the two children, could easily have held her own in any family squabbles had not her mother always sided against her. In retaliation the young girl tried to dominate the family spotlight by acting the role of *grande dame* or *femme fatale*. Such adolescent pretensions only served to aggravate George all the more, especially when she noted that many of her friends actually preferred the impish pomposity of Solange to the drab aloofness of Maurice.

With Chopin, Solange did not have to struggle hard for recognition. He was easily beguiled by her attentions and amused at the mischievous sparkle with which she could carry off a piece of impudence. To him she was a bewitching little sorceress, but to her mother she remained an obstreperous vixen. Searching for a scapegoat on which to blame her daughter's irascible behavior, George lashed out at the child's piano teacher, Mlle de Rozières. "There comes a time," she sternly informed the young lady, "when little girls are no longer little girls, when it is necessary to beware of the effect on their character which can be produced by the words they hear." Therefore, she insisted, "Not a word, *however casual,* about the *masculine sex.*" Blithely disregarding her own kaleidoscopic past, George was suddenly beginning to sound like a paragon of prudery! Unconscious of any inconsistency in her preaching, however, she continued to lecture the stunned girl in a startling crescendo of righteous indignation. "In the past you were not a flirt," she said, "but now, my little feline friend, your eyes have taken on a terribly voluptuous expression. . . . Men are noticing it, but, of course, if that doesn't bother you, why should I care? . . . Still I must explain to you why I don't want Solange around you" (p. 887).

Perhaps it was envy on George's part which prompted her to criticize the "voluptuous-eyed" piano teacher so harshly. At age forty Mme Sand was in the midst of that strenuous transition from youth to middle age when order and tranquillity gradually become more essential to one's existence. While she was content, on the whole, to have exchanged the role of mistress for that of mother, she still found the adjustment a bit difficult, one reason being that the less intimate she was with Chopin, the more possessive he became with her. As a result she often found herself having to endure the aggravation of a lover's jealousy without the compensation of a lover's embrace.

Sometime in the early part of 1845 the small, slender Louis Blanc lent her his embrace during a brief and well-concealed liaison. He was a handsome thirty-four-year-old socialist writer whose radical viewpoints George eventually came to share much more enthusiastically than she did his bed. Within a few months, pleading (prematurely) the encroachment of age, she terminated their affair although the two remained friends for years to come.

To fill the void of physical passion Mme Sand now substituted philosophical fervor, and during much of 1844 and 1845 she campaigned actively for her long-time idol, Pierre Leroux. Proclaiming herself "a fanatical disciple" of his doctrines, she decided to become his spokesman to "the people" and undertook a new genre of novel, the *roman champêtre,* in which she glorified the peasant and his simple way of life. Having lost her publisher due to the socialistic flavor of one of these novels, she began serializing others in the more liberal journals of the day. So intense were her convictions at this time that she even took the liberty of making them known to Prince Louis-Napoléon Bonaparte who was then a political prisoner in the fortress at Ham. "We shall never recognize any other sovereignty than that of the people" (p. 710), she announced emphatically to the future emperor of France.

Chopin, who had known the tyranny of Russian domination in Poland, was not unsympathetic to many of his mistress's views, but philosophical credos and political manifestos, no matter how noble in sentiment or lofty in phraseology, had little power to stir him. He did not share George's dissatisfaction with the July Monarchy of Louis-Philippe; he lacked her republican zeal and was not actively concerned with the problems of a down-trodden proletariat. His range of interest was largely limited to his lessons, his compositions, an occasional concert, and the perennial social whirl of the damask-covered salons in the elegant faubourgs.

Since the winter of 1844–45 was an exceptionally bitter one, Chopin was not able to pursue even these few interests as actively as before. "The terrible cold we have been having here has especially gotten him down" (p. 830), George commented in March, and Chopin himself wrote that "The temperature has dropped lower than ever. This is the first day there has been no snow in the courtyard garden. Spring is forgetting us." [8]

Unfortunately when spring finally did arrive it brought an epidemic of typhus to the region about Nohant, preventing the inhabitants of the Square d'Orléans from setting out for the country as early as they had planned. "The air everywhere is polluted and dangerous," [9] they were advised by George's physician in Berry that May.

While waiting for the epidemic to subside, Mme Sand kept her household diverted by entertaining P.T. Barnum's famous midget, Tom Thumb, and taking them to see a touring band of Iowa Indians. The latter fascinated her so much that she brought their chief, White Cloud, and his wife several lengths of red cloth and some glass beads in order to bribe an interview out of them.

Not until mid-June did George and Frédéric finally set out in Mme Sand's new carriage for Nohant. Accompanied by Pauline Viardot, they were more than glad to leave Paris after one of the longest and most rigorous winters they had ever spent there.

⚜ CHAPTER TWENTY-ONE ﷼

J UNE OF 1845 was bleak and chilly at Nohant. Day after
day the heavy gray skies rumbled and flashed, spewing
out torrents of rain over the dark landscape. The Indre
as well as the little brooks that fed it rose and overflowed their banks. Fields, roads, and villages were inundated
and lay lifeless under the billowy green blanket of turbid
waters swirling above them. Many inhabitants were left home-
less and everywhere the stench of decay filled the air.

Surveying the dismal scene from her house, Mme Sand
wrote Charlotte Marliani: "We are all fine but everyone here is
appalled; it is sickening to see so many unfortunate people
ruined by the floods. No one can ever remember seeing anything like it in our peaceful countryside. Our quiet little
streams have suddenly become rivers with currents and waves
as savage as the sea's. Yesterday the roads were cut off as the
water gushed over them, creating channels as large as the
Loire and as rapid as the Rhône. . . . All the crops along the
river's edge have been lost, and what makes the whole disaster
even worse is the fetid odor of rotting plants which the returning sunshine has produced. The loveliest meadows have become huge polluted swamps and there is considerable fear of
serious epidemics. We are situated somewhat above and away
from the river banks so don't worry about us. The foul air
doesn't reach us. . . . If I didn't love the country with a passion I would be very sorry for having come here."[1]

By early July, the storms finally vanished and the floods receded. The remainder of the month was hot and sultry, but
the change in weather was such a welcome relief that not even
Chopin minded the intense heat. "It suits me perfectly," he

wrote a friend, "and the country is so lovely."[2] Nevertheless he seldom went outdoors except for an occasional carriage ride and usually begged out of the excursions and picnics George often planned for her family "in a wood or amid some ruin"[3] near Nohant.

Away from Paris, Chopin tended to grow moody and listless no matter how much his hostess tried to distract him. He was bad enough when the weather was good, but "on terribly rainy days," George reported, "he becomes so glum and gets positively bored to death. He is not at all amused by the things which delight me and keep me busy in the country. Because of that I would gladly take him up to Paris at the drop of a hat, but on the other hand, I know he would be bored there too unless I stayed. As willing as I would be to sacrifice the country which I love, Maurice doesn't think I should and if I listened to Chopin more than to Maurice there would be some hullabaloo (p. 340). As always the "veritable adoration" (p. 58) between mother and son made it unthinkable for one to go against the wishes of the other.

Although Chopin tired of the country easily, he still had to admit that the change of atmosphere was good for him. "I am not cut out for rural life," he acknowledged, "but the fresh air is a great joy to me."[4] Certainly he must have benefitted from it in order for George to tell Mme Marliani that her friend had been "quite well" during his stay at Nohant that year. "He sleeps and eats and hasn't had any real trouble all summer." Her own physician, Dr. Papet, confirmed this impression after having examined the patient "with the greatest attention and found him perfectly healthy in every respect." His only problem, the doctor felt, was that he "is inclined to be a bit of a hypochondriac."[5]

As well as Chopin appeared to be, however, he still couldn't seem to get much work done. "I don't play a lot," he informed his family, "since my piano is out of tune. I write even less which is why you have received nothing from me for so long."[6] This insidious state of stagnation soon began to alarm the composer and as the summer progressed it became almost a source of panic to him. "Oh! How time flies!" he cried, "I don't know why but I don't accomplish anything worthwhile and yet I don't loaf around. . . . I spend whole days and nights in my room. There are certain manuscripts (Op. nos. 60, 61, and 62) I must finish before I return to Paris since it's impossible for me to compose in the winter" (p. 213).

And yet with all his good intentions he continued to fritter the time away. Little things interrupted his thoughts and took his mind away from his work. He would putter around the house, rearrange his room, daydream, and grow homesick. "I keep getting up and going into your room . . ." he told his sister, Louise. "At this particular moment my mind is not quite all here but off, as usual, in some strange place" (p. 201). When he finally would sit down to compose he almost always ended up erasing more than he had written.

Early each morning his stubborn, hacking cough returned to harass him until around ten o'clock when Solange began to pop in and out of his room. Sometimes she just wanted to chat; other times she brought him some hot chocolate to drink, but most of the time she came to wheedle some favor out of him. "Yesterday," he wrote his family, "Solange interrupted me, wanting to play some duets; today she has asked me to go watch a tree being cut down in the garden" (p. 204).

Elsewhere in the house there were other distractions. Frédéric's Polish manservant, Jan, like his predecessor, proved to be a source of dissension. He was "stupid and humorless"[7] George complained, threatening to throw water on his head the next time he rang the dinner bell so loud and long. Her own maid, Suzanne, fought with the poor man constantly, teasing him and ridiculing his thick Polish accent. Eventually reverberations from these daily storms down in the pantry wafted up to the second floor. "As for what goes on in the kitchen," Chopin claimed, "I would never know if Suzanne hadn't come to complain of Jan. He has been abusing her in French because she took his knife away from the table. . . . He tosses off such lovely epithets as 'ugly as a pig', 'mouth like a *derrière*' and other equally choice remarks. . . . For the sake of peace I may have to fire him which I hate to do. . . . Unfortunately the children don't like him either."[8]

By "the children" Frédéric was, of course, referring to Maurice and Solange. But he soon had to take a third one into account: Augustine Brault, a young cousin of Mme Sand who arrived at Nohant in early September. This new addition to the family was the teenage daughter of a tailor and a coarse woman of rather dubious reputation who was related to Mme Sand through the Delaborde side of her family. On seeing the unwholesome environment in which the poor child was growing up, George could not resist intervening and, in typical motherly fashion, attempted to take charge of the girl herself. The situation proved to be a delicate one since Mme Brault was reluctant to part with her daughter at first. But, being sensitive to money if little else, Adèle Brault quickly consented when George offered certain financial compensation in exchange for her offspring. So it happened that Augustine (or "Titine" as she was usually called) came to live at Nohant during the summer of 1845. "She has everything in her favor," George raved glowingly, "beauty, goodness, youth, honesty, refinement, and simplicity of heart."[9]

Unfortunately Solange did not see eye to eye with her mother in regard to Titine's virtues. On the contrary, she was not at all pleased with her new "sister" whom she promptly looked upon as competition. In Chopin she found an ally who sympathized wholeheartedly with her. He did not care for Titine's plebian background and, according to George, sometimes behaved with "frightful rancor"[10] toward her. Maurice, on the other hand, found the young girl attractive in more than a sisterly fashion. Almost at once he seemed to forget his youthful crush on Pauline Viardot which had begun the summer before. A flirtation developed and the two soon became quite intimate. Day by day it grew more evident that Augustine's presence at Nohant was creating a definite division in the little household, and the longer she remained, the more pronounced it became.

Another difficulty which arose from her arrival was the

added expense that now fell on Mme Sand who not only had to provide food and clothing for the young girl but an allowance of fifty francs a month to her parents for the privilege of assuming their responsibilities. In order to meet these new obligations George sat down in late October and dashed off a new novel which she completed in record time. By the first of November she wrote, offering it to the director of one of the Paris journals, "I have finished my little novel," she told him. "I did it in four days. . . . Its title, unless you have something better to suggest, is *La Mare au Diable*."[11] From a letter written by Delacroix to George Sand it is apparent that the author once thought of dedicating this novel, one of her best-known and most beautiful, to her Polish companion. "You have had a good idea to dedicate it to Chopin," the artist wrote in August 1846.[12] However, for reasons one can only imagine, George changed her mind. It is strange that despite their long association neither Chopin nor Sand ever dedicated one of their works to the other!

Toward the end of November Chopin returned to Paris while George went for a brief visit to her relatives, the Villeneuves, at the chateau of Chenonceaux. Old René Villeneuve, who in 1821 nearly became her guardian, was more than cordial now as her host, but, having grown as "petrified as his collection of sculpture and armor,"[13] he talked about little except his ancestors. Much more fascinating than the Villeneuves themselves was their magnificent chateau. "Chenonceaux is marvellous," George exclaimed. "The decor inside is antique in style and arranged with much taste and elegance." Resting on its graceful arches, the lovely renaissance structure extended out across the river Cher, a feature which combined an exquisite beauty with certain functional conveniences: "One always empties one's chamberpot out the window" (p. 213), George was amused to learn.

Just after her return to Paris Mme Sand came down with the grippe which soon spread to the rest of the family. Surprisingly enough only Chopin escaped. "Everyone in the house is sick with a cold," he wrote his family that December.

"I have my intolerable cough which is nothing extraordinary, but the mistress of the house is suffering from a bad sore throat which keeps her shut up in her room. . . . All Paris is coughing this week. . . . It's not particularly cold but the dampness is awful."[14] The scene at the Square d'Orléans on Christmas Eve, 1845, was scarcely cheery and Christmas Day itself was just as gloomy.

Hemmed in by sickness and bad weather, Chopin grew depressed. He longed for his family and tried to persuade his mother to come to Paris with some friends who were about to leave for France, but she refused. "I should have to spend the whole winter with you," she wrote, "and what would you do with me, my poor child? I would only cause you worry, and knowing how good you are, I am sure you would always be upset. You would feel I was bored, that I wasn't comfortable enough, and a thousand other such things. No, my dear boy that is something I can't do, especially since you are surrounded by people who take such loving care of you, for which I am forever grateful" (p. 232).

By January almost everyone had recovered and George was even feeling well enough to launch into another novel. In contrast to *La Mare au Diable* this new volume was to occupy her for over five months. It was to be given the title of its heroine, *Lucrezia Floriani*. Each morning after she had produced her nightly quota of eight to ten handwritten pages, George left them on her desk, and each day Chopin read and praised them. It was unusual for him to take such an interest in his companion's work and especially strange that this particular novel should win his admiration.

The unlikely plot of the new book concerned the selfish love of a sickly, effete young German, Prince Karol, for a noble-minded, generous Italian actress, Lucrezia Floriani. In her meteoric rise to fame the heroine, who was the daughter of a rough but honest fisherman, had become the mistress of at least three young men: a proud aristocrat, a famous singer, and a poverty-stricken actor. Although her affections had certainly been less than constant she always considered herself faithful and free of deception with each of her lovers. "I have never loved two men at the same time," she asserted virtuously. "I have never belonged in fact or intention to but one man at a given time throughout the duration of my passion. When I no longer loved him, I did not deceive him."[15] These sentiments bore a striking similarity to those George herself had expressed many years before when she first met Chopin: "So far I have been faithful to whomever I have loved," she said then, "perfectly faithful in the sense that I have never deceived anyone and have never ceased to be faithful without very strong reasons which had killed my love through the other's fault. I am not of an inconstant nature."[16]

By her three lovers Lucrezia had had four children to whom she was devoted with a passion that exceeded everything else in her life. Her love for them constituted "chains more sacred than all others . . ." which she vowed "I will never break."[17] Like Lélia she had not really found happiness in physical love and, like George Sand herself, the only affection in which she experienced true fulfillment was maternal love. In fact, so strong was this motherly urge that Lucrezia always "wanted to be the mother of her lovers without ceasing to be that of her children" (p. 255). What the actress merely wished for, George had already achieved, first with Jules Sandeau, later with Musset, and now with Chopin.

At the opening of the novel, Lucrezia, who withdrew from the stage at the height of a brilliant career, has retired to Italy where she is living on the shores of Lake Iseo near her birthplace. There she bought a lavish villa and settled down to bring up her children on Rousseau and nature. Her old father, whom she also looks after, lives nearby in the rude cottage where Lucrezia was born. "Small and slightly plump" (p. 229), the novel's heroine has certain of Mme Sand's physical characteristics and is just as "proud of the plebian blood" (p. 265) that flows in her veins as was the authoress herself.

In marked contrast to the personality and background of Lucrezia are those of Prince Karol. He is an aristocrat, raised by his mother in virtual isolation, and disdainful of all that does not belong to the rarified world in which he exists. Like Chopin, who "obviously avoided society" and had "some slightly misanthropic prejudices,"[18] Prince Karol "detached himself more each day from humanity."[19] There were two main reasons why he shrank from other people in particular and life in general: one was the fragile condition of his health; the other was the sensitive idealism of his nature. Prince Karol, like Chopin, "remained delicate in body, as in spirit. But this absence of muscular development was exactly what preserved in him a charming beauty, an exceptional appearance which showed neither age nor sex" (p. 216).

Although he did, in fact, have a frail constitution, Karol was actually "more nervous and impressionable than really sick" (p. 218). Morbidly he nourished the idea of a premature death "like a poison" (p. 221) in much the same way that Chopin always carried on, "planning his own funeral in advance with a certain degree of pleasure."[20] Death would have provided a welcome escape from the harsh realities of existence which could otherwise be avoided only by retreating into a visionary world of beauty and perfection. Both Chopin and Prince Karol chose the latter alternative and as a result they often tended to drift out of touch with the facts of life. "Always lost in his thoughts," George wrote of Karol, "he had no conception at all of reality."[21] At the same time she complained that Chopin, "devoured by a dream of the ideal . . . did not accept anything of reality. This was his vice and his virtue, his source of greatness and of misery."[22]

So accustomed to their own idealistic realms, both Karol and Chopin looked down on the less perfect world of everyday life with a certain condescension. To accept or adjust to its imperfections implied a compromise which the two men scorned. Unfortunately such attitudes tend to breed self-righteousness in real life as well as in fiction. The prince, like the musician, was prone to spurn what he regarded in his mistress as a "basic bohemian insouciance, a certain vulgar toughness in her make-up."[23] "Karol had no petty faults at all," George claimed. "He had only one single, great, unintentional but disastrous one: his spirit was intolerant" (p. 218). Chopin was similar, she observed: "He could forgive nothing. . . . He would never come to terms with human nature."[24]

Time and again it was inevitable that two such perfectionistic individuals should find themselves at odds with the crass exigencies of mundane living. Often they were irritated, angered, and wounded by it, but pride prompted them to conceal their outrage and their suffering. Both took refuge behind façades of excessive reserve or exaggerated cordiality. Karol possessed a "charming politeness" George wrote, "but one could mistake for a courteous kindheartedness that which was really merely a cold disdain, indeed even an insurmountable aversion."[25] Chopin, when piqued, often disguised his feelings in the same way, according to Liszt. "Happily complacent in outward appearance, he so completely hid the injury to his rightful pride that its existence was scarcely suspected."[26]

The result of such behavior was that few could ever fathom the depths of these two men. "It would take a lifetime to understand such individuals."[27] George wrote of Prince Karol—a lifetime "and a microscope." He was a "walking hieroglyph," she claimed, "moody and enigmatic . . . inconstant and changeable as the clouds" (p. 275). Chopin was equally incomprehensible to her. "He seals himself off hermetically from his best friends,"[28] she complained. His true inner personality was to remain for her, as for Liszt, "apart, unapproached, and unapproachable beneath that smooth and polished surface where it was impossible to gain a foothold."[29]

Overwhelmed by his love for the magnanimous Lucrezia, the shy, young prince grew feverish and swooned. In a state of utter collapse the lovelorn invalid could not be moved and was forced to remain at the actress' villa where, over the following months she nursed him back to health. Like George herself, "Lucrezia had learned at an early age to be nurse and quasi-doctor when the occasion demanded."[30] It seemed that "Providence had in fact sent Karol the person most capable of helping him and saving him in this crisis. Lucrezia Floriani had an almost miraculous instinct for judging the condition of invalids and the treatments they required" (p. 242).

On the shores of Lake Iseo a drama began to unfold, not unlike that on the hillside of Valldemosa. Lucrezia, six years older than Karol,* hovered tenderly over the poor prince throughout his illness and long convalescence. Like Chopin, the tormented young aristocrat was afflicted with nightmares. "Agitated by horrifying dreams, [Karol] sometimes woke up, seized with terror and despair" (p. 243). Touched by his pathetic state, Lucrezia did all she could to cure him. But she soon discovered that Karol was not to be saved by any of the medicinal concoctions or material comforts with which she provided him. What he needed was to be loved. "Love him! Love him! Take pity on him!" his friend, Salvator, cried out one day to the distraught Lucrezia. "Love him, Floriani! Either you are no longer yourself, or a frightful selfishness has dried up the generosity in your breast. He is dying, save him! He has never loved. Make him live or I shall curse you!" What alternative did the noble Lucrezia have but to sacrifice herself up to the suffering prince? "I will love him," she promised, "covering the pale brow of the young prince with a long and ardent kiss; but it will be as his mother loved him" (p. 251).

Many years later there was to be a rather familiar echo of this heroic resignation in Mme Sand's memoires:

> I eventually agreed to the idea that Chopin could rest and regain his health among us for several summers. . . . However, the picture of this sort of familial alliance with a new friend in my life made me pause to reflect. I was alarmed by the task I was about to accept . . . I had a sort of maternal adoration for the artist which was very strong and very genuine but which could not, for an instant, vie with the love of my children, the only pure sentiment that can be passionate at the same time. I was still young enough to have to struggle against love or more properly speaking, desire. . . . Yet after reflecting, this danger disappeared before my eyes. . . . One more obligation in my

* George herself was six years older than Chopin.

life, already so full and so weighed down with fatigue, merely seemed an additional opportunity to live the austere life toward which I felt myself drawn with a sort of religious enthusiasm.[31]

Over the years George had indeed come to be a substitute for Chopin's mother (who was the "only passion of his life,") and behaved toward him much like Lucrezia toward Prince Karol (who also "had but one real passion in his whole life: filial love").[32]

Unfortunately neither George nor Lucrezia could find their mother-son relationships completely satisfying in the absence of more binding ties of mutual interest. Prince Karol's friend, Salvator, tried to show "to the young prince that the harmony of tastes, of opinions, of characters, and of inclinations which is the basis of conjugal tranquillity, could never exist between a man of his age, his position, and nature, and the daughter of a peasant, turned actress, older than him by six years, mother of a family, democratic in her sentiments and memories, etc." (p. 281). The parallel with life at Nohant and the Square d'Orléans was explicit. George had neither Chopin's "tastes, nor his ideas outside of art, nor his political beliefs, nor his appreciation of things at all."[33] He, in turn, George complained, was a "stranger to my works, my studies, and consequently to my convictions" (p. 468).

Lucrezia's life with Karol ultimately degenerated into long years of petty antagonisms and jealousies. Faithful, devoted, and self-effacing, Lucrezia bore it all. But the truth of the matter was that "she, in fact, no longer loved Karol."[34] Under the heavy yoke of her suffering, Lucrezia's youth and beauty faded and, crushed by the weight of her sacrifices, she eventually died.

Happily, George proved to be hardier than poor Lucrezia, but, all the same, during the spring of 1846 she began to find her own strength taxed by the delicate thirty-six-year old companion who shared so many of Prince Karol's exasperating traits. Undoubtedly she intended the novel merely as a warning to Chopin in order to let him realize that some day there might well be a limit to her endurance also. Some day her life too might be sapped away in the same parasitic fashion as was Lucrezia's. "The friendship of Chopin," she later wrote, "was never a refuge for me in times of sadness. He certainly had enough of his own misfortunes to support. . . . My true strength came from my son."[35] Appropriately enough, it was Maurice who did the illustrations for *Lucrezia Floriani*.

As self-evident as the origins of her novel were, George persistently denied that *Lucrezia Floriani* had any basis in fact. It was purely a work of fiction she insisted. How could it be otherwise? She had only two children while Lucrezia had four; Chopin was a musician while Karol was not, etc. Such specious arguments were, of course, flimsy and unconvincing to say the least.

Delacroix, to whom George read several chapters of her new novel in Chopin's presence, was appalled. He was as much astonished at Mme Sand's equanimity as at Chopin's enthusiasm. When the reading was over, he walked back across the courtyard of the Square d'Orléans with the musician and discovered, to his surprise, that his friend really admired the book and completely failed to grasp its message.

Even more indignant than Delacroix was George's colleague, Hortense Allart, who wrote Sainte-Beuve: "I haven't told you how outraged I was by *Lucrezia*. . . . Mme Sand portrays Chopin in the most disgracefully intimate details and with a cold-blooded detachment that nothing can justify. Women can never condemn such betrayals of the boudoir enough. They do nothing but alienate lovers. . . . There is no excuse for *Lucrezia*. . . . How can such a marvellous genius let herself sink to such bad taste?"[36]

Half amused and half astounded by the book, Heinrich Heine commented on its author: "She has shamefully mistreated my poor friend Chopin in a detestable novel divinely written."[37] Even Liszt was disgusted when he read it. "Her talent doesn't compensate sufficiently for the vulgarity of this confession,"[38] he wrote. In his opinion George had acted as if Chopin were merely another butterfly snared in her net whom

she dissected, stuffed, and added to her collection of heroes
for novels.

The *Revue des Deux Mondes,* commenting on the new work,
tactfully avoided any discussion of the personalities involved
and stated simply that *"Lucrezia Floriani* is a study in the disenchantment that follows love." [39]

Whatever it was George had hoped to convey to Chopin
through *Lucrezia Floriani,* she apparently did not intend to
precipitate a rupture between them—at least not just at that
time. Late in the spring of 1846 she wrote Frédéric's sister,
Louise, that she hoped to be able to take Chopin away for the
coming winter. "His health," she explained, "is bound up with
the state of the weather so much that I am really thinking, if I
can earn enough money this summer to travel with my family, of taking him off to the south of France for the three
worst months of next winter. If one could protect him from
the cold for a whole year, with the following summer, he
would have eighteen months' respite to cure his cough. I shall
have to torment him about it because he loves Paris in spite of
what he says." [40]

Certainly as far as Chopin was concerned, things still remained the same between them. When George prepared to
leave for the country early that May he gave a gala farewell
party for her with "music, flowers, and a grand spread." [41]
Shortly afterwards he himself left Paris for what was to be his
last visit to Nohant.

CHAPTER TWENTY-TWO

"THE WEATHER IS SUPERB," George wrote Chopin's sister in June of 1846. "The countryside is magnificent and our dear boy is going to be as healthy as my children, I hope, with the help of a quiet life and lovely sunshine."[1] "It has been years," she claimed, "since I have seen Nohant so fresh, so full of flowers, and lush with greenery" (p. 344). Unfortunately the heat that summer was almost insufferable. George took it all in stride by cooling off in the nearby river whenever the weather became too sticky. Lying on her back in the sand with the water up to her chin, she would relax and smoke a cigar while Solange and Augustine "paddled around like a couple of sylphs or ducks" (p. 370).

For the fastidious Chopin, however, the muggy summer months were a torture, and he suffered pathetically from the stifling heat. "Chopin is absolutely astonished to see himself sweat," George teased. "He is desolate over it. He claims that no matter how much he washes he still *stinks!* We laugh until our eyes are full of tears to see such an ethereal being not wanting to admit that he sweats like everyone else. . . . If people knew . . . that he sweated he would never live it down. He reeks of eau de Cologne but we all tell him he smells like . . . a carpenter and he dashes off to his room as if to flee from his own odor" (p. 379).

Chopin was good-natured enough to tolerate this sort of ribbing, but there were other things going on at Nohant that summer which began to disturb him seriously. He was irked to see Maurice exercise more and more authority around the house and felt himself gradually being excluded from the

family circle. The son, in turn, resented Chopin's participation
in any domestic matters. Little by little the tension between the
two men was mounting, and on the twenty-ninth of June, just
a day before Maurice's twenty-third birthday, the explosion
came. It occurred at the dinner table and was triggered by the
fact that Maurice had received a breast of chicken while Chopin was given only a leg. Vexed at what he considered a delib-
erate slight, Chopin announced indignantly that he would
never consent to being treated like an object of charity in Mme
Sand's house. To this Maurice replied that he would gladly
leave as there was obviously not room enough for both of
them under the same roof. George, of course, immediately
stood up for her son, declaring flatly that there could be no
question of his leaving the house. "I could not and should not
allow it . . ." she declared. Stung to the quick, Chopin remained silent. He "could not bear my interference, as justifiable and necessary as it was," his mistress observed. "He hung
his head and murmured that I didn't love him any more.
What blasphemy after eight years of material devotion!"[2]

As it turned out, nobody left Nohant and life there gradually resumed its normal tenor. To George it seemed that the
air had finally been cleared once and for all. "It was a good
thing that I got a little angry with him," she said that July, "It
gave me the courage to tell him a few basic facts and let him
know that I had had enough. Ever since then he has behaved
more sensibly."[3]

Chopin had certainly been "put in his place" and for some
time he remained subdued. But he no longer felt comfortable
at Nohant. Upset, he found it difficult to work. "I do my best
. . ." he wrote Franchomme, "but nothing comes of it—and if
things go on this way, my new productions won't sound like
the warbling of birds or even the clanking of broken china."[4]
When the summer ended he had, in fact, accomplished less
than usual. What he did write, however, was exquisite.*

---

*The compositions of 1846 (most of which would have been created during the sum-
mer months, as was Chopin's custom) include the two Nocturnes of Opus 62 (B Major

Recognizing this George commented to a friend, "As always Chopin keeps on composing masterpieces . . . although he insists that he has done nothing worthwhile."[5]

Mme Sand also had trouble writing that summer. The stormy events of June had left the atmosphere charged with tension which disrupted her powers of concentration. "I am not working myself . . ." she said, "I can't put my heart into it. When there is a secret anxiety gnawing away at your brain it saps all your inspiration (p. 455). Perhaps she felt she had been too harsh on Chopin. Or perhaps she had an uneasy suspicion that she would probably have to deal even more harshly with him in the future. In any case, whatever might come, there was not the least doubt in her mind that her first obligation would always be to her son.

After the episode at the dinner table Chopin began to withdraw more and more from the rest of the household. "They spent the summer going off on hikes and excursions to out-of-the-way parts of the *Vallée noire*," he wrote his family in the fall. "I never went along since such things tire me more than they are worth and when I am exhausted I am hardly cheerful which keeps the young people from having a good time."[6]

Of the many guests who came to Nohant that summer there were only two with whom Chopin spent much time. One was an old friend from Warsaw, countess Laura Czosnowska, and the other, Eugène Delacroix. In neither case were their visits very pleasant. Finding the family's behavior toward Chopin tactless and disagreeable, Delacroix left in disgust. As for the countess, "the cousin [Augustine Brault] didn't like her and so, of course, neither did the son." Chopin reported to his family. "As a result they made jokes which got more and more vulgar until they saw how aggravated I was. Since then nobody has mentioned her (p. 246).

---

and E Major), the three Mazurkas of Opus 63 (B Major, F Minor and C-sharp Minor), and the fourth Mazurka of Opus 67 (A Minor). In addition he finished the Polonaise-Fantaisie of Opus 61 and the piano-cello Sonata, Opus 65. During the same season he began work on the three Waltzes of Opus 64 (including the famous "Minute" or "Little Dog" Waltz).

Even his favorite, Solange, tended to neglect Chopin that summer. At eighteen she had found herself a handsome new beau among the Berry gentry, a young man named Fernand de Preaulx. George seemed quite pleased. "He is a country gentleman," she informed friends in Paris, "a man of the woods who is as simple as Nature herself. He dresses like a gamekeeper, is as handsome as an ancient statue, and as hairy as a savage."[7] "You wouldn't exactly call him brilliant, especially when it comes to talking," she admitted, "but he is a good soul with both feet on the ground and a fine sensible outlook on everything. I love him with all my heart in spite of myself. He will make a worthy and devoted son for me though he isn't anyone to set Paris on fire (p. 517).

In reality he had not set Solange on fire all that much either. "The Princess" simply wanted to get married for the sake of being called "Madame," her mother claimed somewhat unfairly. Perhaps it never occurred to George that Solange might have been anxious to marry for exactly the same reason that she herself had—to get away from a mother whom she could not stand. At any rate if this thought ever entered her mind she did not dwell on it for long. As always, her main concern was Maurice who continued to manifest considerable interest in his young cousin, Augustine. This was a match which Mme Sand was highly in favor of and she did all she could to encourage it.

Chopin was permitted to observe these developments from the side-lines but his opinions were never solicited and he wisely refrained from expressing them. This was clearly the way George wished things to be. As she had explained in *Lucrezia Floriani,* "a lover should not conduct himself like a husband and install himself in his mistress' home like a guardian of a fortress!"[8]

By October Frédéric was making plans to leave for Paris and wrote Mlle de Rozières to see that the carpets were laid and the curtains hung in his apartment. "I shall soon have to start thinking about my 'mill,' that is to say my lessons," he told his family. "Probably I will be going back to Paris with

Arago, leaving the mistress of the house here for some time as her son and daughter are in no hurry to return to the city. There was some question of spending this winter in Italy, but the young people prefer the country here. However by spring if either Solange or Maurice get married (both affairs are in the works) they will most likely change their minds."[9] A short while afterwards, in the crisp autumn chill of early November, he set out for the city, leaving Nohant behind forever.

Back in Paris everything was "damp and gloomy." "It is impossible to keep from catching cold" (p. 254), he wrote George toward the end of the month. Within a few weeks biting winds began to hurl gusts of snow through the brittle air as the first blizzards of winter arrived. "I am well," Chopin assured the household at Nohant, "but I don't dare leave my fireplace for an instant" (p. 257).

In reality he was often out wading through the snow and slush on some errand for George. "Tomorrow I will send you the fur and other things that you wanted," he wrote in answer to one of her frequent requests. "Your piano will cost 900 francs. . . . Aren't you going to send me your cape to have it fixed here? Or do you know a dressmaker there who can do it? . . . I haven't gotten around to taking care of your cigar lighter. I don't know if there is enough tinder in it or not. . . . Borie dropped by to see me and I will have the piece of cloth you mentioned sent to him" (pp. 255–56). He longed constantly for news of Nohant and always worried about his mistress's health. "I am glad you haven't had any of our bad weather . . ." he would write her. "I hope your migraine has gone away and you can get out in your garden for a stroll. . . . Please write me whenever you have a chance, so I will know you are well" (p. 259).

George, however, did not have too much time to write as she was busy on a new novel, *Le Château des Désertes*. Although the cold was not as severe at Nohant as in Paris, she kept a fire burning in the drawing room practically all the time. When she was free in the evenings she would devote herself to the family's little theatrical productions which became a veritable obsession with the entire household that winter. Dinner was usually eaten on the run while George hurriedly sketched the outlines of a plot on which the evening's drama was to hang. Then the children rushed off to put together some costumes and improvise their dialogue. Within half an hour everyone reassembled in the salon where a makeshift stage had been set up, and the commedia dell'arte-like production began. Seated at the piano, George provided direction and accompaniment for these little scenarios. "All this goes on until midnight," she described, "after which we have a late supper, a good laugh, and go to bed." [10]

There was more to these lively winter nights, however, than George's innocent account would indicate. A frequent guest in her home now was Victor Borie, a twenty-eight-year old friend of Pierre Leroux's, who had recently settled at La Châtre to become editor of *L'Éclaireur de l'Indre*. After the evening's theatricals he often stayed the night—eventually in George's bedroom.*

At Christmas the Nohant actors put on a melodrama called *The Cavern of Crime* to which they invited the whole neighborhood. "I can't imagine anything more fascinating!" Chopin wrote from Paris. "Enjoy yourselves all you can," [11] he told them. He himself remained alone and miserable in the Square d'Orléans during the holidays.

On February 5 George and her family returned to Paris for the signing of Solange's marriage contract. Although Chopin was "sick as a dog" (p. 262) when they arrived, the elation of seeing George again was enough to put him back on his feet. Soon he was out with her, ambling through the Luxembourg gardens, dashing off to dinner or the theater, and planning parties for her in his small apartment.

One day while Mme Sand was still in Paris, an energetic young man with broad shoulders and a bushy auburn beard appeared on her doorstep. After rendering effusive homage to the author he requested permission to carve marble busts of both her and her daughter. This garrulous intruder turned

* Exactly when this intimacy began is uncertain—possibly in 1847, certainly by 1848.

out to be Auguste-Jean-Baptiste Clésinger, a sculptor who had already made himself known to Mme Sand the year before through a note he had written her in March of 1846. Out of the hundred or more letters which she received each month his had been particularly memorable because of its gushing sentimentality and atrocious grammar. What he had wanted at the time was to name one of his works after the heroine of her novel, *Consuelo.* Mme Sand consented then and gave the matter no further thought until she now found herself face to face with the man eleven months later. Flattered by his interest George could see no harm in letting Solange and herself pose for him. Indeed she was quite intrigued by the gruff naïveté and infectious enthusiasm of her exuberant admirer, and over the next few weeks she and Solange began to make frequent trips to his atelier. There the "monumental mason" chisled and chatted away, charming his new subjects by the whirlwind force of his restless, driving personality.

The two women had not gone for many sittings before Clésinger began making advances to Solange, who, despite being engaged, still enjoyed playing the coquette. Soon the susceptible young girl found herself "violently taken"[12] by the handsome sculptor, fifteen years her senior. Like the clouds of marble dust which floated up to the hazy reaches of the lofty atelier, Solange's emotions soared tremulously off to vertiginous heights. If Fernand de Preaulx had never really succeeded in setting her aglow, Clésinger, on the contrary, seemed *"all* fire and flame" (p. 686) to her now.

Sometime in February when he was visiting the Square d'Orléans, the young sculptor was introduced to Chopin and Delacroix. "I did not care much for him,"[13] the painter commented. He felt that his work, for the most part, showed a "lack of proportion and . . . no intelligence in the lines" (p. 77). Chopin, on the other hand, ranked Clésinger among the "new talents"[14] at the annual exposition of painting and sculpture that year. However, as a person he was not impressed by him. "God knows," the finicky Pole sniffed, "what sort of a background he comes from" (p. 282).

None of these opinions, of course, had any effect on Solange who remained ecstatic over Clésinger. As for George, she tolerated everything calmly until her daughter suddenly announced that she no longer intended to marry de Preaulx. With the signing of the marriage contract only one day off Mme Sand was completely stunned. Needless to say, so was de Preaulx. But to everyone's relief, the jilted fiancé retired gracefully from the scene "like a *true French cavalier.*" [15]

With the field all to himself now, Clésinger pressed his suit even more aggressively. Worried because she did not know exactly how far things might go George decided she had best hustle her daughter back to the country as quickly as possible. Indeed she feared events might already have passed beyond her control.

Borrowing Chopin's carriage she rushed Solange back to Nohant at the end of the first week in April, only to be followed a few days later by the resolute sculptor. In an explosive *tour de force* he swooped in and out of Nohant in the space of three days, shattering all resistance in his path and leaving both mother and daughter limp from his onslaught. "Clésinger arrived here like Caesar," George wrote breathlessly, "with a firmness, a determination, and an obstinacy that would brook no indecision or delay. We had to tell him *yes* or *no* within twenty-four hours. . . . In the three days he was here he didn't sleep more than two hours the whole time and never seemed to wear out for a minute. Such endurance amazes me. I like it!" (p. 659).

By April 16 definite plans for the wedding were underfoot. Knowing Chopin's distaste for Clésinger, George tried to keep everything from him until the last moment. "It doesn't concern him," she told Maurice, "and once the Rubicon is crossed all the ifs, ands, and buts can only make things worse" (p. 661).

Later, when Chopin broached the subject of returning to Nohant that spring, she wrote him to wait for her in Paris until the end of May. "It must have something to do with Solange's wedding," he surmised in a letter to his family, "(but not to the young man I wrote you about). May God protect them . . ." he added with a vague premonition that all was not well. "If anyone deserves happiness it is Mme Sand."[16]

By the sixth of May matters were progressing smoothly enough for George to confide everything to Charlotte Marliani.

> I want you to know before anyone else. Solange is getting married two weeks from now to Clésinger, a scuptor and a man of great talent who has a big income and can give her the brilliant sort of life she craves.* He is madly in love with her and she is delighted with him. She has been as sudden and firm in her determination this time as she was capricious and irresolute before. Apparently she has found her dream. May God grant it to be so. As for me I like the boy very much and so does Maurice. He is not too polished at first glance but he is full of divine inspiration. For some time I have been observing him without his being aware of it. . . . What gives me the most confidence is his remarkable sincerity which almost verges on brusqueness. He is somewhat too naïve but he is industrious, courageous, energetic, determined, and persevering.[17]

Not everyone who knew Mme Sand's future son-in-law, however, shared her enthusiasm for him. He was a "noisy, disorderly individual, a former cavalryman turned big-time sculptor, who doesn't know how to behave outside of a tavern or a loft,"[18] some claimed while others regarded him as "dissipated, brutal, and vulgar in both language and manners, excessively bohemian in his way of life, and certainly not made for marriage."[19] George chose to ignore such reports, dismissing them all as malicious gossip. "I have undertaken a veritable inquest in regard to Clésinger," she informed Mme Marliani, ". . . and I am convinced that Clésinger has been an irreproachable man in every sense of the word."[20]

As the wedding grew near, George observed that Solange was not feeling well. Jumping to conclusions she pictured herself on the verge of becoming a grandmother and immediately

---

* George was deceived in this. The truth was that Clésinger had upwards of 24,000 francs' worth of debts.

jotted off a panicky note to Maurice, who was in Guillery visiting his father. "Come on Maurice, come on. . . . You must
start right away. If your father can't come with you then bring
his consent and his instructions for the marriage contract but
hurry! Our situation is impossible. Get here fast!" (p. 690).

The same day Clésinger himself wrote Maurice: "Solange is
sick with anxiety and suspense. She also has other feminine
reasons which are upsetting me and making me ill myself. I
only hope M. Dudevant will simply come right away and not
ask any further questions! . . . In case your father is short of
money I am giving your mother 300 francs to send you so
there won't be any excuse."[21]

No sooner had Clésinger mailed this letter than George
received word from Princess Czartoryska that Chopin was
seriously ill. The news couldn't have come at a worse time.
With matters as they were she could scarcely rush up to Paris
just then. "I am sick with anxiety," she wrote Mlle de Rozières,
"I can't leave my family under the circumstances without even
Maurice here to save appearances and protect his sister from
all sorts of wicked suspicions. . . . Tell Chopin whatever you
think best in regard to me. I don't dare write for fear of upsetting him. I am afraid Solange's wedding is going to aggravate him a great deal."[22]

A few days later a reassuring letter came from Delacroix,
saying that Chopin's illness had been "a most violent attack of
asthma," but that he had recovered from it. With this news
George could now rest more easily. "At last he is saved
again," she wrote with relief to Grzymała, "but the future
looks grim to me . . . I will be in Paris for several days toward
the end of this month and if Chopin can be moved I will bring
him back here" (p. 699). Somewhat embarrassed at the way
she had treated her old friend she tried to explain to
Grzymała why she had had to act as she did.

I think Chopin must have been hurt at being kept in the dark
and not being allowed to give any advice [in regard to Solange's
marriage], but it's impossible to take his advice on practical mat-

ters seriously. He has never seen things as they really are and doesn't understand human nature at all. His soul is all poetry and music and he can't tolerate anything else. Besides, his interference in the affairs of my family would mean the loss of all dignity for me and the loss of all love between my children and myself. Talk with him and try to make him understand in a general way that he ought not to concern himself with them. If I tell him that Clésinger (whom he doesn't like) is worthy of our affection he will only hate him the more which in turn will make Solange mad at him. All this is a difficult and delicate affair. I don't know any way to calm or reassure a sick individual who is irritated by the very efforts one makes to cure him—The disease which racks this poor creature in body and soul has been killing me for a long time now and I picture him continuing to go on this way without my ever being able to do him any good, since it is his restless, jealous, and suspicious attachment for me which is the main cause of his unhappiness. (p. 700)

It was as if George were echoing the words of Lucrezia Floriani. Like the martyred heroine of her recent novel, she saw herself a victim of her own generosity. "For the last seven years I have lived like a virgin with him as well as *with all others*" she told Grzymała.

I have grown old before my time, but it really didn't cost me any effort to sacrifice since I was so tired of passion and so hopelessly disillusioned. If ever there were a woman on this earth who should have been able to inspire him with complete confidence I was the one, but he never understood. I know many people accuse me of having either exhausted him with the violence of my passion or driven him to desperation with my thoughtlessness, but I think you know what the real story is. As for him, he complains that I have killed him with my abstinence while I was certain that I would have been the death of him otherwise. You see what a predicament I am in with this disastrous friendship in which I have made myself his slave whenever I could without showing him an impossible and unfair preference over my children. . . . In this respect I have been incredibly patient which I never thought I could be—I who was never cut out to be a saint . . . I am at the point of martyrdom but heaven is implacable toward me as if I had some great crimes to atone for. . . . (p. 700)

What Mme Sand wrote Grzymała this time was not all hypocritical hyperbole, designed merely to justify her behavior.
She was indeed distraught and depressed that spring. In addition to Solange's wedding and Chopin's illness she had other
problems to worry about. The previous year had not been a
good one financially for her. There had been a drought at
Nohant and now in Paris, for the first time since the beginning
of her literary career she was having difficulty finding a publisher. She was, in fact, so near the brink of despair that the
thought of suicide crossed her mind more than once that May,
as she recorded in her *Journal Intime*.[23] Only her sense of maternal obligation seems to have saved her. "May God in His
goodness grant that my children at least may be happy,"[24] she
pleaded as she pulled herself together and struggled on for
their sake.

In Solange's case it certainly seemed as if happiness were
imminent with her wedding scheduled to take place at Nohant
on the nineteenth of May. Hurriedly the announcements were
sent out, haphazardly printed on cheap paper, and on May 18
the baron Dudevant arrived just in time for the ceremonies.
In order to avoid any gossip about the haste with which the
whole affair had been whipped into shape, George spread the
word that Clésinger had threatened to elope with Solange if
she did not rush the wedding through. At the signing of the
marriage contract which took place after the baron's arrival,
George gave the young couple her property in Paris, the
Hôtel de Narbonne which was worth an estimated hundred
thousand francs and yielded an annual income of six thousand. As for the father of the bride, he brought nothing to the
event other than his presence.

Then, on the very eve of the wedding, Mme Sand, in the
midst of rushing about, fell and sprained her ankle. By the
next morning it had become so swollen and painful she could
not stand to walk on it. However, fearing to risk any further
delay she insisted on being carted "like a parcel" to the church
in a sedan chair. "Never was a marriage carried off with such
speed and determination," she wrote afterwards. "We called

up the Mayor and the curé when they least expected it and the wedding took place as if by surprise (p. 712). In lieu of a large reception George decided to contribute a thousand francs "to the poor of the parish," victims of the past year's famine. So, amid an atmosphere devoid of gaiety and cluttered with confusion, the wedding of the "grande princesse" and the "beau diable" took place at last. It had turned into quite an ordeal for all concerned, but on the twentieth George could sigh with relief, "It is all over now and we can catch our breath again" (713).

Meanwhile in Paris, Chopin, who had not been informed of the event until the last minute, was far from pleased with the news. "I don't give them a year together after the first child," he prophesied sourly. The rumors going around Paris concerning Clésinger were scarcely complimentary. "Marliani, Delacroix, Arago, and myself have heard the most deplorable reports about him," he told his family. According to these accounts the man was in debt and behaved like a brute. It was even said that he "struck his mistress whom he abandoned in order to get married just when she was pregnant." Furthermore, Chopin went on, "he drinks (we have all seen that—but it was simply written off as part of his genius). In short, all the artists who know him (speaking in terms of the man, not the sculptor) don't consider him as any great prize and are terribly astonished that Mme Sand chose him for a son-in-law."[25]

Chopin, like George, conducted his own private investigation of Clésinger's background but came up with quite different findings from hers. The man's father, he discovered, was "a sculptor at Besançon, but not too well known elsewhere . . . Cardinal Rohan took the son under his protection in order to make him a priest, but after six months the boy left him and turned to drawing and sculpture. At this point his life became rather shady—all sorts of unsavory things—he was run out of one place then another and went to Italy where he had to flee again because of the debts he ran up in Florence. Since his father would have nothing to do with him he joined the cavalry but didn't stay in it long. . . . He has no friends or associates. His father didn't even come to the wedding. He merely sent a note. Mme Sand has never seen him; she has only heard her son-in-law speak of him" (p. 287).

All in all, Chopin concluded, "This unfortunate marriage . . . has made a painful impression on me" (p. 286). In fact, he added, it had exactly the same effect on "all Mme Sand's old and true friends," and made "no better impression on Paris society" in general. "So many people are bewildered that a young girl like Sol[ange] should fall head over heels in love with an artist who exhibits such voluptuous, not to say lewd works. . . . He is the kind who would even chisel his wife's little derrière in white marble. *He certainly has nerve enough to do it*" (p. 284).

Naturally the secrecy with which everything had been handled annoyed Chopin. "They were rather ashamed to write me about it" (p. 283), he figured. "It was a moment of sheer madness . . . and there wasn't anyone around to pour cold water on things. . . . What a pity" (p. 285). His criticism was aimed more at George than Solange. "She hasn't got a penny's worth of common sense (p. 282), he regretted to say, and worse still, "she does not always tell the truth—but that is the privilege of a novelist" (p. 285), he concluded sadly. Thinking it all over he decided it was just as well he had missed the wedding. "I don't know how I would have reacted in the face of everything" (p. 282). Under the circumstances it was really much easier just to send a short note of congratulations and forget the whole affair.

In light of all that happened he was no longer certain whether he still wanted to return to Nohant or not that summer. "To tell the truth," he admitted, "I am not too anxious" (p. 284). Unhappily now, as far as his life with George was concerned, a "grain of sand had disrupted the tranquil lake and little by little the pebbles and rocks were to fall one by one." [26]

❦ CHAPTER TWENTY-THREE ❧

ONLY FOUR DAYS after she had gotten Solange married, George again found herself in the midst of wedding preparations. A friend of Clésinger's, the painter, Théodore Rousseau, had become interested in Augustine Brault and on learning that she returned his feelings, he proposed. "It's just one wedding after another,"[1] George chirped merrily as she awaited Rousseau's arrival at Nohant on the twenty-third of May. On the whole she was very pleased with this match: "I would like to have seen Maurice marry Augustine," she wrote her half-sister, Caroline Cazamajou, "but they simply weren't in love" (p. 737). The truth was, Maurice, with his "irresolute character," couldn't really make up his mind whether he was or wasn't in love, so George finally had to make the decision for him. "You don't really love A[ugustine]," she told him. "And she deserves something better than that. You haven't contracted any obligation toward her since you haven't had *any sort of intimacy* which would make it your duty to marry her. But you have been guilty of certain faults in mentioning love to her and asking her to become your wife—only to tell her the next day that you were not the man to marry her—and later acting jealous and trying to discourage other suitors who approached her. Even to this day you keep telling her *yes* and *no* at the same time." Quite naturally Augustine herself got disgusted with Maurice's wishy-washy behavior and let his mother know it. "She still retains a sisterly affection for you," George informed her son, "but she *does not wish* to marry you now, not even if you genuinely wanted it."[2] When he realized that he had lost his chance, the vacillating lover began to feel sorry for himself and sulk, but for once George remained firm with him. "Maurice regrets the way he acted, but it's too late now. He couldn't decide what he wanted and so now the poor child is simply going to have to swallow his own medicine, as bitter as it is."[3]

At the end of May Mme Sand rushed up to Paris with Augustine to make some last minute arrangements. "I am about to lose my head, I have so many things to do . . . and I have hardly finished with all the business and bother of the last wedding,"[4] she scribbled in a hurried post-script to a letter Chopin was writing his sister. Within a few days the marriage banns were posted in both the church of Notre-Dame-de-Lorette and the mayor's office in Paris. Everything seemed to be progressing smoothly when, without warning, catastrophe struck.

"One fine morning, just before the second publication of the banns," George was shocked to find the bridegroom suddenly acting "like a madman, half-crazed with a violent love for Aug[ustine], coupled with outrageous suspicions of her, of me, and of Maurice. . . . He felt he had been *deceived* and *tricked*. He had been carried away beyond reason by an anonymous letter which was unbelievably vicious. He kept saying over and over, 'I love her', 'I will marry her as *sullied* as she is, but I want some *money* and a *confession*.' The explanation of these peculiar demands was simply this," she related. "Cl[ésinger] had urged him into the marriage by telling him that I had a considerable sum at my disposal and that I promised to give Aug[ustine] a large dowry,* all the while he was telling me that Rousseau didn't want anything, had no need of anything, was thinking of nothing but love and preferred not even to talk about *finances*. . . . As for the *confession*, someone had succeeded in persuading him that she had had a child by Maurice and that before coming to live with me she had been highly promiscuous."[5]

* George did, in fact, plan to give Augustine 100,000 francs as a dowry but because much of this was to come from business contracts which she was still negotiating, the total amount was not to be available to the couple for some time.

"Who knows where the anonymous letters and the slanders came from?" George wondered. She had her suspicions and feared it was all too likely they had come from Solange and Clésinger. "It's certainly the most plausible hypothesis. Even today," she wrote one of her friends, "Sol[ange] says she will see to it that Aug[ustine] *never marries,* that she will *pursue her all the way to hell* if necessary and other such sweet things" (p. 32).

After an explosive scene, full of accusations and recriminations, on the fifth of June, it was apparent that there would be no wedding. "I pity you," George told the young painter, "for having lost all reason, goodness, delicacy, and affection in the space of a single day. I don't understand your behavior at all. . . . Be careful, Rousseau," she warned, "Don't say anything malicious or untrue about George Sand and Augustine."[6] For the sake of saving face she then announced that the engagement had been broken off because of the artist's debts and poor health—a statement which itself smacked of malice and untruth.

Disgruntled, the two women set out for Nohant on the seventeenth of June. Chopin, whom they had seen in the city, was still undecided about returning to the country and remained behind in Paris for the time being. From what George had seen of him he seemed to be "getting along rather well" (p. 742), which was certainly more than she could say for herself just then.

The Rousseau affair had had a double impact on Mme Sand in that it not only disillusioned her with the painter but also alienated her from the Clésingers whom she held responsible for the whole disaster. She now began to open her ears to a great many things about her son-in-law that she had never bothered to listen to before. Appearances to the contrary the sculptor was, in fact, deeply in debt, she learned—so much so, it turned out that he and Solange now tried to persuade Mme Sand to mortgage Nohant in order to help them out. Incensed, George sent back a scorching reply to Clésinger. "I am sorry I cannot give you what you ask for," she wrote

In addition I have some serious complaints to register. I knew full well that you were badly in debt; everyone has told me so, and the aplomb with which you denied it two or three times in Paris when I tried to talk to you about it only made me all the more suspicious. I don't understand people who lie and I have caught you lying more than once. . . . In regard to all those commissions from the government which are supposed to be so lucrative, but which you never have the time to do since you have so many better offers, why is it that you toss them to one side unless you are making the whole story up? . . . In your situation, being in debt and with no guaranteed income from your work during the year, you still go around talking about buying land, building, etc. . . . I am afraid you don't quite have all your wits about you when it comes to business matters and I'm alarmed now about Solange's future which you paint to me so brilliantly and confidently. All this is to let you know that I don't trust you and wouldn't take out a mortgage on Nohant for anything in the world! (pp. 771–74)

Another thing that upset George about Clésinger was that he did not seem to be able to control Solange as she had expected. It was apparent while she was in Paris that her daughter was no more subdued in character since her marriage than she had been before. "I found her petty and mean again," George noted, "acting in a jealous manner which is ugly, stupid, and hardly excusable at her age. . . . Instead of lifting her up to your level," she told her son-in-law, "you have let her become a malicious, *wheedling*, deceitful little girl again" (p. 771).

But despite all this George was not about to deny the couple room and board when they decided to alight at Nohant for a while that July. Considering what had just taken place in Paris, Solange must have realized that she could hardly expect a very warm reception from either her mother or her cousin. Nevertheless their visit might have been tolerable had the Clésingers come prepared to be a little conciliatory. But Solange was her usual arrogant self and Clésinger was as brash and blustering as ever. "During the two weeks they spent here," George reported, "their behavior was the most scandalously unheard-of that you could imagine. The scenes which forced me not only to *show them* the door but literally to *throw* them out of it are not to be believed: they are simply indescribable. It can all be summed up in a few words," she wrote Mlle de Rozières.

> We nearly had a slaughter here. My son-in-law attacked Maurice with a hammer and would probably have killed him if I hadn't thrown myself between the two, slapping Clésinger in the face while he struck me on the chest. If the curé, some friends, and a servant who were there had not restrained him, Maurice, who was armed with a pistol, would have killed him on the spot. Solange fanned the flames with her vicious disdain, having already been the cause of these deplorable outbursts by her idle gossip, lies, and incredibly filthy stories. . . . The diabolical couple left yesterday evening, riddled with debts, triumphantly flaunting their impudence, and stirring up such a scandal over the countryside around here that they will never be able to live it down. . . . I don't ever want to see them or let them set foot in my house again. They have gone beyond the pale. My God! What have I done to deserve such a daughter![7]

Back in Paris, Chopin remained unaware of all that was taking place at Nohant but this time George did not dare leave him completely in the dark. "I have had to write part of all this to Chopin," she explained to Mlle de Rozières. "I was afraid he might arrive in the midst of a great cataclysm and would die from the pain and shock of it. But," she cautioned, "don't tell him just how far things have really gone. It's better to hide it from him if possible" (p. 12).

Meanwhile the Clésingers, having been evicted from Nohant, took refuge in nearby La Châtre. After their stormy departure George was irate to find they had carried off furniture, bedspreads, candelabra, and other articles from her house. "They are *thieves* of the first order," she raged. "With the most amazing brazeness they would have left me without so much as a bed" (p. 13). She was equally indignant when she caught the couple trying to make off with Chopin's carriage with no thought whatsoever of a "by your leave" from either herself or its owner. Adamant in her refusal to let the carriage off her property, she forced her daughter and son-in-law to provide other transportation for themselves.

The Clésingers now found themselves in a genuine predicament. Solange was pregnant and unable to stand a long, rough journey in public conveyances. From La Châtre, where they stopped to rest and nurse their grievances, Solange sent a note to Chopin. "I am sick," it read. "The trip by diligence to Blois* will exhaust me greatly. Would you lend me your coach for my return to Paris? Please let me know immediately. In order to leave I am waiting for your answer at La Châtre where I am very upset. I left Nohant for good after the most atrocious scenes instigated by my mother. Wait for me, I beg you, before you leave Paris. I want very much to see you as soon as possible. Your carriage was positively refused me. So if you would like me to be able to use it, write me a note with your permission and I will send to Nohant for it."[8]

Still ignorant of what had really happened, Chopin did not know what to make of this letter, but he had no doubt as to what he should do about it. He could scarcely say no to his longtime favorite. As Solange knew full well, she could always count on Chopin's indulgence. "I am very upset to hear of your trouble," he replied, "I hasten to place my carriage at your disposal. I have written your mother about it. Take care of yourself" (p. 295).

When George received Chopin's note she reacted as though struck in the face. She felt betrayed. Grudgingly she relinquished the carriage and then, in the heat of her anger, dashed off a scathing letter to its owner. Exactly what she said is not known; the note was apparently destroyed but not before Chopin had shown it to Delacroix. The painter was utterly astounded. "I must admit," he confided in his journal, "it is an atrocious letter. Bitter passions and long-suppressed impatience are plainly discernible, with a contrast that would be almost funny if the whole affair were not so sad; from time to time she plays the woman's part and bursts into tirades which might have been taken straight from a novel or a sermon on philosophy."[9]

Chopin, having heard only Solange's version of the recent

---

* From there the couple could travel comfortably by train to Paris.

scenes at Nohant, wrote back defending himself and the Clésingers. In regard to her daughter, he informed George, "I cannot remain indifferent. You will remember that I used to intercede with you for both your children, without preference. I did this whenever I had the chance, being certain that it is your destiny to love them *forever*—since that is the only affection which never changes. Misfortune may obscure it at times but never destroy it. Such misfortune must be very overwhelming today since it prevents you from wanting to hear anything about your daughter just as she is on the threshold of her true vocation, just when her physical condition demands more than ever a mother's solicitude. Considering the gravity of a matter such as this which affects your most sacred feelings, I will not let my own personal sentiments intrude. Time will take care of things. I shall wait—as always, your most devoted Ch." [10]

With these words, written July 24, 1847, the thirty-seven-year-old Chopin closed the last letter he ever wrote Mme Sand. "Time will take care of things," he had hoped with pathetic resignation, but tragically enough time was running out.

The next day, as this very letter was on its way to Nohant, George was beginning to get alarmed over what had become of Chopin. She still expected him to spend the summer as usual with her in the country but it was already late July and as yet there was no word from him. Even after the galling experience of having to turn his carriage over to the Clésingers she was still willing to let him come back to Nohant and invited Delacroix to join him. "Chopin is coming," she wrote the painter, "His carriage is waiting for him in Blois [where the Clésingers had left it]. If you could come with him it would be more pleasant for you and the two of you could be together." [11]

To find out what had happened to her friend she wrote Marie de Rozières on the twenty-fifth.

I am disturbed and frightened since I have not received any news of Chopin for several days. I don't know just how many days . . . but it seems to me it has been too long. He was about to leave and then all of a sudden he didn't arrive and hasn't written. Is he on his way? Was he held up or is he sick somewhere? . . . I would already have set out for him if it weren't for the fear of our crossing en route as well as the horror I have of going to Paris and exposing myself to the hatred of that one [Solange] whom you think is so good and affectionate toward me! . . . But if I haven't heard anything by tomorrow I think I will leave anyway. It is just too much to suffer so many troubles all at once and I assure you that without Maurice. . . . I am certain I would end this poor life of mine. (p. 17)

Her apprehensions regarding Chopin were soon resolved as the next morning's mail brought his letter to Nohant. Politely but emphatically he made it clear to George that he had no intention of siding with her against the Clésingers. As for returning to Nohant he simply avoided any reference to the matter at all. Stung by this attitude George became thoroughly infuriated. "I see that as usual I have been duped by my own stupid heart," she exploded to Mlle de Rozières. "While I spent the past six nights awake tormenting myself about the state of his health he has been busy thinking and saying the worst things about me to the Clésingers. Isn't that a pretty picture! His letter was ridiculously pompous and the sermons of this *fine paterfamilias* have served as a lesson to me. . . . From now on I shall not let myself get worked up over him. . . . Everything is finally clear to me!—and I shall act accordingly" (p. 50).

The more George thought the matter over the less surprised she felt by Chopin's letter. After all for some time she had suspected that it was really Solange and not herself that Chopin had always been fond of. No wonder he was standing up for her now. "I remember those bursts of furious jealousy of which I was supposed to be the object," she wrote her old friend, Emmanuel Arago,

I was obviously only serving as a pretext since it could hardly have been on my account that he became jealous of all the men who courted Solange. . . . For the past two years I have seen and told myself quite clearly that his pretended love for me is, in fact, really hatred. . . . What a relief for me to see this chain broken! I have been tied down to a cadaver for nine of the best years of my life, fighting against his narrow and despotic spirit but always remaining chained to it out of pity and fear of making him die from unhappiness otherwise. He and his friends were forever holding that threat over my head. "Alas! If you do one little thing to displease him, if you say one little word that upsets him, he will die and you will have killed him!" . . . Thank God it won't be me who kills him now. Finally I can begin to live after having been the one who was being killed by incessant pinpricks over the past nine years. Well, now I am going to get some work done, go out as I please and sleep for a change! (p. 47)

It was not until two days later that George got around to taking up the matter directly with Chopin. "I was going to order some post horses for yesterday and set out by cabriolet in this frightful weather, sick as I am, to spend a day in Paris to find out what had become of you," she began in a martyred tone.

Your silence made me worry about your health. And all the while you were taking the time to think things over. From your reply I gather you are not the least bit upset. So much the better, my friend. Do whatever your heart tells you now. Go by your instincts and consider them the voice of your conscience. I understand perfectly well. As for my daughter . . . she has the bad taste to say that she needs the love of a mother whom she detests and vilifies. . . . It seems to please you to listen to and perhaps believe all that. I will not get involved in any such arguments. They fill me with horror. I would rather see you side with the enemy than defend myself against one nourished at my breast with my own milk. Take care of her since she is the one you feel obliged to devote yourself to. I would not wish it on you but you understand that I only see things from the point of view of an outraged mother—all the more so now than before. . . . It is enough to be a dupe and a victim. I forgive you and will not reproach you anymore in the future, since you have said sincerely what you believe. It astonishes me a little but if you feel more free and comfortable that way then I won't let your strange change of face bother me. Farewell my friend. May you soon be cured of all your ills as I hope you are by now (I have

my own reasons for thinking so). After nine years of unswerving
devotion I can only thank God that it has all finally come to an
end in this incredible way. Let me hear from you from time to
time, but it is useless to think we can ever relive what is past. (p.
54)

The stabbing finality of this letter stunned Chopin. He
never replied and there was no further correspondence between the once-intimate couple. Characteristically, George had
had the last word.

৫% CHAPTER TWENTY-FOUR %৩

THROUGHOUT the latter half of 1847 Mme Sand remained at Nohant. The summer ended dismally with overcast skies, chill winds, and torrents of rain. Exhausted by her recent tribulations, she could no longer muster up her usual optimism. With forty-three years of highly active life behind her she now began to feel age creeping up and viewed its approach morosely. At least she hoped it might bring her some tranquillity, some "recompense for the great sacrifices, the endless work, and fatigue of a life given over entirely to devotion and self-denial. I don't ask for anything," she wrote modestly that August, "but to be able to give happiness to those I love. And yet, I have been paid back with nothing but ingratitude. . . . Right now it is all I can do to force myself to go on living." Fortunately Maurice was with her and as always proved to be a great pillar at strength. "He sustains and consoles me,"[1] she wrote. In fact without him, she claimed, she certainly would have ended her wretched life then. But thanks to her "faithful Maurice" she had no fear of being abandoned because she knew he would "never love any woman as much as his mother" (p. 97).

In order to distract herself George went back to writing, and by October she was able to complete the manuscripts of two new novels, *Le Château des Désertes** and *Francois le Champi*. Shortly afterwards she began another project which she had first contemplated as early as 1844: an autobiography to be

---

* Not published until 1851, the novel was originally entitled *Célio* since it deals with Célio Floriani, the son of Lucrezia Floriani.

entitled *Histoire de ma Vie*. This, she explained, was to consist of

> a series of recollections, professions of faith, and meditations, gotten together in such a manner as to give the details a certain poetry combined with great simplicity. However I don't plan to reveal *all my life*. I don't care for the pride and cynicism found in typical *confessions*. I don't think one should bare all the mysteries of one's heart to people worse than oneself who would tend to derive a bad lesson from them rather than a good one. . . . Far be it from me to accuse or bring sadness to anybody. That would be offensive and do me more harm than any of my victims. I believe therefore that I am writing a useful book, free from any insidiousness or scandal, and without any vanity or baseness. It is a pleasure to work on. (p. 188)

Around the same time she also began to collaborate on a deluxe edition of Rabelais with her son and Victor Borie, who was now, more than ever, a frequent visitor at Nohant. Her plan was to edit the sixteenth-century satirist in such a way as to edify a nineteenth-century public by censoring "all that is *ugly*" and preserving "all that is *beautiful*" in his work. Like her memories, this was a project Mme Sand had long entertained: "Twenty years ago I thought . . . about expurgating Rabelais" she wrote, "and was always tempted to tell him, 'Oh, divine master, what an atrocious pig you are!' " Behind her sophisticated screen of cigar smoke, George was, after all, very much a convent-bred product. "I believe," she declared piously, "that we shall have rendered a great service to truth and art by placing in the hands of virtuous women and clean-minded young people a masterpiece which has been justifiably forbidden to them up to now" (p. 187).

All these literary undertakings succeeded in soothing Mme Sand's troubled mind to a certain extent. "I am working and have become calm again" (p. 164), she announced in November of 1847. But underneath this new-found calm there was a lingering sadness. "The more I succeed in distracting myself at any time," she confessed, "the more somber and painfully unhappy I feel later" (p. 186).

She still brooded over Chopin and constantly tried to convince herself that everything had really worked out for the best. "I can tell you truthfully," she wrote Mme Marliani,

that I am not at all annoyed that he has taken his life out from under my control. Both he and his friends expected me to assume far too much responsibility. He was growing more and more sour each day and indulged in spiteful, jealous temper tantrums in front of all my friends and children. Solange took advantage of all this with her typical cunning and Maurice was beginning to get aggravated with him. Since he knew and could see the innocence of our relationship it was clear to him how this poor, sickly creature (not willfully, but perhaps because he couldn't help it) posed as my lover, my husband, and the master of all my thoughts and actions. He was on the brink of exploding and telling him face to face that he was making me—at forty-three years of age—look ridiculous, and that he was abusing my goodness, patience, and pity in his sick, neurotic condition. . . . Seeing the storm that was brewing, I took advantage of Chopin's preference for Solange to let him sulk without making any effort to get him back. . . . I don't know how this cooling off of our relationship will end. I don't plan to do anything to alleviate it or make it worse since I have done no wrong . . . but I cannot, should not, and do not want to lapse back under that subtle tyranny which was stabbing the life out of me with those continual pinpricks, some of which struck pretty deeply. . . . The poor child could no longer even maintain that outer decorum of which he was a slave both in principle and in practice. Everyone, men, women, young, and old, became objects of horror because of his furious, unreasoning jealousy. If he had controlled himself to the point of exhibiting all this just to me I could have tolerated it but his outbursts took place in front of my children, my servants, and other people who, on seeing it, lost all respect for me—respect to which my age and conduct for the past ten years have entitled me. I simply couldn't stand it any longer. I know his friends will judge matters differently. They will make him the martyr and find it more convenient to believe that I have kicked him out for a new lover than to accept the truth. (p. 112)

How imperceptibly this profile of Chopin merged into that of Prince Karol, a man "supremely polite and reserved"[2] but one who tended to "take everything to excess, likes and dislikes, happiness and sorrow," a man "of an artistic nature" (p. 234), but one who "could be sarcastic and cutting in the sweetest manner, inflicting wounds which could penetrate to the very heart" (p. 298), a man consumed with jealousy—jealous even of his mistress' children and the rugged health she enjoyed. How different, though, were the fates of the real-life characters!

Except for brief trips to Ville d'Avray in the spring and to the Rothschild's at Ferrières in the fall, Chopin remained in Paris throughout the rest of 1847. He kept in close contact with the Clésingers, who were still wandering about since their recent eviction from Nohant. They traveled first to the baron Dudevant's in Guillery and then to Clésinger's father's in Besançon, since the sculptor's staggering debts kept them constantly on the move in an effort to avoid creditors. "For some days now," Solange wrote Frédéric late in September, "we have hardly been able to think of anything else but filthy money matters. . . . What a predicament after four months of marriage, and with names like ours!"[3]

When he learned of their plight Chopin loaned the couple 500 francs out of his own meager funds. To Solange's credit she was very conscientious in seeing that it was quickly repaid. "You know only too well for me to remind you what a valuable service you rendered," she acknowledged.

> Without you we should have been in a sorry state. . . . It seems we are always punished according to our sins. Look at me, with my luxurious tastes! I who would have found a coach-and-six barely good enough to ride in, I who counted on living in a fanciful realm full of poetic dreams, floating on clouds, surrounded by flowers, here I am now—more dreary and downtrodden than the lowest of the low. I'm sure I shall become a miser, I who could easily have tossed away millions. There are few women my age who have been brought up like a princess as I was, that could stand up under such harsh trials in such a calm manner. On the one hand financial worries, on the other hand a mother who abandons me before I have learned to cope with life, and a father, more severe than affectionate, a father without tenderness—such things just don't happen every day to girls of nineteen. . . . (p. 300)

In November when the couple was visiting friends again at La Châtre, Solange went to Nohant twice, hoping for some sort of rapprochement with her mother. "I found her greatly changed," she wrote Chopin, "as cold as ice, really hard-bitten. She began by saying that if I should have a falling-out with my husband I could always return to Nohant. But, as for him, she no longer even acknowledges his existence. What do you think of that for a how-do-you-do? Afterwards you can imagine how difficult it was for me to find anything affectionate to say in return." Maurice did not behave any more cordially. He merely "went through the motions of politeness," fondling his little dog, Bébé, the whole time "with his selfish, know-it-all expression" (p. 303).

"How badly I feel about the results of your two visits to Nohant," Chopin wrote back. "However, the first step has been taken. You have made a show of good will and that must have had some effect in bringing the two of you together. . . . Time will do the rest . . ." (p. 307). For the Clésingers he had no doubt there would be a reconciliation with Mme Sand; for himself, though, he had given up hope and resigned himself to permanent exile from Nohant.

As much as he had always loved the city, Chopin now found the Square d'Orléans a lonely place. Nearby at No. 7, the Marliani's, who were in the process of getting a divorce, had vacated their apartment. Across the courtyard at No. 5, George's quarters continued to go unoccupied. What she planned to do with them remained a mystery. Weeks and months passed without any news at all from Nohant.

As fall approached, the trees in the garden turned brown and began to shed their leaves. Beneath the maze of barren branches which swayed and crackled in the November wind the neat little gravel walks criss-crossing the courtyard stood silent and empty in the pale autumn sunlight. The Square d'Orléans, once the scene of so much gaiety, had now grown sadly deserted. Chopin longed to move away but could not find a suitable apartment. So day by day he sat in his rooms watching the warmth of summer slip by and the crisp fall air give way to the damp chill of winter.

By December all of Paris was buried under a stark white mantle. "It's snowing and looks very gloomy" (p. 316), Chopin wrote Solange on the thirty-first. Because of the cold he seldom went out and then only in a carriage. Whenever he had any business to be transacted his publishers were usually kind enough to come out to the carriage so he would not have to exert himself. Often he took his meals away from the square with Gutmann or Grzymała but hardly ever attended the lavish soirées, dinners, and musicales which he used to adore so much. "I take a whiff of my homeopathic bottles from time to time" (p. 313), he told his family. But even this did little to preserve his failing strength.

In December he heard from the concierge that George and her family had decided to give up their apartment but planned to keep a few rooms temporarily at No. 3. Just prior to this his Pleyel piano had been returned to him from Nohant where he had left it the year before. "I have no desire whatsoever for Chopin to make me a present of his piano," George told his one-time pupil, Mlle de Rozières. "I do not like being under any obligation to those who hate me, and what Chopin has said to his friends in confidence—which, like all confidences, have been passed along—proves to me where we stand from here on out. . . . I always knew his friendship for me would turn to aversion since he never does things halfway. . . . The last thing in the world I want now is *any favor from him.*" [4]

As the year drew to a close Christmas came and went "in the most prosaic manner" at the Square d'Orléans. "This *horrible year* has got to end," [5] Chopin cried out miserably. Unfortunately when it finally did, his creative genius all but ended with it. Only three more short compositions were to come from his pen in the little time remaining to him.*

At Nohant George, too, was glad to see the end of 1847. It had been a year which she described as "perhaps the most hectic and unhappy" [6] in her life.

With the dawning of the new year Chopin found himself very much alone and depressed. His mind was obsessed with

---

*The Waltz in B Major (without opus number, composed for Catherine Erskine), and the Mazurkas in G Minor (Op. 67, no. 2) and F Minor (Op. 68, no. 4).

thoughts of George, and unable to hold back his bitter anguish, he poured it all out to his sister. "What an odd creature in spite of her intelligence!" he exclaimed.

> Some sort of madness has gotten hold of her. She is making a wreck of her life and ruining that of her daughter as well. The son is headed for a bad end too. . . . To justify herself in her own eyes she has tried to find fault with those who wish her well, who had faith in her, who never caused her the least bit of trouble, but whom she can't stand around her since they only serve to mirror her true self. That's the reason she hasn't written me a single word; that's why she won't come back to Paris this winter; and that's why she hasn't said a thing about me to her daughter. I have no regrets for having helped her through the eight most difficult years of her life, those when her daughter was growing up and she was raising her son. I don't regret a thing I had to put up with . . . Mme Sand can find nothing in all that but good memories of me whenever she looks back over the past. Right now she is playing the mother role to a ridiculous extreme, acting like a far better and fairer one than she actually is—it's a fever for which there is no cure. . . . There's talk of her *Mémoires* . . . this is really a bit premature since dear Mme Sand will still have many more adventures, some good and some bad, before she gets to the end of her road.[7]

"I hope all this doesn't upset you," he went on, "It happened quite a while ago. Time is a great healer, but I still haven't gotten over it yet" (p. 320).

A number of friends tried to intercede with Mme Sand on Chopin's behalf. Pauline and Louis Viardot, like many others, had ceased to hear anything from Nohant for some time after Solange's wedding, but when George herself finally broke the long silence, they immediately took the opportunity to urge her to reconsider Chopin's position. "In your letter there is another passage I simply can't let pass without comment," Pauline wrote in this regard.

> It is the one where you say that Chopin belongs to Solange's *clique*, which makes her look like a victim and reflects badly on you. I swear to you that this is absolutely untrue, at least as far as he is concerned. On the contrary, this dear and excellent friend is only absorbed in, or rather afflicted by one single

thought, that is the harm which this unfortunate affair must have done, and is still doing to you. I have not noticed the least change in him—he is still as kind and devoted as ever—adoring you as always, rejoicing only in your happiness and burdening himself only with your griefs. For heaven's sake, darling, don't ever believe those officious friends who come to you with foolish gossip. (p. 305)

In the note which Louis added to his wife's letter he also spoke up for Chopin: "I ought to assure you in all fairness and truth," he told Mme Sand, "that the animosity which you think he bears you without any sense of gratitude was never shown—not to us at any rate—by a single word or gesture . . . I am afraid *it is only the whispering of evil lips that has come between you.* May God protect you from it" (p. 306).

Despite these pleas George remained unmoved. "He has dreamed up and attributed faults to me that I never even conceived of, faults I couldn't possibly be guilty of (all conscience aside) simply because they are not part of my nature,"[8] she answered the Viardots.

In February when Maurice went up to Paris to close the apartment in the Square d'Orléans she instructed him:

If you have anything to leave with Chopin, give it to the porter without any note. That's the best way to handle things. If you happen to run into him, say 'Hello' as if nothing were the matter. 'You're fine? Well so much the better then.' Don't say anything more and go on your way. In case he avoids you, then do the same. If he should ask about me, tell him I have been very sick as a result of all my griefs. Don't spare any words with him about that and say it in a rather curt manner so as not to encourage him to talk about Solange. If he does speak of her, which I doubt, tell him it is not your place to go around offering explanations. (p. 286)

As for bumping into Mme Marliani, however, that was quite a different matter. "Tell her all she wants to know," George told Maurice, seeing a good opportunity to turn her voluble friend's incessant chatter to her own advantage. "You know how nosy she is and how it simply kills her not to have every detail . . . Mrs. [*sic*] Clésinger and Chopin are sounding their trumpets against us, so blow the truth through Mme Marliani's horn" (p. 289).

On the very evening George was writing these instructions Chopin was sitting down at the piano on the stage of the Salle Pleyel. It was February 16, 1848, the date of his final concert in Paris. He still abhorred performing in public as much as ever, but financial necessity now forced him back on the concert stage for the first time in nearly four years. His health had slipped to the point where he could no longer teach much, and not having his usual productive summer at Nohant there was little income from his publishers that winter. For these reasons he let Pleyel and other friends persuade him to give a concert in February. The limited number of tickets was completely sold out more than two weeks in advance—even though they cost twenty francs each, eight more than the most expensive seats at the Opera. "The King has requested ten tickets," Chopin wrote his family. "The Queen and the duc de Montpensier also want ten apiece."[9] As the royal family was in mourning then due to the death of Mme Adélaïde, the king's sister, none of them could actually attend but their tickets would doubtless go to other members of the court. From as far as Brest and Nantes people wrote in for seats. "Such a rush surprises me," the pianist commented five days before the concert. "I had better begin to practice . . . I feel I am playing worse now than ever" (p. 322).

All these preparations produced a great strain on Chopin who was just recovering from a bout of influenza. To make matters easier Pleyel sent the piano for the concert over to his apartment for him to practice on while one of his pupils, Miss Jane Stirling, arranged for the green room to be specially heated and assured her teacher that she would have the auditorium aired at intermission. Still Chopin continued to worry over every little detail all the way down to which one of his dozen tail coats he should wear for the concert.

Surprisingly enough, at 8:30 on the night of the sixteenth, when the pianist threaded his way among the baskets of flowers on the stage of the Salle Pleyel, few in the audience were able to detect any traces of the previous week's anxiety on his face or in his carriage. Few suspected he hardly had the strength to finish his program. Exhausted as he left the stage for the last time (after having been called back to repeat the final waltz) Chopin all but fainted in the green room. Meanwhile, out front, his listeners descended the flower-draped stairway of the concert hall, unaware of the supreme effort the performance had cost the sick artist. They were overcome by the shimmering beauty of his delicate, almost inaudible pianissimos and the subtlety of his shading. The latter, in fact, had been so remarkable that few actually realized Chopin never played a single loud note the whole evening, so great were the contrasts between his "pianos" and "pianissimos."

The following day an amazed and admiring Paris was at his feet. "It was as if one were alone with you in the midst of a crowd," his friend, the marquis de Custine, wrote, "as if there were no piano present at all—only a soul, and what a soul!" (p. 325).

"A concert by the *Ariel* of pianists" the *Revue et Gazette Musicale* raved on February 20. Besides "the fine flower of the most distinguished feminine aristocracy," it proclaimed, "there were also present the aristocracy of artists and music lovers, happy to capture this musical sylph in mid-flight. . . . It is easier to write about the reception he received and the raptures he aroused than to describe, analyse, and divulge the mysteries of an execution which has no equal in our earthly realm. Even if we had that pen which traced the delicate wonders of Queen Mab at our disposal . . . it would not be adequate to give you any conception of a talent so purely ideal in nature that matter hardly seems to enter into it." [10]

It was hoped that Chopin would follow this success with another but the pianist showed no enthusiasm to repeat it. "A subscription has been started for a second concert," he wrote his family, "but I'm sure I won't go through with it, I'm so sick of this one already." [11] Even if he had planned another concert it would never have materialized, for the rumblings of revolution were already audible in the streets of Paris that February.

THE UNREST which troubled Paris in February of 1848 was soon to make itself felt throughout all France and across the entire breadth of Europe. Unemployment was widespread in both the cities and the rural areas, while the price of grain rose steadily everywhere—a combination of events which proved to be highly explosive. Resentment was growing against the government headed then by a conservative faction under Guizot, but for much of the population the real focus of resentment was the stodgy figure of Louis-Philippe. His prosaic appearance and lusterless personality left him devoid of the vital charismatic qualities essential for a hero. This was an especially serious defect in a man who governed a nation that still remembered Napoléon.

In February of 1848 a number of opposition journals began organizing political banquets which threatened to fan the sparks of this smoldering discontent. Alarmed, M. de Rambuteau, Prefect of the Seine, brought the matter to the attention of the king. Louis-Philippe, however, remained unruffled and replied calmly that such fears were foolish. Paris did not remain as calm as the king. As the month progressed, the talk at the banquets became more and more inflammatory until Guizot finally took measures to prohibit one such gathering at which fifteen hundred people planned to assemble near the Étoile on February 22. Although the event was officially canceled, many did not receive the news in time, with the result that crowds of workers and students arrived only to find themselves left to mill idly about in the gray drizzling atmosphere. From time to time chants and cries of "Long live reform" or "Down with Guizot" rang through the air. Proceeding from the Madeleine a band of several hundred students began to march and sing down the rue Royale. In the Place de la Concorde where more crowds had gathered a band was playing waltzes and polkas while in the Champs Élysées a cold, restless throng began smashing and burning Punch and Judy stalls to keep warm. Throughout the city the streets started to fill up with agitators and onlookers. For the most part their mood was boisterous and their movement aimless. But as the day wore on, scattered scenes of violence erupted. Near the rue Saint-Honoré one demonstrator was wounded by a saber. On other streets the pavement was ripped up, stones were hurled, and barricades erected. In the Place du Théâtre Français and on the rue de la Bourse several shops were broken into. Later a mob of students invaded the empty Chamber of Deputies and then suddenly near the Louvre the noisy crowd fell back in shocked silence as they watched the removal of a limp body, the first victim of the impending revolution.

Despite the pouring rains that followed on the twenty-third the crowds remained in the streets, more barricades were flung up, and cannons hauled over the broken pavements. Later in the day the National Guard was called out and the air snapped with sporadic volleys of gunfire. In the rue Montmartre a red flag went up while an armed mob with torches and candles stuck in their rifle barrels gathered in the rue des Capucines and tried to break past the guards in front of the Foreign Ministry. Heckled by the angry mob, a frightened soldier fired impusively into the crowd. Immediately a series of shots shattered the gray gloom and fifty-two dead were left littering the steps of the ministry. The bodies were quickly piled on top of a nearby carriage and the somber cortège headed across the city toward the Bastille leaving a stream of blood and indignation in its path. The crowds in the streets were now implacable.

At this point Louis-Philippe could no longer remain unperturbed. Panicky, he dismissed Guizot and hastily tried to reorganize his government. But Paris was in such a state of turmoil that news of his reforms did not spread swiftly enough to the people.

On the afternoon of the twenty-fourth, after a plateful of chicken and an earful of advice, the king decided to leave the Tuileries to review his troops, hoping to boost their morale and quiet the fears of the people with a show of confidence. However, seeing his reception vary from mere indifference to outright hostility, the seventy-five-year old monarch broke off his review and returned to the Tuileries where he announced his abdication. Tired, discouraged, and with only fifteen francs in his pocket, he fled with the queen through a passageway leading on to the Place de la Concorde where they hurriedly climbed into a court brougham and departed unobtrusively, leaving the government in chaos and the city in shambles.

No sooner had the royal couple slipped away than the mob invaded the Tuileries, smashing mirrors and breaking statues. Some ransacked closets, stealing clothes and jewelry, while others headed for the cellar where they punctured the wine barrels and drank themselves into a stupor. The following morning several of the rioters were found dead on the cellar floor, having drowned in the two feet of wine that flooded it.[1]

Throughout these tumultuous days Chopin remained in bed with a severe attack of "neuralgia." George, far away in Berry, received the disturbing news slowly in piecemeal fashion. She welcomed the collapse of the July monarchy but worried about Maurice, who had stayed in Paris while all these upheavals were taking place. If Louis-Philippe's throne were to topple she did not want her son engulfed in its rubble.

When the first reports of the "banquet business" arrived, she tried to stave off her fears. "It's all just an intrigue between ministers who are tumbling out of power and those scrambling up to grab it," she assured Maurice. "Write me what you are able to see *from the sidelines,* but," she cautioned, "don't poke around in any *melées* if they occur."[2]

By the twenty-third of the month she had grown much more alarmed and tried to persuade Maurice to leave Paris immediately. "You must come home at once . . ." she wrote him. "You know full well I wouldn't advise you to act cowardly, but your place is here if there is to be any serious trouble. A revolution in Paris would have instant repercussions in the provinces, especially here where news arrives in a matter of hours. You therefore have an obligation to fulfill in your own home which would make it inexcusable for you to be anywhere else" (p. 304).

Her son, however, had no intention of returning just then. Events in Paris were far too exciting. "Maurice is absolutely radiant," Delacroix wrote George. "He went out of here looking as if he were completely intoxicated. I never thought him capable of such elation."[3] This state of affairs was too much for Mme Sand who could not stay put any longer. Prodded by curiosity she dashed off to the capital, arriving in Paris on the twenty-seventh.

There she found her son unharmed and discovered that her old friend, Lamartine, had established a provisional government and appointed another friend (and former lover) of hers, Louis Blanc, to head the commission on labor problems. Both men were vociferous in their promises of reforms which kindled George's socialist-oriented sympathies. Eager to participate in the molding of their new utopia, Mme Sand moved in with her son, took her meals at a nearby restaurant, and promptly went around to call on all the new members of the make-shift government. Soon she was volunteering her services for the drafting of bulletins and brochures. Fired with energy and consumed with dedication, she exclaimed exuberantly, "My heart is bursting and my head is aflame. All my physical ailments and personal sorrows are forgotten. I am alive, strong and active, and don't feel a single day over twenty."[4]

With a fervor equal to that of an ancient Athenian battling for democracy, she plunged into the course of revolutionary events. Among the numerous tasks which she now assumed was that of director of the *Bulletin de la République*. In addition she began working on her own weekly newspaper, *La Cause du*

Peuple, and set about writing letters to the "children of the republic" whom she considered her own by adoption. As late as one or two o'clock in the morning she could be found conferring with various government officials and even went so far as to assist in arranging for a revision of the Marseillaise!

In the midst of all this, unknown to Mme Sand, Solange gave birth to a premature baby girl on February 28 at the baron Dudevant's estate in Guillery. Almost immediately the young mother scribbled off a note to Chopin, informing him of the great event. Delighted, he replied on the third of March: "As you can imagine, the arrival of your little girl brought me more joy than the arrival of the republic. Thank God your sufferings are over. A new world is beginning for you. Be happy and take care of yourself." As for the situation in the capital, "Paris is quiet with fear," he told Solange. "Everyone is up in arms and joining the National Guard. The shops are open but there aren't any customers. Foreigners are waiting with passports in hand for the damage to the railroads to be repaired so they can start operating again. Clubs are being formed. But I'll never finish if I try to write you all the things that are happening here."[5]

The following day was Saturday, the fourth of March and in her new apartment on the rue de la Ville-l'Évêque, Mme Marliani was receiving guests. As the bleak winter sun fell across the gray façades of the buildings lining the street, Mme Sand's carriage clattered to a halt in front of the ionic-columned portico of the large house where Charlotte Marliani lived. Inside the vehicle, beside George, was a young man, Eugène Lambert, a painter and close friend of her son. Alighting from the carriage Mme Sand and her companion climbed the five or six steps up to the glass-panelled entrance where they waited for a few moments while the concierge opened the door. Then turning to their right, past the graceful bronze and crystal sconces of the foyer, they walked between the pillars of a tall archway to the spiral staircase that led to Mme Marliani's rooms. At the head of the stairs two men were about to descend just as George and Lambert started up. Instantly Mme

Sand recognized one of the faces. It was clearly Chopin's despite the fact that he looked somewhat older and more gaunt than when she had last seen him less than a year before. In her surprise she scarcely noticed the other man, Edmond Combes, the French vice-consul to Rabat in Morocco. On the narrow staircase it was impossible for the estranged couple to avoid each other. What occurred after the first awkward moment of silence is uncertain. Mme Sand's recollection was that Chopin rushed past her without speaking. "I wanted to talk to him," she asserted, "but he slipped away." Only when she sent Lambert after him did he finally return against his will and as they exchanged greetings his manner seemed curt, almost hostile. "I offered him my hand," George recalled and as he took it she noted he was cold and trembling. "It was my turn to tell him that he no longer loved *me*," she had wanted to say but restrained herself and went on leaving "everything in the hands of Providence and the future.[6]

Such was Mme Sand's account of the event which contrasts considerably with Chopin's description, written the following day to Solange. "I went to Mme Marliani's yesterday," he told her,

> and at the vestibule door as I was leaving I ran into your mother who had just arrived with Lambert. I said hello to her and immediately asked how recently she had heard from you. "A week ago" she told me. "Nothing yesterday or the day before?"— "No"—"Then allow me to tell you that you are a grandmother. Solange has a little girl, and I am very pleased to be able to be the first to give you the news." I took my leave then and went downstairs. Combes . . . was with me, and as I had forgotten to say that you were doing well, a very important point, especially for a mother . . . I asked Combes to go back upstairs to say that everything was fine with both you and the child. It would have been too much for me to hobble up those steps again. While I was waiting below your mother came down and with great concern asked me all sorts of questions about your health. I replied that you *yourself* had jotted off a brief note in pencil to me the day after your child was born. I told her you had suffered a great deal but that the sight of your little girl had made you forget everything. She asked whether your husband was with

you, and I said that the address on your letter looked as if it were in his handwriting. She inquired how I was—I told her I was fine—I then summoned the concierge to open the door, said good-bye and walked back to the Square d'Orléans.[7]

All the way home Chopin seemed very sad and depressed according to Combes who accompanied him back to his apartment. Seeing George again had affected him deeply. That unexpected encounter on the steps at Mme Marliani's was to be the last time their paths would ever cross. "I was never to see him again,"[8] George recorded in her memoires.

⳼ CHAPTER TWENTY-SIX ⳥

THREE DAYS AFTER she had run into Chopin on the stairs at Mme Marliani's, George was back at Nohant. She was now quite heady with the revolutionary spirit of Paris and eager to spread its ideals throughout the quiet province of Berry. "Long live the republic!" she exclaimed. "It's all so incredible, so intoxicating, and so marvellous to have gone to sleep in the mire and then to wake up in heaven. . . . The republic has triumphed; it is secure now and we will all die rather than lose it. . . . I have returned here to help my friends insofar as I can to revolutionize Berry which needs a little prodding."¹ One of her first projects was to install Maurice as mayor of Nohant. The fact that he had no political background and was not yet even of legal age to assume the office did not restrain his exuberant mother in the least. Buoyed up with confidence she proceeded to have several of her friends appointed Commissaries of the Republic at Châteauroux and La Châtre.

Only one event blighted her happiness at this point: Solange's infant died less than a week after birth and was buried on March seventh. News of this softened Mme Sand's feelings toward her daughter. Saddened, she wrote Solange several letters of sympathy and encouragement which marked the beginning of an improvement in their relationship. In Paris, Chopin was pleased to hear of George's new attitude and wrote Solange, "I am very happy about the nice letters Madame, your mother, has written you. Look out for your health now and everything will turn out as well as can be."²

Despite her sorrow George remained undaunted and dashed back to Paris a few weeks later intent on bolstering up

Lamartine's wobbly government. There she set about writing reams of propaganda, causing the satirical journals, *La Lanterne* and *Le Charivari* to scornfully dub her the Egeria* of the new republic. Oblivious to their taunts, George did not relax for a moment, but continued energetically contributing to such journals as the left wing *La Reforme* and her own *Bulletin de la République*. It amused her to know that her proclamations in the latter would be issued with government authorization and go out addressed "To All Mayors," including her son at Nohant. Unable to resist teasing Maurice about this she wrote him, "You are going to be receiving through official channels your *mother's* instructions! Ha, ha, Mr. *Mayor*," she chuckled, "you had better watch your step."[3]

There could be no doubt that George relished her position of authority that lifted her a bit above the crowd. But at the same time she was wholly—almost humbly—dedicated to the people whose infectious spirit of brotherhood pervaded the streets of Paris during those days of buoyant optimism. The course of mankind was changing and she felt that liberty, equality, and fraternity were at last becoming realities for France. Unfortunately this illusion of brotherly love was short-lived. The radicals and socialists who had grown increasingly dissatisfied with Lamartine's moderate government, began to show their unrest. Even George herself began to find Lamartine too lukewarm and bourgeois. He was, after all, perhaps more of an artist† than a statesman, she felt and did not hesitate to say so directly to his face. It was not long, in fact, before he was forced to include more radical leaders in his government. But even this did not prove enough to pacify the restless populace.

By April the people had taken to the streets again. At night the boulevards flickered with the glow of torchlight parades and resounded to the beating drums, the crackle of gunshot,

---

*Egeria was a nymph who, in classical mythology, acted as legal adviser to Numa, king of ancient Rome.
†Lamartine is remembered today more as a romantic poet than a revolutionary statesman.

and cries of "Down with————!" or "Death to————!"
Then a great wave of fear spread over the city following which
the streets became empty once more. Not a soul was to be seen
at night, "not even a cat, only patrols every twenty feet or so,"
George reported. "When a poor pedestrian appears at the end
of the street, the patrol cock their rifles, turn, and watch him
pass. . . . All the clubs sit in vigil throughout the night,
armed, and barricaded. None of their members is allowed to
set foot outside the door for fear of being assassinated. Since
everyone shares the same fear, they all stay shut up and nobody budges. . . . No one dares to close more than one eye at
a time when they sleep here" (p. 422).

With so much excitement in Paris George did not bother to
attend her adopted daughter's wedding, which took place at
Nohant on April twelfth. Poor Augustine, having suffered
such humiliation from her previous suitors, had finally found
a worthy husband in Karol de Bertholdi, a thirty-six-year old
Polish art teacher. Ironically enough, in Mme Sand's absence
it was Maurice, who once gave the girl up so off-handedly,
who now had to give her away officially.

As political events in Paris headed in a more radical direction George found her own sentiments also swinging further
toward the left. In fact, she even went so far as to call herself a
communist—provided she was allowed to define the word in
her own terms. "If by communism," she wrote, "you mean the
desire and determination to employ every legitimate means
sanctioned by the public conscience, to abolish from this day
hence the atrocious inequality of extreme wealth and extreme
poverty, and to replace it with the beginnings of true equality,
then yes, we are communists indeed, and dare to say so."[4]

In the sixteenth number of the *Bulletin de la République*,
dated April 15, she shocked both the government and the
public alike by threatening a *coup d'état* if the ensuing elections
scheduled for April 23 did not support the existing moderate-
radical coalition. "If these elections," her incendiary article
declared, "do not bring about the triumph of social truth, if
they express only the interests of a select caste and violate the

confidence and loyalty of the people, then instead of being, as they should, the salvation of the Republic, they will signal its defeat. There can be no doubt about this,"[5] she emphasized, and urged the masses to take to the streets in protest if that occurred.

A socialist uprising on the following day, April 16, led by Blanqui, Cabet, and Raspail, was immediately put down with cries of "Long live the Republic" and "Death to the Communists." George, whose actual philosophy was hardly as inflammatory as her words, was quite relieved to see the socialists squelched. Only a few days later all rifts seemed to have healed and the people staged a colossal exhibition of solidarity which George considered "the most glorious in all history. One *million souls*" she asserted with suspicious extravagance, "forgetting all resentment, all conflict of interest, forgiving the past, and taking no thought for the future, embraced one another throughout the length and breadth of Paris, crying *'Long live Fraternity!'* * It was sublime. . . . The sky, the city, the horizon, the green countryside, the domes of the great buildings, viewed from the top of the Arch of Triumph, in the rain and in the sunshine, what a setting for the most gigantic scene of humanity ever assembled! . . . It was absolutely out of this world! . . . I watched for twelve whole hours and never got my fill of it even then" (p. 430).

Scarcely had the uproar from this tumultuous "Feast of Fraternity" died down than the results of the April 23 elections led to further disruptions. With the franchise extended to more of the population than ever before, the French people overwhelmingly rejected the radicals and socialists and called for a complete change in the complexion of the Assembly. Outside Paris the feeling was clearly that the revolution had been carried too far. The conservative provincial was alarmed by the disorders which had wrought so much havoc in the capital. The new representatives chosen by the people therefore included a group of more moderate Liberals and Republicans

* The whole event was labeled somewhat pretentiously the "Feast of Fraternity."

along with many who had even been former supporters of Louis-Philippe. Lamartine remained but Louis Blanc fell. George, whose views by this time had become too radical to suit most of the newly-returned Assembly, was disappointed in the elections. "The masses," she lamented, "have no faith at all in their own people and have just proved it" (p. 513). Nevertheless she remained in Paris, conferred daily with the members of the new government, and continued to pour out her political views in print. Many a warm spring day found her lounging on the Chamber of Deputies lawn with such prominent politicos as Ledru-Rollin stretched out beside her and a sentry posted nearby to see that no one disturbed them.

On May 15, less than a month after the elections, Paris again erupted in violence. It was as if the people had taken seriously Mme Sand's advice in her sixteenth *Bulletin de la République* and refused to accept the results of the balloting. During the three days of demonstrations that ensued, the socialist and radical elements, headed by Blanqui, Barbès, and Blanc tried to stage a second revolution. Mobs swarmed over the boulevards and the whole city once more became the scene of bloody fights. The Palais Bourbon was invaded and the Assembly dissolved. While George admired both Barbès and Blanc she did not sympathize with their coup d'état. "My faith is not weakened but my heart is certainly sick," she announced. "That insane affair on May the fifteenth wiped out all progress since the beginning of time" (p. 473). While she took no part whatsoever in the riots, she did mill around the streets observing the spectacle and to her surprise found everywhere that people were blaming her for the uprising because of her notorious *Bulletin* of April 15. At one point she claimed she even "saw a very raucous female hanging out of a cafe window haranguing the mob. Some of the men in the crowd around her assured me she was George Sand, but I can vouch for the fact that she most certainly was not" (p. 461).

By May 17 the abortive rebellion was over. Blanqui and Barbès were thrown into prison while Louis Blanc fled. George emerged physically unscathed but politically stigmatized. "They say that I was an *accomplice* in something, what though I haven't the least idea . . . I was there as an astonished and distressed spectator and since when has it been *forbidden* by the law to be part of a group of idlers?" (p. 498).

With the failure of this ill-timed coup, the socialists suffered a severe setback. Anticipating arrest at any moment, George hastily burned everything in her possession that might be construed as compromising and planned to flee immediately to Nohant. But then instead of leaving, she changed her mind and decided to remain. To run, she reasoned, would look cowardly and so she stayed on where she was, resolutely awaiting her fate. As the turmoil subsided, however, she found to her chagrin that she was completely ignored. "After spending two days in Paris without any incident taking place," she confessed deflatedly, "I left" (p. 473). As matters stood she really had no choice but to return to Nohant; she was out of money.

Back in the country she encountered a hostile reception which surprised and wounded her. "Here in this picturesque, gentle, good, and quiet Berry, in this spot which I love so much, where I have shown the poor and simple that I recognize my obligations to them, I am regarded as an enemy of the human race."[6] There were threats to burn her house and wherever she showed her face in public there were cries of "Down with the Communists!"[7] "I have been strongly advised to go into hiding," she wrote a friend, ". . . I am no longer really safe here. The bourgeoisie have made the peasants believe that I was the ardent disciple *of Father Communism,* a very wicked rogue who creates havoc everywhere in Paris and who wants all children under the age of three and all old people over sixty put to death. . . . Outside of my own neighborhood people believe it, and threaten to bury me in some ditch" (p. 482).

With relatively little to do for a change, Mme Sand now found her thoughts wandering back to Chopin from time to time. In June she inquired of Mme Viardot how he was. "Do you see Chopin?" she asked. "Tell me about his health. I cannot bring myself to repay his fury and hatred in the same manner. Many times I think of him as a sick child who has gone astray and turned bitter" (p. 495). Since she was still on less than cordial terms with her daughter she resented the fact that Chopin and Solange remained in close touch with each other. On several occasions she had seen the latter in Paris but their encounters had not been particularly pleasant. The girl, she was thoroughly convinced, possessed "only a stone" (p. 495) where her heart should have been.

On June 23 more riots broke out in Paris. At the base of the July Column in the Place de la Bastille a fanatical agitator named Pujol whipped up the crowd into a frenzy that threatened to begin the revolution all over again. The following days witnessed a series of bloody atrocities which left the entire city aghast. "During these cruel days," Prosper Merimée wrote, "we have been confronted with every sort of heroism and viciousness that you can imagine. The insurgents massacred their prisoners, cutting off their hands and feet. In one convoy of prisoners which my company led up to the Abbaye there was a woman who had slit the throat of an officer with a kitchen knife and a man whose arms were red up to the elbow, having bathed his hands in the open belly of a wounded guard.[8] When the uprising was finally quelled there were 5,000 dead in the streets!

At this point the pendulum swung and a mood of reaction settled over the populace which had at last grown disgusted with the excesses of revolution. The clubs were suppressed, working hours increased, and freedom of the press restricted.

At Nohant George was appalled by the whole debacle. "What days of tears and indignation," she groaned, "I am ashamed now to be a Frenchwoman, I who was once so thrilled by it."[9] She began to feel that the bloody gulf between proletariat and bourgeoisie could never be bridged. About this time she published in the *Vraie République* one of the last of the political articles she was to write that year. Afterwards she no longer wished to contribute anything to the socialist cause she had once espoused so ardently. "You ask me in what papers I am writing," she replied to a friend at the end of the summer,

"I am not writing at all just now. . . . For some time past I have felt discouraged and broken in spirit. I am still sick at heart and must wait until I am cured" (p. 637).

The cure was simpler than she realized. *"Work, that's the great panacea,"* [10] she once preached in her youth, and work indeed proved to be her salvation now. One day on a stroll through the countryside near Nohant, her old friend, François Rollinat, urged her to write another of the pastoral novels she had created so successfully with *La Mare au Diable* and *François le Champi*. At first she resisted, pleading fatigue and disillusionment. "All this will pass I know," she said, "and the future will be ours but for the time being our ranks are decimated. God will always reign but just now it seems he has turned his back on us." [11] Rollinat insisted, however, that she forget Paris and the revolution. Turn back to nature, he told her: "Listen to the song of the plow" (p. 8). "As afflicted and unhappy as we are," he admitted, "no one can take away from us the sweetness which Nature offers and the repose that we find in her poetry. Therefore since we cannot contribute anything else to those who are unfortunate, let us take up Art again as we once understood it. In other words, let us render joyful homage to this poetry (of Nature) which is itself so joyful. Let us pour it forth on the wounds of humanity like a balm from some nourishing plant" (p. 10).

"In that case," George replied, "we shall return to our flock and wend our way back to the sheepfold" (p. 10).

With this resolution the author resigned her role of revolutionary reformer and sat down at her desk once more to write another chronicle of the rustic Berry peasantry she had known and cherished since childhood. The result was *La Petite Fadette,* a touching novel which regained for her that popularity she had almost lost among her fellow countrymen. If she was now no longer the "Muse of the Revolution," she was still at least the "Poet of the People."

THE UNSETTLED EVENTS of 1848 had an entirely different effect on Chopin than they had had on George Sand. Where they threw the one into a frantic burst of activity they left the other in a fretful state of idleness. The revolution brought the musical season in Paris to an abrupt end, and as many of the aristocratic families (from whom most of his pupils came) fled the capital, it greatly reduced the number of lessons he gave each day and severely cut down on his income.

During the first troubled weeks after Louis-Philippe's abdication the young musician remained confined to his rooms in the Square d'Orléans recuperating from attacks of "influenza" and "neuralgia." Dr. Molin, a homeopath in whom he had great confidence, tended him during these illnesses, and by March his health began to improve, but his spirits remained low. With the course of the revolution so uncertain, his future in Paris did not look promising. And yet if he were to leave Paris where could he go? All of Europe was beginning to quake with revolutions and counterrevolutons. Only England seemed relatively calm, although even there Queen Victoria found it expedient to withdraw from public view for a while when the Chartists took to demonstrating in the streets.

It was to this refuge that one of Chopin's pupils, a forty-four-year old Scottish spinster, Miss Jane Stirling, had been urging him to go for some time. Well-bred, kind-hearted, and generous, she came from an aristocratic family that had made its fortune in trade with India and the Orient. Chopin had known her for many years and was fond of her. In 1844 he had even dedicated two of his nocturnes (Op. 55) to her, and it was now at her insistence that he finally agreed to set out for the British Isles in mid-April of 1848.

At that time of year the musical season in London was still in full swing, offering Chopin opportunities to give concerts, teach, and earn some money which he badly needed. All his close friends approved of the journey and Dr. Molin gave his consent. So, on the evening of April 19, Chopin left Paris by train and took the channel boat to England. The next day in London he was met by Miss Stirling and her older sister, Mrs. Erskine, a widow in her mid-fifties.

The two women were incredibly meticulous in their preparations and provided for their guest's every comfort. They even remembered his favorite kind of drinking chocolate and had monogrammed stationery waiting for him on the desk in his rooms at No. 10 Bentinck Street, Cavendish Square.

A few days later he moved into more spacious quarters at No. 48 Dover Street near Picadilly. The new rooms must indeed have been large since he managed to fit three pianos into them, an Erard, a Broadwood, and a Pleyel. "But," he complained, "what good do they do me since I don't have any time to play? There are so many social calls I have to make and receive that the days go by like lightning." [1] Miss Stirling and her sister, in their eagerness to show off their new celebrity, scarcely gave him a moment's peace. "My dear Scottish ladies shower me with affection," he wrote, "I am always at their place when I am not invited out. But they are used to jolting around all day in a carriage, traipsing from one end of London to the other, leaving their calling cards everywhere. They want me to go and see all their friends when, in fact, it is almost more than I can do just to keep body and soul together" (p. 348).

London's murky spring weather was not good for Chopin's lungs and he suffered constantly from shortness of breath. "I have not yet got used to this London air—" he wrote back to Paris, "and this life of dinners and soirées is very hard on me. I have been spitting up some blood these last few days—and I have not been able to eat anything but ices and lemonade" (p. 345).

Despite their guest's obvious weakness, Chopin's avid hostesses, "the good Scottish ladies," did not slow their pace one bit and seemed totally oblivious to how exhausted he was becoming on their relentless treadmill of social activities. Not only were these incessant functions tiring for Chopin, they were frequently boring, and with his poor command of English, they were often completely bewildering. London society, as far as he could make out, seemed to be composed of an endless "quantity of *Ladies* . . . whose names go in one ear and out the other as soon as they are introduced" (p. 345).

If their names did not stick with him, however, the ladies themselves certainly did; he could not escape them. At the dinner table or in the drawing room they constantly gushed over him with a stream of vapid remarks. Familiar with his works under the saccharine titles popular in England then, they would beg him to play his "Sighs" and "Murmurs of the Seine" (the Nocturnes of Opus No. 9) or bubble enthusiastically over his "Souvenirs of Poland" (Mazurkas). "All their compliments," Chopin declared, "invariably end with the words: 'Leik water'; in other words the music seems to flow like water. I have never yet played for an English woman," he swore, "without having to listen to her say 'Leik water'." When, as often happened, some aspiring young lady induced Chopin to hear her out at the piano, the effect was scarcely as liquid. "They all look at their hands and play one wrong note after another in the most soulful manner," he observed. "What an odd lot! God bless them!" (p. 387). "Old lady Rothschild" particularly offended Chopin one evening when she came over and asked him with astonishing bluntness, how much he cost. The English, he complained, "calculate everything in terms of pounds sterling and would have no respect for art if it weren't considered a luxury" (p. 378).

With his entrée into the best circles Chopin met a number of celebrities including Thomas Carlyle, Charles Dickens, Ralph Waldo Emerson (lecturing then at Exeter Hall), and

Guizot who had fled to England with Louis-Philippe. But Jenny Lind, who was singing at the Italian Opera in Haymarket that season, probably impressed him more than any other. They dined together several times and Chopin found her delightful. "She is a Swede beyond comparison," he remarked admiringly. "She has a radiance that does not come from any earthly light. She seems to be illuminated by the aurora borealis itself" (p. 342). Less fascinating was lady Byron whom he also met that summer. "I get along with her quite well," he commented. "We chat together like a goose and a piglet; she quacks along in English while I squeal away in French. I am not at all surprised that she bored Byron" (p. 369).

On three occasions Chopin played at private gatherings in London, charging, as he had informed "Old lady Rothschild," twenty guineas a performance. The first of these took place at lady Gainsborough's, a former maid of honor to the queen, while the second occurred at the Marquis of Douglas' where he met the queen's aunt, the duchess of Cambridge. The third, which proved to be the most brilliant of all, was given by the duchess of Sutherland in her sumptuous residence, Stafford House on May 15. There Chopin performed "in the presence of the queen, Prince Albert, the prince of Prussia, Wellington and all the cream of the Garter—on the occasion of a christening" (p. 346). He was graciously received and treated like an distinguished guest rather than a paid performer. "The duchess presented me to the queen," he wrote with delight. "She was very cordial and spoke to me twice. Prince Albert came over and stood beside the piano. These are supposed to be rare favors here I am told" (p. 367).

A further honor Chopin received in London was an invitation to play with the Philharmonic. He declined, however: "It wouldn't work out well," he claimed. "Their orchestra is just like their roast beef and turtle soup, hearty and highly touted, but that's about all" (p. 343).

Although he did not play with the Philharmonic that summer, the English public did get a chance to hear him twice in small recitals, the first of which he gave on June 23 to an audience of 150 in a large second floor salon at the home of Mrs. Sartoris, No. 99 Eaton Place.* The second took place on July 7 at the house of lord Falmouth, No. 2 St. James's Square. There Pauline Viardot sang several of his mazurkas (to which she had written words!) and according to the *Athenaeum* and the *Daily News* the recital was a great success—even more outstanding than the earlier one at Mrs. Sartoris'.

In spite of the warm welcome which met him everywhere, Chopin was not really happy in "this abyss called London" (p. 340). Fundamentally he just could not understand the English. They struck him as pretentious, pompous, and tedious. "Whatever is not boring here," he sputtered one day "is not English!" (p. 357).

Besides his irritation with the city and its people there were other matters that disturbed him during the summer of 1848. The unrest in Poland at that time made him anxious about his family. "Things are bad at home," he wrote his pupil, Adolphe Gutmann, "I am terribly worried about it all" (p. 341). "Awful reports about what's going on in the Grand Duchy of Poznań have reached me here. . . . Horror upon horror! It has absolutely crushed me" (p. 344).

He was also upset by what he heard about George Sand. Many unpleasant rumors were circulating about her. "Lately she has been wallowing in a good deal of mud and has been the source of embarrassment to a lot of people," he wrote his family, repeating all the gossip he had heard. "They have printed and are passing out on the streets a biography of her, written and signed by *Augustine's father*, who accuses her of corrupting his daughter and forcing her to be Maurice's mistress. After all that he claims she married her off to the first man who came along despite the objections of her parents to whom she had promised Maurice as a son-in-law . . . In a

---

* Mrs. Sartoris, who was the sister of the famous actress, Fanny Kemble, daughter of the actor, Charles Kemble, and wife of a "wealthy man of fashion," had had some success in her own right as a singer during her early years. Chopin had known her previously in Paris.

word it is a nasty mess. . . . It's a dirty trick on the father's part but it happens to be true" (p. 377). Undoubtedly Chopin's wounded pride derived some perverse pleasure from his former mistress' adversities, but the very harshness of his comments conveys how deeply he still felt about her. He could not forget George or ever be indifferent toward her.

As midsummer arrived and the musical season drew to a close, Chopin found fewer and fewer diversions to ward off the phantoms of the past that depressed him. Exhausted by the strenuous activities of the preceding three months, he no longer had the physical strength to cope with a strange environment any more. "Some mornings I think I am going to give up the ghost in a fit of coughing. I am so miserable. . . . My nerves are all to pieces and I am tortured by a feeling of homesickness. Despite all my efforts to accept things as they are, I am so upset. What is going to become of me?" (pp. 354–55). He would have liked to return to Paris but could not go back now that the riots of the June Days had thrown the city into confusion again. Miss Stirling and her sister tried to cheer him up, but their constant hovering and suffocating attention nearly drove him to distraction. "Heavens! Will they never stop telling me what to do? I don't know which way to turn!" (p. 357) he stewed.

By the end of July, London had become oppressively hot. As usual the queen left for Scotland, and fashionable society followed in her wake. When Miss Stirling and Mrs. Erskine set out for Midlothian to visit their brother-in-law, Lord Torphichen, Chopin found himself suddenly alone. Rather than stay behind he finally decided to accept their invitation and join them up north.

In Scotland the weather was pleasant and the countryside beautiful. As before, the two sisters surrounded Chopin with kindness and did not allow him to want for anything. "They even bring me the Paris newspapers every morning" (p. 375), he burbled. The gracious surroundings of Lord Torphichen's estate, Calder House, and its restful pace pleased Chopin. Country life in Britain could be "most delightful" he discovered. But after a few relaxing weeks he had to leave for Manchester where he was scheduled to give a concert on the twenty-eighth of August. There he played before an audience of 1,200 but was too weak to perform as he would have liked. Still, he claimed, "I had a very good reception" (p. 382). A friend who heard him that day, however, reported that he played too softly to arouse any enthusiasm and was truly pathetic.

From Manchester Chopin returned to Scotland to visit another sister of Miss Stirling, a Mrs. Houston who lived at Johnston Castle near Glasgow. While there he gave a concert in the city's Merchant Hall on the afternoon of September the twenty-seventh. By now fall was approaching and the country began to grow damp and foggy, but Chopin seemed indefatigable. Moving on to Loch Lyne where a former pupil lived, he then proceeded to Keir in Perthshire to stay with Sir William Stirling-Maxwell, an uncle of his "good Scots ladies." It was here that he eventually began to succumb to the exertion of his travels. "All morning up to two in the afternoon I am not good for anything," he wrote Grzymała.

> Later, after I have dressed, everything irritates me and I can only gasp until dinner time, after which I have to stay at the table with the men, watching them talk and listening to them drink. Seated at the table my mind wanders despite all their attempts to be polite and their stabs at *conversing* in French. Finally, bored to death, I go to the salon where it takes all the energy I can muster up to revive myself since everyone is curious to hear me play. When it is all over my good Daniel [his valet] carries me upstairs to my bedroom . . . undresses me and puts me to bed, leaving a candle behind. Only then am I free to gasp and dream until it has to begin all over again. (p. 389)

On the fourth of October he was back in Edinburgh and gave still another concert, this time at the Hopetoun Rooms. Weary to the point of collapse, he did not even bother to inspect the hall before his performance. When he walked on stage that night he was greeted by a "select and fashionable" audience to whom he played beautifully, but the frailty of his execution was conspicuous. For Chopin the whole event amounted to scarcely more than "a little success and a little money" (p. 394).

After a few short excursions to the country homes of some local gentry, Chopin returned to Edinburgh where he took refuge in the house of Dr. Lyszczyński, a Polish homeopath and his English wife. There he could speak Polish, relax, and feel secure in the presence of a physician and compatriot. Mrs. Lyszczyński, however, found her guest extremely difficult, complaining that he always got up late, insisted on breakfast in his room, behaved more vainly than any woman, and couldn't bear to be contradicted or told what to do.

Chopin, it is true, was growing peevish. He could not stand the Scots any more than he could the English. Although they were kind he did not find them attractive, and as for their taste, they even excelled the English at being philistine and provincial. "They play the most outlandish pieces, carrying on as if they were works of art," he wrote disdainfully. "It is pure folly to try and interest them in anything serious. Lady ———— is one of the most prominent ladies back in London and said to be very musical. Well, I spent several days in her castle here and one evening, after I had played and this great Scottish lady had sung a multitude of ditties, someone brought out a sort of accordion and she proceeded in all earnestness to render the most horrible tunes on this contraption. What can you do? It seems that all these creatures are a little batty. . . . Another one, for the sake of being unique, accompanies herself standing at the piano while she sings a French romance with an English accent: 'J'aie aiimaiie' (j'ai aimé)!!! The princess of Parma even told me that one of them is known to whistle with a guitar accompaniment!" (p. 394).

If anything could possibly be worse than their music, he railed on, it was their conversation. "Everybody here is a cousin of some noble family with an illustrious name no one has ever heard of on the continent. They talk incessantly about their genealogical lines: it's just like the Gospels where such-and-such-a-one begat so-and-so, and he begat another, et cetera, et cetera for page after page right up to Jesus Christ himself" (p. 384).

As fall progressed the Scottish climate began to irritate Chopin as much as the people did. "I am choking now more than I was a month ago in this beautiful homeland of Walter Scott" (p. 391), he wrote in October. When rumors reached him that he was about to marry Jane Stirling, he choked indeed! "She might as well marry death,"[2] he gasped. "I am nearer a coffin than a nuptial bed."[3] He was, in fact, feeling so miserable by this time that he sat down and wrote out a will with instructions on how to dispose of his "old rubbish" if he should give up the ghost somewhere. The months of constant running around to keep up with his "good Scots ladies" had become too much for him. If only he could escape them now just long enough to rest and recuperate he felt he might survive. But the irrepressible Miss Stirling with her unflagging devotion— and her inseparable sister—would not give him a minute's peace. "They are nice but so boring. God forgive them!" he sighed wearily. "They write me everyday; I never answer, but no matter where I go they pop up whenever possible" (p. 397).

Miraculously, at the end of October, he finally eluded them for a while and fled to London where he arrived on the thirty-first. There he secluded himself at No. 4 St. James's Place and, for eighteen days, remained in bed suffering from a "cold, headaches, suffocations, and all my awful symptoms" (p. 399). Only once did he drag himself out and then only because he had been asked to play for a Polish benefit in the Guildhall on November 16. The event was a lavish ball, attended by a society more intent on dancing than listening to a recital.* His

---

*It is disputed whether Chopin actually played in the Guildhall proper or in the Common Council Chamber adjacent to the main hall. The Guildhall itself has no records to confirm one version or the other. The archives show a petition on October 19, 1848, "from Lord Dudley Coutts Stuart, M.P. and others in which they asked for the use of the Guildhall on some day after November 9th for the purpose of a ball for the relief of Polish refugees." This was "laid before the Common Council. The Council complied with the prayer of the petition and the proceeds were to be in aid of the funds of the Literary Association of the Friends of Poland [*Journal of Common Council,*

performance was treated as little more than background music and few paid any real attention to him. Such was Chopin's last public performance—"a final expression of love extended to his country, a final glance, a final sigh, and a final sorrow!"[4] It passed virtually unnoticed; only one newspaper even bothered to review it.*

Back in his rooms at St. James's Place Chopin stayed indoors most of the short while he remained in London. The weather had grown chilly and he had no energy to venture out. He seldom even took the trouble to dress during the day. As soon as his Scottish angels heard where he was they hurried off to hover over their sickly charge. Although their intentions were kindly their presence was annoying. "My fine Scots ladies are getting on my nerves again," the invalid complained. "Mrs. Erskine, who is a very dedicated Protestant, the good lady . . . brings me her Bible, speaks to me of my soul and checks off psalms for me to read. . . . She never stops telling me that the next world will be better than this one."[5] Poor Chopin! He was discouraged enough without having to put up with the morbid consolation of Mrs. Erskine's Calvinistic litanies.

As the long gloomy days wore on, the sick man's patience and resignation began to falter. He could scarcely breathe, the future looked hopeless, and death seemed imminent. The thought of dying frightened him, but the effort of living seemed even more intolerable. "Why should I bother to return?" he asked Grzymała, the only one to whom he could confide his anguish.

"Why does God do things this way? Why doesn't He just kill me outright instead of making me die little by little?" Not since the terrible winter in Majorca had Frédéric been so sick

126:383]. However, there is no further reference to the ball, and the recital and even the date is not recorded." (Personal communication from Betty R. Masters, Deputy Keeper of the Records of the Guildhall, May 23, 1979.) The one newspaper account, *The Illustrated London News,* November 18, 1848, does not specify where Chopin actually played.

* The *Illustrated London News* (November 18, 1848) alone seems to have felt it worth writing up. And then it stated simply that "M. Chopin, the celebrated pianiste [*sic*] was also present and performed some of his beautiful compositions with much applause."

and desperate. How tenderly he remembered all that George had done for him then and how bitterly he missed her now. Crushed by an overwhelming agony that he could no longer bear, he suddenly lashed out at this woman he had once adored: "I have never cursed anyone," he cried, "but I am so utterly miserable now, I think I would feel easier if I could only bring myself to curse Lucrezia" (p. 400).* "Oh what has become of my art?" he moaned, "and where have I squandered my heart?" (p. 397).

Having vented his anguish, the exhausted invalid grew calm again. His "fever of indecision" passed and with a final burst of determination he resolved at all costs to return to Paris. "Please give instructions to have the bedclothes and pillows aired," he told Grzymała, "Have the carpets and curtains put back . . . and tell Pleyel to send me any sort of piano by Thursday evening. . . . Have a fire lit, make the place warm and dust it; perhaps I may still recover" (p. 402).

On Wednesday, November 22 he sent a letter to Solange Clésinger, informing her: "Tomorrow I leave for Paris, hardly able to drag myself around and more feeble than you have ever seen me . . . I am all swollen with neuralgias and unable either to breathe or to sleep" (p. 404). In this pathetic condition he boarded the train for the channel the next day, accompanied by his valet, Daniel, and a Polish refugee, Niedzwiedzki. As the train pulled out of the station he had a sudden convulsive attack which subsided within a short while but left him very much weakened. For most of the trip he had to keep his legs propped up on the seat opposite him. In Folkstone the three stopped for a meal before crossing the channel and then resumed their journey, getting as far as Boulogne where they rested for the night. The next morning they headed on to Paris and arrived there some time around noon on Friday.

As Chopin entered the drawing room of his apartment in

* It is apparent that Chopin now understood the intended significance of the characters in George's novel, *Lucrezia Floriani*.

the Square d'Orléans his eyes fell upon a small bouquet of violets which stood on one of the tables. Grzymała had not forgotten his request: "At least let me find a little poetry whatever it may be when I come home and go to my room where I will undoubtedly remain for a long time to come" (p. 403).

𝓬𝕩 CHAPTER TWENTY-EIGHT 𝕩𝕤

A S CHOPIN PREDICTED, he stirred very little from his bedroom in the Square d'Orléans during the rest of 1848. In Berry George Sand remained secluded also; not, however, for reasons of health as in Chopin's case, but because of fear. Many of her socialist friends had recently been packed off to jail or forced into exile and she herself had been the object of numerous threats. The uprisings of June had inaugurated a wave of conservatism that left most of the nation hostile to the liberal theories she once touted so loudly. Those "June Days" had frightened both the people and the government into equating a socialist republic with the appalling spectacle of mob rule. Quick to see her unpopularity, Mme Sand decided to withdraw from the public eye and maintain silence on all political matters for the time being. "I detest what they call politics today," she said. "It is a stupid and insincere business."[1] Adhering to the philosophy that still waters run deep, she justified her silence by claiming the sincerest are often the quietest.

Like her contemporary, Karl Marx, she considered socialism an inevitable stage in human evolution and as far as she was concerned, it could triumph now on its own without her assistance. "Heaven is conspiring and we mortals have only to let ourselves be carried along by the stream of progress,"[2] she assured her socialist friend, Barbès whom the tide of progress had carried off to prison that year.

It was all very fine for George to take a vow of silence, but it was not to last for long. As with almost all resolutions of abstinence, the temptation to violate it became irresistible in time. Soon Mme Sand was back at work with Victor Borie on a pamphlet entitled *Travailleurs et Propriétaires*. Not happy with the new constitution adopted by the Second Republic in November, she was even less satisfied with the subsequent elections which brought Louis-Napoléon into power that December. "The institution of the presidency is bad," she wrote, ". . . it is a sort of semi-monarchical restoration."[3] To bring back a Bonaparte reflected too much of an "infatuation for the Empire" she felt, and was clearly the "worst aspect of the public sentiment" (p. 722). While past experience had taught George to be more temperate in the expression of her opinions, she could no longer suppress them altogether and on December 22 she once again put her political views on paper, this time in an article for *La Reforme* entitled *À propos de l'Élection de Louis Bonaparte à la Présidence de la République*.

Three days after the appearance of this article, death struck Mme Sand's family: on Christmas day her half-brother, Hippolyte, died at his home in nearby Montgivray. Rather coarse but jovial, this hearty country squire had gradually drunk himself to death over a period of many years. His slow deterioration had become a source of great sadness to George who watched him progress pathetically to his inevitable end. "It was suicide" (p. 744), she claimed. "For some time," she wrote in her memoires, "his reason had left him; drunkenness had ravaged and destroyed that wonderful creature and left him wavering between idiocy and madness. . . . He began to hallucinate and spent his last months haranguing me and writing me the most unimaginable letters. . . . He wrote me that he knew from *an infallible source that my political friends wanted to assassinate him*. My poor brother!"[4]

During January of 1849 while George Sand was still in mourning at Nohant, Chopin remained virtually bedridden at the Square d'Orléans, so weak that the least exertion completely exhausted him. "I have to lie down ten times a day," he informed Solange who was constantly in touch with him. Since Dr. Molin's death the previous November he had never been able to find another physician to suit him. "Dr. Molin," he avowed, "had the secret of getting me back on my feet again.

For the past two months I have been seeing Mr. Louis and Dr. Roth . . . and now Mr. Simon who has a great reputation as a homeopath. But they only fumble about without bringing me any relief. They all agree about climate—quiet—rest. Rest!" he exclaimed sick with discouragement, "I shall have that one day without their help." [5]

Irritable and discontented, he continuously shifted from one doctor to another. Dr. Oldendorf was followed by Fraenkel from Warsaw, who in turn was followed by Blache and then Cruveilhier. They pumped him full of herbal infusions, lichen concoctions, and Pyrennées water, charged him ten francs a visit and called on him once or twice a day. "But for all that," he complained, "they give me very little relief" (p. 407). His condition was truly heartbreaking according to Delacroix who visited him frequently at that time. "His suffering prevents him from taking an interest in anything," the artist wrote, "least of all in his work." [6]

The previous December George wrote Pauline Viardot twice asking about Chopin's health. It was not until the following February that Pauline answered and the news she relayed was not good. "You ask me for word of Chopin. Well, here you have it. His health is deteriorating slowly. Some days are so-so, such that he can get out in a carriage while there are others during which he spits up blood and has fits of coughing that nearly suffocate him. He never goes out in the evenings now. However he can still give some lessons and, on his good days he can even be cheerful." Then she added, "He always speaks of you with the greatest respect and I must emphasize again as in the past that he *never* speaks *otherwise*." [7]

It was true indeed that Chopin spoke often of Mme Sand, but his remarks were now edged with bitterness and not always as respectful as Mme Viardot had claimed. One evening when Delacroix visited him their conversation went on until ten in the evening. "We talked of Mme Sand," the artist reported,

> of her strange life and extraordinary mixture of virtues and vices. All this was in reference to her Mémoires. Chopin says

that she will never be able to write them. She has forgotten the past; she has great outbursts of feeling and then forgets very quickly. For instance, she wept for her old friend, Pierret, and then never thought of him again. I was saying to Chopin that I foresaw for her an unhappy old age, but he does not think so. She never appears to feel guilty about the things for which her friends reproach her. Her health is extremely good and may well continue to be so. Only one thing would affect her deeply, the death of Maurice, or his going wholly to the bad.[8]

In addition to Delacroix, Chopin had many other regular callers during the months that he was confined to the Square d'Orléans. These included Franchomme, Pleyel, the Viardots, Prince and Princess Czartoryski, Grzymała, Mme Rothschild, and Adolphe Gutmann. From time to time the irascible Clésinger would burst in. Even Jenny Lind, whom Chopin had met in London, came once and sang for him. Countess Delphine Potocka and her sister, Princess de Beauvau, were also frequent visitors. Chopin was especially fond of the countess whose singing never failed to move him. Delacroix saw her many times at Chopin's and considered her an "enchantress," "I had heard her sing twice before," he wrote on one visit, "and thought that I had never met with anything more perfect, especially the first time, when it was dusk and the black velvet dress she was wearing, the arrangement of her hair, in fact everything about her, judging by what I could see, made me think she must be as ravishingly beautiful as her movements were certainly graceful" (p. 93).

These attentions from his friends meant a great deal to Chopin. Without them he would have faced endless hours of boredom, which, as he told Delacroix, "was the worst evil he had to suffer" (p. 97). In April he went to the opening of Meyerbeer's new opera, Le Prophète, but for the most part, "I do not go out," he said, "except now and then to the Bois de Boulogne."[9] Occasionally Delacroix accompanied him on these rides through the park but it was more common for the artist to arrive at the Square d'Orléans and find his friend "in a state of collapse, scarcely breathing."[10]

As the months progressed Chopin's financial situation gradually went from bad to worse. Unable to teach or compose any longer he eventually reached the point where he could not continue to meet his expenses for doctors, medicines, and other necessities. Early in 1849 Miss Stirling and her sister, Mrs. Erskine, always sensitive to Chopin's needs and yet aware of his delicate pride, sent him an anonymous gift of 25,000 francs. For the sake of discretion they had it delivered to Mme Étienne, the concierge at the Square d'Orléans. Unfortunately the absent-minded woman tossed the valuable package into a drawer and promptly forgot all about it. Meanwhile Chopin managed to struggle by, thanks to gifts of 1,000 francs from the Rothchilds, 2,000 from his mother, and a number of other contributions from generous friends.

With fitful bursts of sun and showers spring finally arrived. Despite muddy streets and drafty rooms Chopin began to feel better. "I hope the *spring sunhsine* will be my best doctor,"[11] he wrote Solange, showing the first traces of optimism in many months. Through her reply, he was delighted to learn that the Clésingers had just been blessed with a "great big baby girl."

On the bleak side, spring also brought with it cholera, death, and the Scots ladies. It was around the first of June when Miss Stirling and her sister returned to Paris and settled down in Saint-Germain. Chopin, ignorant of the 25,000 francs they had sent him (which still remained in Mme Étienne's apartment) could only comment: "They will bore me to death, yet" (p. 414). Shortly afterwards, as if in retribution for Mme Étienne's negligence, her son was stricken by cholera. With incredible swiftness the disease spread throughout Paris and before the epidemic had subsided it carried away two of Chopin's outstanding colleagues, the pianist Kalkbrenner and the famous singer, Angelina Catalani.

These disastrous events prompted some of Chopin's close friends to move him out of the city until the cholera had been checked. Through their efforts a comfortable second-floor apartment was found in the suburb of Chaillot. The expense was great—400 francs a month—but Chopin was led to believe the rent was only half this amount since the difference was secretly made up by a devoted friend, Mme Obreskoff. The new apartment was situated high on a hill overlooking all of Paris. The view was magnificent. "From the five windows of my salon," Chopin wrote, "I can see all the high buildings, the Tuileries, the Chamber of Deputies, the Church of Saint-Germain-l'Aux [errois], Saint-Étienne-du-Mont, Notre-Dame, the Panthéon, Saint-Sulpice, the Val-de-Grâce, and the Invalides—and from here to there nothing but gardens" (p. 418).

At Chaillot Chopin was able to work a little and completed his last two compositions, the Mazurkas in G Minor and F Minor (Op. 67, no. 2 and Op. 68, no. 4). For a while he seemed to improve. "I feel stronger," he told Grzymała, "because I am well fed and have stopped taking all my medicines. I am always gasping and coughing as usual but it doesn't bother me too much now" (p. 414). Soon, however, he began to slip again and Dr. Fraenkel, who was attending him, appeared unable to do anything about it. "He finally got to the point where he didn't even take the trouble to test my urine," his disgruntled patient complained and eventually the poor doctor stopped visiting the sick man altogether. "Maybe if I am left to myself I'll get better all the faster" (p. 416), Chopin conjectured. But instead matters grew worse and he continued to cough and spit blood more each day. In order to see that he was adequately cared for, the Czartoryskis sent their old servant, Matuszewska, to stay with him at night. Her copious honey and flour plasters applied with quantities of religious assurance availed little as Chopin became weaker and weaker.

At last on June 25 he broke down and begged his sister, Louise, to come visit him. "I am sick," he confessed after having tried for so long to hide it, "and no doctor will do me as much good as you" (p. 417). At the time he was not aware that Princess Czartoryska had already been working for over a month to obtain a passport for Louise and her family. As early as May 16 she had written a relative, "Go to Mme Kiseleff's [wife of the Russian ambassador to Paris]. I have asked her to have a letter sent to Warsaw regarding a passport for Chopin's sister and brother-in-law. Find out what's going on" (p. 411).

Because of the political situation at that time a passport was difficult to acquire. In order for Louise to leave Poland the Czar's express permission was necessary. As late as the tenth of July her departure was still uncertain.

By this time Chopin's friends were becoming seriously concerned over his condition. Mlle de Rozières who was vacationing in Belgium with a friend, Mme Grille de Beuzelin, got so upset that her companion brashly took it upon herself to write George Sand about the situation. Although she had never met the author, Mme de Beuzelin presumptuously urged her to hurry to Chopin's bedside. Earlier that May, George had, in fact, been to Paris briefly on business. If Chopin would have "called me to him" then, she claimed, ". . . I should have gone. Had he but written or had someone write an affectionate word I should have replied."[12] But then the fear of political violence along with the threat of cholera caused her to leave the city abruptly after only three days. Back at Nohant she basked in the Berry sunshine, swam in the river Indre, and grieved over the loss of her dear friend, Marie Dorval, who had died prematurely that month. Now in July George had no intention of returning to Paris since she felt Chopin did not really want to see her. Indeed her presence might actually make him worse, she reasoned, by stirring up pangs of self-reproach over the way he had treated her in the past. The truth of the matter was, she did not believe Chopin was really as sick as everyone insisted. "I have seen him so many times on the point of death that I never despair of him" (p. 221).

While these letters were being exchanged, events at Challot had embroiled Chopin in another exasperating situation with his two Scots ladies. His obvious lack of money had finally made it clear to them that their anonymous gift had never reached him. Through an extraordinary series of circumstances involving consultations with a famous medium named Alexis it was eventually determined that the money was still in Mme Étienne's drawer in the Square d'Orléans. When the perplexed concierge was confronted with the matter she immediately produced the missing package which had remained sealed with the full 25,000 francs inside it. At this point Mrs. Erskine was forced to confess the whole affair to Chopin. "She handled it all so stupidly," he complained angrily, ". . . that I couldn't resist telling her a thing or two. I let her know that I could never accept such a gift from anyone less than the Queen of England. . . ."[13]

What had been intended as a tactful and unobtrusive gesture became an acutely embarrassing one. "They are kind-hearted, no doubt," Chopin admitted, "but at the same time they're a bit too theatrical" (p. 433). While he refused to accept any of the money at first, necessity eventually forced him to take 15,000 of it in order to pay his ever increasing debts.

Happily the arrival of Solange Clésinger around the first of August and the even more welcomed appearance of his sister, Louise, on the eighth of the month took the invalid's mind off the blundering incident with the Scots ladies. After considerable trouble, Louise had at last obtained passports for herself, her husband Kalasanty, and her fifteen-year old daughter, both of whom accompanied her to Paris. While Chopin was overjoyed to see his family again, the emotional strain was great. "I am quite exhausted," he wrote Mlle de Rozières, "and they are too." But, he added, "I wish you as much happiness as I have at this moment" (p. 434).

On hearing of Louise's arrival, George Sand decided to write her directly to find out about Chopin. But then she hesitated, fearing what Louise had probably been led to think of her. Finally, however, she enclosed a note for her in a letter to Mme de Beuzelin. "Dear Madame," she wrote the latter,

> I understand that the sister of the friend about whom we have spoken is with him. I hope this will restore him, for this sister is an angel and he loves her dearly. The situation now gives me the opportunity to do what you wished, without upsetting the sick one. By asking Mademoiselle [sic] Louise for news of her own health I will be able to show an affectionate remembrance of her brother. The more I recall all that I suffered, the less I am able to convince myself that he really wants to remember me. Louise will be the best judge of that and can either tell him of my letter or not. . . . People have written me that he was

much better, but others who see him at different times and in different conditions think otherwise so that I don't know what to believe.[14]

The enclosed note which Mme de Beuzelin subsequently forwarded ran as follows:

Dear Louise, I hear you are in Paris—I was not aware of this before. Now at last I shall have some accurate news of Frédéric. Some say he is much worse than usual while others write that he is only weak and not feeling well as I have always seen him. Drop me a line if I may take the liberty of asking, for one can be misunderstood and abandoned by one's children without ceasing to love them. Tell me about yourself also and believe me, a day never passes since we met that I don't think of you and cherish your memory. The memory you carry of me in your heart has undoubtedly been tarnished but I don't believe I have deserved all I have suffered. Yours with all my heart, George. (p. 255)

The letter was posted September the first. As the days and weeks passed George waited in vain for an answer. Louise did not reply.

Toward the middle of September Chopin wrote Franchomme in Tours, "I am rather worse than better. Messrs. Cruveilhier, Louis and Blache have decided in a consultation that I should not undertake a trip now [to a warmer climate] but I should find an apartment with a southern exposure and stay in Paris. After much searching an apartment has been found which meets all the requirements desired although it is very expensive—No. 12 Place Vendôme."[15] Ironically enough this was the site of the former Russian embassy.

For a brief while the thought of the move revived Chopin, who began to take a lively interest in his new quarters. But no sooner was he settled in the Place Vendôme apartment than he began to fail rapidly. Propped up on a stack of pillows in his curtained bed he could barely speak at times for hoarseness and had to resort to sign language. Often his friends read aloud to him.*

---

* One of his favorite books was Voltaire's *Dictionnaire Philosophique,* from which the chapter on taste was said to be the last thing ever read to him.

On October 12 his condition became so critical that his former schoolmate from Warsaw, the abbé Alexandre Jełowicki, was summoned to give him the last rites of the Church. As the priest arrived in the early hours of the morning Chopin at first refused to see him, but later consented. When Jełowicki entered the bedroom he was stunned at Chopin's death-like appearance. "His face looked like alabaster, icy pale and transparent. His eyes were usually clouded except for a momentary flash that illumined them from time to time. Invariably sweet and amiable, sparkling with wit, and affectionate in the extreme, he hardly seemed to belong to this world. But alas!" the poor abbé bewailed, "he was not thinking of heaven" (p. 446). Chopin's only response to his old friend was an extended hand and a perfunctory, "I love you very much, but don't say a word. Just go to sleep" (p. 447).

"A leaden cloud of doubt" had overcast his childhood faith Jełowicki surmised, somewhat miffed that Chopin seemed to resist his religious consolations. "The piety which he had suckled along with milk from the breast of his Mother Poland was no longer but a memory of the past for him. . . . Only his exquisite sense of propriety, kept him from ridiculing everything holy" (p. 446).

Undaunted, however, Jełowicki returned the next day and this time spoke at length with Chopin on matters of faith, urging him to take the sacraments. "I took advantage of his weakened condition," the young cleric wrote, "to speak to him of his Mother. . . . and to try to reawaken in him the faith which she had instilled in him—Oh! I understand you, he told me, I don't want to cause my dear mother any grief by dying without the Sacraments . . . but I cannot receive them because I do not regard them as you do. . . . If you want, I can confess to you because of our friendship but not for any other reason" (p. 446). The abbé, however, was persistent. "My dear friend," he said, "today is the nameday of my brother, Edouard [a friend recently assasinated in Vienna]. . . . For the sake of my brother," he implored, "grant me a gift—I will give you whatever you wish Chopin replied and I said to him: Give me your soul . . . I know what you mean, Chopin answered and sat up on the edge of his bed. . . ." Jełowicki then sank to his knees. "In silence," he reported, "I placed the crucifix in his hands. The tears flowed from his eyes. Do you believe? I asked him. He answered: I believe—As your Mother taught you? As my Mother taught me, he replied. Then staring down at the crucifix he confessed in a flood of tears, and immediately afterwards received Communion and Extreme Unction . . ." (pp. 446–48).

Following the sacraments Chopin asked Princess Czartoryska and Franchomme for some music. They began but had to stop when a spasm of coughing overcame the invalid.

The next days were full of agony. At times Chopin was lucid; at other times, barely conscious. Periodically he roused himself to utter a few last requests with what little strength was left to him. Turning to Pleyel who was at his bedside one of these days, he begged that none of his remaining compositions be published. To Louise he gave instructions that his heart should be taken to Warsaw after his death and requested that Mozart's Requiem be performed at his funeral.

On Sunday the fifteenth Delphine Potocka arrived in Paris from Nice, having heard that Chopin was dying. When she slipped quietly into the room where he was dozing fitfully, the listless expression on his gaunt face brightened. Turning toward the lovely countess who stood at his side wearing a loosely flowing white gown he smiled and asked her to sing for him. The piano was rolled from the living room to the door of the bedroom and the "unhappy Countess, mastering her grief and suppressing her sobs had to force herself to sing. . . . I, for my part," wrote a friend who was present, "heard nothing. I do not know what she sang* . . . I remember only the moment when the death rattle of the departing one inter-

---

*What Mme Potocka actually sang is a subject of much debate. Grzymała claims she sang three airs by Bellini and Rossini; Liszt and Karasowski were told she sang Stradella's "Hymn to the Virgin" and a Psalm by Marcello, while Gutmann maintains she sang the Marcello Psalm and an aria by Pergolesi. Franchomme, on the other hand, states that she sang only one number, an aria from Bellini's opera *Beatrice di Tenda,* an assertion with which Chopin's niece concurs.

rupted the countess in the middle of the second piece. The instrument was quickly removed and beside the bed remained only the priest who said the prayers for the dying and the kneeling friends around him."[16]

Throughout the night of the fifteenth and during the following day Chopin frequently sank into such a stupor that he no longer seemed to be breathing and everyone feared he was gone. Then suddenly he would be shaken by a convulsion. "All at once," Jełowicki wrote, "Chopin would open his eyes and, recognizing the crowd around him would say: What are they doing? Why aren't they praying? And everyone would fall on their knees along with me while I recited the Litany and even the Protestants joined in the responses."[17] From time to time, the abbé claimed, he would mutter the words, "Jesus," "Mary," and lift the crucifix to his lips. During his lucid moments he seemed aware of the fact that he was dying and said good-bye to those present. Twice he asked for music, especially Mozart's.

As news of his impending death spread over the city a horde of curiosity seekers thronged the Place Vendôme. Their vulgarity shocked Pauline Viardot who reported that "all the *grandes dames* of Paris felt obliged to come and swoon in his room which was already packed with would-be artists hastily making sketches. There was even a photographer who wanted to move the bed over near the window so he could have some light on the dying man . . . At this point, the good Gutmann threw the whole lot of publicity hounds out the door in a fit of indignation (p. 450).

The ensuing agony that stretched into the early hours of the next day cannot be related objectively. Those who witnessed it were too immersed in their own emotions to recall anything that did not relate to them personally. We cannot even be sure who was actually present at Chopin's bedside during his final moments. However, among the few family members, friends, and pupils we know stayed with him to the very end was Solange Clésinger. Her mother, having failed in her attempt to communicate with Chopin's sister, apparently made no fur-

ther effort to come to Paris. How her arrival would have affected Chopin remains uncertain. Two days before his death
he reportedly told Franchomme, "She had said to me that I
would die in no arms but hers."[18] And on the sixteenth of October, Charles Gavard, the brother of one of his pupils wrote
that George Sand sent a "Mme M." to inquire after Chopin at
the Place Vendôme. Another pupil, Adolphe Gutmann, however, claimed that it was Solange herself who did the inquiring
in order to determine whether her mother would be welcome
if she came.* While it is doubtful that George ever left Nohant
during this time, Solange insisted to Mme Marliani that she
had seen her mother in Paris five or six days before Chopin
died. "I think she's crazy," Mme Marliani wrote George.[19] But
Solange stuck to her story and assured her that others also saw
her mother walking along the quays that day.

Although some of Chopin's friends remained bitter toward
George Sand and claimed that she had "poisoned his entire
existence,"[20] and shortened his life there is no indication that
Chopin himself still wished to curse Lucrezia on his deathbed.
On the contrary, the abbé Jełowicki describes Chopin telling
those at his bedside, "I love God and all mankind. . . . To die
this way is welcomed . . . I am happy. I have no fear. Pray for
me" (p. 449).

As the hours passed he sensed death drawing near. "Leave
me alone," he told Dr. Cruveilhier, "Let me die. God has
forgiven me. He is already calling me to Him. Don't bother
anymore. I want to die." Then, according to the pious abbé,
"at the moment of death he repeated once more the sweet
names of Jesus, Mary, and Joseph. . . . He pressed the cross
to his lips, then to his heart and with a last breath uttered
these words: 'I have already reached the fount of eternal joy' "
(p. 449).

At least, these were the last words the abbé considered
worth recording. Others with different perspectives witnessed
a different drama during those dark moments early in the

---

* His story was not consistent, varying from one telling to the next.

morning of October 17, 1849. According to Adolphe Gutmann, who claims to have been present then,* it was in his
arms that Chopin died. "When he no longer had the strength
to open his eyes," Gutmann reported "he asked: 'Who is holding my hand?' And on recognizing my voice he tried to kiss
my hand. Then we embraced and he placed a farewell kiss on
my cheek, saying 'Dear Friend!!!' Afterwards his head fell
forward on to his chest and his soul departed . . ." (p. 451).

When his breathing could no longer be detected, according
to still another eyewitness, Charles Gavard, "Dr. Crueveillé
[sic] took a candle and, holding it before Chopin's face, which
had become quite black from suffocation, remarked to us that
the senses had already ceased to act. But when he asked Chopin whether he suffered, we heard, still quite distinctly, the
answer, 'No longer' [plus]. This was the last word I heard from
his lips. He died painlessly between three and four in the
morning."[21]

---

*Chopin's niece (who was fifteen years old at the time of her uncle's death) stated
many years later that Gutmann had not been present at the deathbed. However, Grzymała and Pauline Viardot, who wrote of the event immediately afterwards, refer to
his presence.

⟨⟨ CHAPTER TWENTY-NINE ⟩⟩

During the night of Tuesday to Wednesday,
the 17th at 2:00 A.M.

Oh! my darling, he is gone. Little Louise and I are fine. I love
you with all my heart. Look after Mother and Isabelle.

Adieu . . .[1]

WITH THESE BRIEF WORDS Louise informed her husband and family of the passing
of her brother. She could write no more; the
long vigil at his bedside had left her weak and
numbed. In the early hours of the morning the heavy atmosphere of death hung oppressively over the darkened room.
The candle on the table at which she wrote flickered unevenly
as it cast its quivering light on the few intimate friends who
remained hushed and choked in the shadowy stillness.

Seeing Louise hesitate, Princess Marcelina Czartoryska slid
softly to her side, slipped the pen from her trembling hands
and finished the page: "Our poor friend has left this life," she
wrote

> He suffered terribly before he reached that final moment, but
> he endured the ordeal with patience and angelic resignation.
> Your wife nursed him most admirably. God gave her the great
> physical and moral strength she needed. She has asked me to
> tell you that she will write all the details in a few days and begs
> you not to worry about her. Chopin's friends will help her with
> everything, and as for the trip home, they assure her it will be
> safe for her to travel alone. I don't have the strength to write
> more now, but I tell you from the bottom of my heart that I will
> faithfully fulfill the promise I made to you and to our dying
> friend and will take care of your wife as if she were my own sis-
> ter. (p. 440)

Little by little the mourners recovered from the dazed reverie into which the shock of death had plunged them. Except for the few who stayed behind to comfort the grieving sister, they slowly departed one by one.

With the approach of morning, daylight began to seep through the thick curtains of the silent room and the somber stillness soon gave way to noisy bustle. There were innumerable arrangements to be made prior to the funeral. Before the body was removed, Clésinger arrived to take casts of the dead man's face and hands while another artist, Kwiatkowski, scurried back and forth doing pencil sketches of his head which still rested pale and hollow-cheeked on the white pillow where it had sunk in death only a few hours before. Later, according to Liszt, flowers began to pour into the room, inundating the bed on which Chopin lay and converting the entire apartment into a fragrant garden of delicate hues.

Before the end of the day the body was taken away so that an autopsy could be performed. In his last hours, the dying composer, too weak to speak, had scribbled on a piece of paper, "As this cough is about to kill me I beg to have my body opened so I won't be buried alive."* At the time of the autopsy his heart was removed, and in keeping with his request, was transported to the Church of the Holy Cross in Warsaw on the Krakowskie Przedmiescie, the street where he had lived in his youth.

On the third day after his death Chopin's body, "embalmed and in full dress, was laid out amid flowers for friends and acquaintances to take a last look at the Great Master" (p. 444). Later it was taken to the basement of the Madeleine where it remained for well over a week while the elaborate preparations for the funeral were completed. Part of the delay was due to the Archbishop of Paris' refusal to permit women to sing in the Requiem. Only at the urging of Father Deguerry,

---

*Some authorities claim the handwriting on this note indicates that it was written by Chopin's father, Nicholas, and not by the composer. Nevertheless Frédéric's body was opened after his death and a postmortem examination performed by Dr. Cruveilhier.

vicar of the Madeleine and a great admirer of Chopin, did the archbishop finally relent.

For the performance of the Requiem, the orchestra of the Conservatoire was engaged. The soloists chosen included Pauline Viardot-Garcia, Jeanne Castellan, Alexis Dupont, and Lablache, who had sung the bass role in the same work twenty-two years earlier at Beethoven's funeral. The Mozart Requiem itself had not been heard in Paris since 1840 when Napoléon's body was brought back from St. Helena to be enshrined in the Invalides.

To Grzymała's outrage the chorus demanded 2,000 francs before they would "render Chopin the homage which their own self-respect should have impelled them to offer rather than sell to his memory" (p. 445). As a result of these expenses Louise found herself compelled to accept Jane Stirling's offer of 5,000 francs to defray the enormous cost of her brother's funeral.

Between three and four thousand invitations were sent out for the occasion. "Your presence," they read, "is requested at the funeral service, procession and interment of M. Frédéric Chopin, deceased the 17th of this month, to be held in the Church of the Madeleine, Tuesday the 30th of October at 11:00 o'clock in the morning."

When the day finally arrived it dawned bright and sunny, Théophile Gautier reported in La Presse. "All nature exuded a festive air and a golden ray of sunlight, streaming through the open doors of the Madeleine, darted joyfully throughout the crowd at the funeral service." Gleaming in bright silver above the lintel of the main door were the initials F.C. centered in swags of black drapery hung from the entrance. Not a vacant seat or a square foot of standing room was available by the time the service began. The galleries over the porticos and behind the choir as well as the organ loft and even the aisles of the nave were crammed with spectators. The only empty space remaining was that reserved for the deceased himself in the "lofty mausoleum" erected at the juncture of the nave and choir. Also draped in black and silver it rested imposingly in the midst of the filled church awaiting the solemn procession of pallbearers.

"At noon," Gautier wrote,

the grim servants of death carried the casket of the great artist through the entrance of the sanctuary. At the same time there resounded from the choir of the church a funeral march [Chopin's own Funeral March from the Sonata in B-flat Minor] so well known to all the admirers of Chopin and orchestrated especially for this solemn event. A deathly shudder fell over the entire congregation and there was not a soul present, no matter how mundane and indifferent his thoughts may have been the instant before . . . who did not experience the sensation of a shivering chill.

Slowly and majestically the coffin was borne up the aisle and placed on the great catafalque near the high altar, after which the Requiem began. On two occasions Gautier mentioned, "during interruptions required by the liturgy of the office of the dead," the organist, M. Lefébure-Wély, performed the Chopin Preludes in E Minor and B Minor. At the close of the service he played a medley of Chopin themes as the congregation left their seats and departed. Many were weeping openly.

From the Madeleine the cortège proceeded at a slow pace along the broad boulevards to the cemetery of Père Lachaise. Meyerbeer and Prince Adam Czartoryski, who led the procession, walked the entire distance behind the hearse. When they reached the cemetery, the pallbearers, Prince Alexander Czartoryski, Delacroix, Franchomme, and Gutmann* lowered the casket from the hearse and bore it through the crowd of mourners to the graveside. In accordance with Chopin's wishes there was no ceremony at the interment. The priest merely murmured a short prayer in Polish as he scattered a handful of Polish soil over the coffin. With these simple tokens of farewell the composer was laid to rest and the crowd dispersed in silence.

Back in the Place Vendôme, as Louise went through the few

---

* Some claim that Pleyel rather than Gutmann served as pallbearer.

possessions of her late brother, she came across a small black notebook full of memoranda from preceding years. Among its pages was a silk envelope embroidered with the initials G-F (George-Frédéric). Inside lay a lock of black hair which Mme Sand had once given Chopin. After their long years of attachment this was the only thing of hers that remained to him except for memories.

During his last hours, as he lay dying in Paris, George had been busy at Nohant writing a new article for Victor Hugo's journal, *L'Événement*. It was a plea addressed *To the Moderates* for clemency on behalf of those deported after the eruptive "June Days" of 1848. When news of Chopin's death reached her she paused in her work.* While imbued with that stoic strength so necessary for survival, Mme Sand had never grown inured to sorrow. Chopin, she was told, had called her, missed her, and loved her like a child up to the very end. How much of this was true she had no way of knowing but all the same, a shadow fell across her thoughts as she recalled their many years together. Outside Nohant the dry October leaves floated through the clear autumn air. Softly they drifted to the ground like dying memories and swept in gusts across the lawn. Once more the tragedy of death had littered George's life with its debris.

Alone in the privacy of her home, Mme Sand preferred to keep her feelings to herself. For days she felt sick at heart and wrote a friend that she had been deeply affected by Chopin's death. However, one can only calculate the depth of her sorrow by the extent of her silence. Not until years later, when speaking of Chopin in her memoires did she acknowledge, "I have been repayed for my years of care, of anguish, and of devotion by years of tenderness, trust, and gratitude which a mere hour of injustice or separation cannot possibly destroy in the sight of God."[2]

With a poignant mixture of sadness and regret George took

---

* The news presumably arrived in a letter (now lost) from Charlotte Marliani, written on October 17.

up the lock of hair Frédéric had once exchanged for hers so long ago, enclosed it in an envelope and reaching for her pen, jotted on the back of it: "Poor Chopin! October 17th, 1849." With that the forty-five-year-old novelist resumed the full life which yet lay ahead of her. As she had learned years earlier in her youth, "Happiness passes, our worlds change, and the heart grows old."[3]

NOTES

✣

INTRODUCTION

1. Franz Liszt, *Frédéric Chopin*, trans. Edward N. Waters (New York: Free Press of Glencoe, 1963), p. 168.
2. Curtis Cate, *George Sand* (New York: Houghton Mifflin, 1975), p. xxi.
3. Liszt, *Chopin*, p. 135.

CHAPTER ONE

1. George Sand, *Correspondance*, ed. Georges Lubin (Paris, 1967), 3:570.
2. S. Rocheblave, "Une Amitié Romanesque: George Sand et Mme d'Agoult," *La Revue de Paris*, December 15, 1894, p. 814.
3. George Sand, *Histoire de ma Vie* (Paris, 1928), 4:405.
4. Franz Liszt, *Frédéric Chopin*, trans. Edward N. Waters (New York: Free Press of Glencoe, 1963), p. 152.
5. Marie d'Agoult, *Mémoires (1833–1854)* (Paris, 1927), p. 208.
6. Liszt, *Chopin*, p. 158.
7. d'Agoult, *Mémoires*, p. 207.
8. Liszt, *Chopin*, p. 158.
9. Frédéric Chopin, *Correspondance de Frédéric Chopin*, ed. Bronislas Sydow, Suzanne and Denise Chainaye, and Irène Sydow (Paris, 1954), 2:208.
10. Sand, *Correspondance* 3:196.
11. Liszt, *Chopin*, p. 90.
12. Joseph Brzowski, *Journal*, quoted by Arthur Hedley in *Chopin* (London, 1963), p. 72.
13. Ferdinand Denis, *Journal (1829–1848)* (Paris, 1932), p. 69.
14. Brzowski, *Journal*, p. 72.
15. George Sand, *Correspondance*, ed. Georges Lubin (Paris, 1966), 2:597.
16. Sand, *Correspondance*, 3:539.
17. *Ibid.*, 2:409.
18. Charles Didier, *Journal*, quoted by John Sellards in *Dans le Sillage du Romantisme* (Paris, 1933), p. 66.
19. Liszt, *Chopin*, p. 144.

CHAPTER TWO

1. George Sand, *Correspondance*, ed. Georges Lubin (Paris, 1966), 2:608.
2. George Sand, *Correspondance*, ed. Georges Lubin (Paris, 1967), 3:476.
3. George Sand, *Histoire de ma Vie* (Paris, 1928), 2:72.
4. George Sand, *Correspondance*, ed. Georges Lubin (Paris, 1964), 1:215.
5. Heinrich Heine, *Lutèce* (Paris, 1855), p. 47.
6. Sand, *Correspondance*, 1:267. Subsequent references to this work will appear in the text.
7. George Sand, *Histoire de ma Vie* (Paris, 1928), 4:122.
8. Heinrich Heine, *Works of Heinrich Heine*, trans. Charles Godfrey Leland (New York: Croscup and Sterling, 190–), 8:298.
9. Sand *Correspondance*, 2:120.
10. Antoine Fontaney, *Journal Intime* (Paris, 1925), p. 174.
11. Sand, *Correspondance*, 2:880. Subsequent references to this work will appear in the text.
12. *Correspondance de George Sand et d'Alfred de Musset* (Monaco, 1956), p. 70.
13. Sand, *Correspondance*, 2:811.
14. George Sand, *Correspondance*, ed. Georges Lubin (Paris, 1967), 3:89.
15. Sand, *Histoire*, 4:316, 317.
16. Sand, *Correspondance*, 3:713.

CHAPTER THREE

1. According to Bernard Gavoty in his book *Chopin* (Paris, 1974) the actual dedication was intended for Mlle Charlotte de Rothschild.
2. Frédéric Chopin, *Correspondance de Frédéric Chopin*, ed. Bronislas Sydow, Suzanne and Denise Chainaye, and Irène Sydow (Paris, 1954), 2:150–52. Subsequent references to this work will appear in the text.
3. George Sand, *Correspondance*, ed. Georges Lubin (Paris, 1967), 3:699.
4. *Correspondance de Liszt et de la comtesse d'Agoult* (Paris, 1933), 1:184.
5. Chopin, *Correspondance*, 2:218.
6. Fryderyk Chopin, *Selected Correspondence of Fryderyk Chopin*, ed. and trans. Arthur Hedley (London: Heinemann, 1962), p. 148.
7. Chopin, *Correspondance*, 2:225.
8. Charlotte Moscheles, *Life of Moscheles*, ed. and trans. A. D. Coleridge (London: Hurst and Blackett, 1875), 2:29.
9. Chopin, *Correspondance*, 2:228.
10. Frédéric Chopin, *Correspondance de Frédéric Chopin*, ed. Bronislas Sydow, Suzanne and Denise Chainaye, and Irène Sydow (Paris, 1960), 3:41.
11. *Ibid.*, 2:219.

CHAPTER FOUR

1. George Sand, *Histoire de ma Vie* (Paris, 1928), 4:356.
2. Edgar Sanderson, J. P. Lamberton, and John McGovern, *Six Thousand Years of History* (Philadelphia: E. R. Dumont, 1900), 9:208.
3. Marie d'Agoult, *Mémoires (1833–1854)* (Paris, 1927), p. 84.
4. George Sand, *Correspondance,* ed. Georges Lubin (Paris, 1967), 3:622.
5. Sand, *Histoire,* 4:362.
6. Sand, *Correspondance,* 3:401.
7. George Sand, *Correspondance,* ed. Georges Lubin (Paris, 1969), 5:757.
8. d'Agoult, *Mémoires,* p. 75.
9. Sand, *Correspondance,* 3:658.
10. George Sand, *Journal Intime* (Paris, 1926), p. 55.
11. Frédéric Chopin, *Correspondance de Frédéric Chopin,* ed. Bronislas Sydow, Suzanne and Denise Chainaye, and Irène Sydow (Paris 1954), 2:217.
12. Sand, *Journal,* p. 45. Subsequent references to this work will appear in the text.
13. John Sellards, *Dans le Sillage du Romantisme* (Paris, 1933), p. 71.
14. George Sand, *Correspondance,* ed. Georges Lubin (Paris, 1968), 4:174.
15. George Sand, *Correspondance,* ed. Georges Lubin (Paris, 1964), 1:168.

CHAPTER FIVE

1. Franz Liszt, *Frédéric Chopin,* trans. Edward N. Waters (New York: Free Press of Glencoe, 1963), p. 108.
2. *Ibid.,* p. 79.
3. "Le Journal de Chopin," *Le Guide Musical* September 8 and 15, 1907, p. 552.
4. George Sand, *Correspondance,* ed. Georges Lubin (Paris, 1968), 4:293.
5. S. Rocheblave, "Une Amitié Romanesque," *La Revue de Paris* December 15, 1894, p. 824.
6. Aurore Sand, "Une Correspondance inédite de George Sand avec Balzac," *Les Nouvelles Littéraires,* July 26, 1930, p. 8.
7. Honoré de Balzac, *Lettres à L'Étrangère* (Paris, 1899), 1:461.
8. Sand, *Correspondance,* 4:711.

CHAPTER SIX

1. George Sand, *Correspondance,* ed. Georges Lubin (Paris, 1968), 4:315.
2. Franz Liszt, *Frédéric Chopin,* trans. Edward N. Waters (New York: Free Press of Glencoe, 1963), p. 84.
3. Ernest Legouvé, untitled review, *Revue et Gazette Musicale de Paris,* March 25, 1838, p. 135.

4. Robert Schumann, *Gesammelte Schriften Ueber Musik und Musiker* (4 vols.; Leipzig, 1854), 2:104.

5. Heinrich Heine, *Works of Heinrich Heine*, trans. Charles Godfrey Leland (New York: Croscup and Sterling, 190–), 4:278.

6. Frédéric Chopin, *Correspondance de Frédéric Chopin*, ed. Bronislas Sydow, Suzanne and Denise Chainaye, and Irène Sydow (Paris, 1954), 2:262.

7. Liszt, *Chopin*, p. 110.

8. Chopin, *Correspondance*, 2:234.

9. Sand, *Correspondance*, 4:437. Subsequent references to this work will appear in the text.

10. Chopin, *Correspondance*, 2:237.

CHAPTER SEVEN

1. Frédéric Chopin, *Correspondance de Frédéric Chopin*, ed. Bronislas Sydow, Suzanne and Denise Chainaye, and Irène Sydow (Paris, 1953), 1:49.

2. *Allgemeine Musikalische Zeitung*, November 18, 1829, p. 757.

3. Chopin, *Correspondance*, 1:134. Subsequent references to this work will appear in the text.

4. Frédéric Chopin, *Correspondance de Frédéric Chopin*, ed. Bronislas Sydow, Suzanne and Denise Chainaye, and Irène Sydow (Paris, 1954) 2:39. Subsequent references to this work will appear in the text.

5. Felix Moscheles, ed., *Letters of Felix Mendelssohn to Ignaz and Charlotte Moscheles* (Boston: Ticknor, 1888), p. 129.

6. Charlotte Moscheles, *Life of Moscheles*, ed. and trans. A. D. Coleridge (London, Hurst and Blackett 1873), 1:316.

7. Chopin, *Correspondance*, 2:147.

8. George Sand, *Journal Intime* (Paris, 1926), p. 127

CHAPTER EIGHT

1. Frédéric Chopin, *Correspondance de Frédéric Chopin*, ed. Bronislas Sydow, Suzanne and Denise Chainaye, and Irène Sydow (Paris, 1954), 2:255.

2. George Sand, *Correspondance*, ed. Georges Lubin (Paris, 1968), 4:487.

3. Chopin, *Correspondance*, 2:286.

4. George Sand, *Histoire de ma Vie* (Paris, 1928), 4:435.

5. George Sand, *Les Majorcains* (Paris, 1843), p. 32.

6. Chopin, *Correspondance*, 2:287.

7. George Sand, *Winter in Majorca*, trans. Robert Graves (Valldemosa Edition, Mallorca, 1956), p. 30.

CHAPTER NINE

1. George Sand, *Correspondance,* ed. Georges Lubin (Paris, 1968), 4:512.
2. George Sand, *Winter in Majorca,* trans. Robert Graves (Valldemosa Edition, Mallorca, 1956), p. 7. Subsequent references to this work will appear in the text.
3. George Sand, *Un Invierno en Mallorca* (Palma, 1902), p. 209.
4. Marcel Godeau, *Le Voyage à Majorque* (Paris, 1959), p. 48.

CHAPTER TEN

1. George Sand, *Winter in Majorca,* trans. Robert Graves (Valldemosa Edition, Mallorca, 1956), p. 32.
2. George Sand, *Correspondance,* ed. Georges Lubin (Paris, 1968), 4:522.
3. Sand, *Winter,* p. 33.
4. Sand, *Correspondance,* 4:517.
5. Sand, *Winter,* p. 35.
6. Sand, *Correspondance,* 4:516.
7. Sand, *Winter,* p. 34.
8. Sand, *Correspondance,* 4:522.
9. Bartolomé Ferra, *Chopin and George Sand in Majorca,* trans. James Webb (Palma de Mallorca, 1936), p. 58.
10. Marcel Godeau, *Le Voyage à Majorque* (Paris, 1959), p. 39.
11. Sand, *Winter,* p. 39.
12. Sand, *Correspondance,* 4:516.
13. Sand, *Winter,* p. 36.
14. Sand, *Correspondance,* 4:521.
15. Frédéric Chopin, *Correspondance de Frédéric Chopin,* ed. Bronislas Sydow, Suzanne and Denise Chainaye, and Irène Sydow (Paris, 1954), 2:265.

CHAPTER ELEVEN

1. George Sand, *Winter in Majorca,* trans. Robert Graves (Valldemosa Edition, Mallorca, 1956), p. 36.
2. Frédéric Chopin, *Correspondance de Frédéric Chopin,* ed. Bronislas Sydow, Suzanne and Denise Chainaye, and Irène Sydow (Paris, 1954), 2:260.
3. Marcel Godeau, *Le Voyage à Majorque* (Paris, 1959), p. 81.
4. George Sand, *Correspondance,* ed. Georges Lubin (Paris, 1968), 4:515.
5. Sand, *Winter,* p. 43.
6. Chopin, *Correspondance,* 2:271.
7. Sand, *Correspondance,* 4:529.
8. Sand, *Winter,* p. 45.

9. Sand, *Correspondance*, 4:516.

10. Sand, *Winter*, p. 46.

11. Chopin, *Correspondance*, 2:274.

12. Sand, *Correspondance*, 4:529.

13. Chopin, *Correspondance*, 2:274.

14. Sand, *Winter*, p. 47. Subsequent references to this work will appear in the text.

15. George Sand, *Correspondance*, ed. Georges Lubin (Paris, 1966), 2:533.

16. Chopin, *Correspondance*, 2:277.

17. Sand, *Correspondance*, 4:534.

18. Chopin, *Correspondance*, 2:277.

19. Sand, *Correspondance*, 4:532.

20. Chopin, *Correspondance*, 2:277.

21. Sand, *Correspondance*, 4:532.

CHAPTER TWELVE

1. George Sand, *Winter in Majorca*, trans. Robert Graves (Valldemosa Edition, Mallorca, 1956), pp. 94–95.

2. Frédéric Chopin, *Correspondance de Frédéric Chopin*, ed. Bronislas Sydow, Suzanne and Denise Chainaye, and Irène Sydow (Paris, 1954), 2:283.

3. Sand, *Winter*, p. 95. Subsequent references to this work will appear in the text.

4. George Sand, *Correspondance*, ed. Georges Lubin (Paris, 1968), 4:518.

5. Chopin, *Correspondance*, 2:282.

6. Sand, *Winter*, p. 109.

7. Sand, *Correspondance*, 4:518.

8. Sand, *Winter*, p. 109.

9. Bartolomé Ferra, *Chopin and George Sand in Majorca*, trans. James Webb (Palma de Mallorca, 1936), p. 27.

10. Sand, *Winter*, p. 103.

CHAPTER THIRTEEN

1. George Sand, *Winter in Majorca*, trans. Robert Graves (Valldemosa Edition, Mallorca, 1956), p. 137.

2. George Sand, *Correspondance*, ed. Georges Lubin (Paris, 1968), 4:555.

3. Sand, *Winter*, p. 136.

4. Sand, *Correspondance*, 4:553.

5. George Sand, *Histoire de ma Vie* (Paris, 1928), 4:307.

6. Sand, *Correspondance*, 4:607.

7. Frédéric Chopin, *Correspondance de Frédéric Chopin*, ed. Bronislas

Sydow, Suzanne and Denise Chainaye, and Irène Sydow (Paris, 1954), 2:284.

8. Sand, *Histoire*, 4:444.

9. George Sand, *Les Majorcains* (Paris, 1843), p. 35.

10. Chopin, *Correspondance*, 2:291.

11. Sand, *Winter*, p. 112.

12. George Sand, *Un Invierno en Mallorca* (Palma, 1902), p. 32.

13. Sand, *Winter*, p. 146.

14. Charles Dembowski, *Deux Ans en Espagne et en Portugal pendant la guerre civile, 1838–1840* (Paris, 1841), p. 301.

15. Sand, *Winter*, p. 135.

16. Sand, *Histoire*, 4:438.

17. Sand, *Correspondance*, 4:531.

18. Sand, *Winter*, p. 164.

19. Sand, *Histoire*, 4:443–44.

CHAPTER FOURTEEN

1. George Sand, *Histoire de ma Vie* (Paris, 1928), 4:443.

2. George Sand, *Winter in Majorca*, trans. Robert Graves (Valldemose Edition, Mallorca, 1956), p. 26.

3. George Sand, *Correspondance*, ed. Georges Lubin (Paris, 1968), 4:585.

4. Sand, *Winter*, p. 165.

5. Sand, *Correspondance*, 4:585. Subsequent references to this work will appear in the text.

6. Frédéric Chopin, *Correspondance de Frédéric Chopin*, ed. Bronislas Sydow, Suzanne and Denise Chainaye, and Irène Sydow (Paris, 1954), 2:310.

7. Sand, *Correspondance*, 4:570.

8. Franz Liszt, *Frédéric Chopin*, trans. Edward N. Waters (New York: Free Press of Glencoe, 1963), p. 160.

9. Chopin, *Correspondance*, 2:303. Subsequent references to this work will appear in the text.

10. Sand, *Correspondance*, 4:589.

11. Chopin, *Correspondance*, 2:323.

12. Sand, *Correspondance*, 4:644.

13. Chopin, *Correspondance*, 2:323.

14. Sand, *Correspondance*, 4:625.

CHAPTER FIFTEEN

1. George Sand, *Correspondance*, ed. Georges Lubin (Paris, 1968), 4:659.

2. George Sand, *Winter in Majorca*, trans. Robert Graves (Valldemosa Edition, Mallorca, 1956), p. 3.

3. George Sand, *Histoire de ma Vie* (Paris, 1928), 4:446.

4. Frédéric Chopin, *Correspondance de Frédéric Chopin,* ed. Bronislas Sydow, Suzanne and Denise Chainaye, and Irène Sydow (Paris, 1954), 2:340.

5. Sand, *Histoire,* 4:470.

6. Chopin, *Correspondance,* 2:348.

7. Sand, *Correspondance,* 4:688.

8. Chopin, *Correspondance,* 2:340.

9. Sand, *Correspondance,* 4:684.

10. Sand, *Histoire,* 4:380.

11. George Sand, *Correspondance,* ed. Georges Lubin (Paris, 1964), 1:715.

12. Sand, *Histoire,* 4:465.

13. Chopin, *Correspondance,* 2:345.

14. Sand, *Correspondance,* 4:715.

15. Chopin, *Correspondance,* 2:350.

16. Frédéric Chopin, *Correspondance de Frédéric Chopin,* ed. Bronislas Sydow, Suzanne and Denise Chainaye, and Irène Sydow (Paris, 1960), 3:38.

17. Sand, *Correspondance,* 4:562.

18. Chopin, *Correspondance,* 2:336.

19. Sand, *Correspondance,* 4:758.

20. Chopin, *Correspondance,* 2:360–62.

21. Sand, *Correspondance,* 4:755.

22. Chopin, *Correspondance,* 2:354.

CHAPTER SIXTEEN

1. Robert Schumann, *Gesammelte Schriften ueber Musik und Musiker* (4 vols.; Leipzig, 1854), 3:121.

2. George Sand, *Histoire de ma Vie* (Paris, 1928), 4:296.

3. George Sand, *Correspondance,* ed. Georges Lubin (Paris, 1968), 4:790.

4. Honoré de Balzac, *Lettres à L'Étrangère* (Paris, 1899), 1:553.

5. *Letters of Elizabeth Barrett Browning* (London: Macmillan, 1898), 2:63.

6. Charlotte Moscheles, *Life of Moscheles,* ed. and trans. A. D. Coleridge (London: Hurst and Blackett, 1873), 2:58.

7. Sand, *Histoire,* 4:456.

8. George Sand, *Correspondance,* ed. Georges Lubin (Paris, 1969), 5:251.

9. *Ibid.,* 4:868.

10. *Ibid.,* 5:251.

11. *Correspondance de Liszt et de la Comtesse d'Agoult* (Paris, 1933), 1:376.

12. Sand, *Correspondance,* 5:251.

CHAPTER SEVENTEEN

1. George Sand, *Correspondance,* ed. Georges Lubin (Paris, 1969), 5:74.

2. George Sand, *Correspondance,* ed. Georges Lubin (Paris, 1968), 4:867.

3. George Sand, *Correspondance*, ed. Georges Lubin (Paris, 1964), 1:880.

4. *Ibid.*, 5:125. Subsequent references to this work will appear in the text.

5. Frédéric Chopin, *Correspondance de Frédéric Chopin*, ed. Bronislas Sydow Suzanne and Denise Chainaye, and Irène Sydow (Paris, 1960), 3:45.

6. Solange Joubert, *Une Correspondance Romantique: Mme d'Agoult, Liszt, Henri Lehmann* (Paris: Flammarion, 1947), p. 170.

7. Escudier, "Concert de M. Chopin," *La France Musicale*, May 2, 1841, p. 155.

8. Joubert, *Correspondance Romantique*, p. 170.

9. Unsigned article by Liszt, *Revue et Gazette Musicale de Paris*, May 2, 1841, p. 245.

10. *Correspondance de Liszt et de la comtesse d'Agoult* (Paris, 1933), 2:105.

11. Sand, *Correspondance*, 5:290.

12. Chopin, *Correspondance*, 3:97.

13. Franz Liszt, *Frédéric Chopin*, trans. Edward N. Waters (New York: Free Press of Glencoe, 1963), p. 112.

CHAPTER EIGHTEEN

1. George Sand, *Correspondance*, ed. Georges Lubin (Paris, 1969), 5:367.

2. Frédéric Chopin, *Correspondance de Frédéric Chopin*, ed. Bronislas Sydow, Suzanne and Denise Chainaye, and Irène Sydow (Paris, 1960), 3:86.

3. George Sand, *Histoire de ma Vie* (Paris, 1928), 4:465.

4. Chopin, *Correspondance*, 3:63.

5. Chopin, *Correspondance*, 3:50. Subsequent references to this work will appear in the text.

6. Sand, *Correspondance*, 5:360. Subsequent references to this work will appear in the text.

7. George Sand, *Horace* (Paris, 1843), p. 122.

8. *Correspondance de Liszt et de la comtesse d'Agoult* (Paris, 1933), 2:186.

9. Chopin, *Correspondance*, 3:88.

10. Sand, *Correspondance*, 5:456.

11. Chopin, *Correspondance*, 3:89.

12. Sand, *Correspondance*, 5:522.

13. Chopin, *Correspondance*, 3:95.

14. Escudier, "Concert de M. Chopin," *La France Musicale*, February 27, 1842, p. 82.

15. Maurice Bourges, "Soirée Musicale de M. Chopin," *Revue et Gazette Musicale de Paris*, February 27, 1842, p. 82.

16. Sand, *Correspondance*, 5:647.

17. Chopin, *Correspondance*, 3:107.

18. Sand, *Correspondance*, 5:648.

19. Chopin, *Correspondance*, 3:81.

CHAPTER NINETEEN

1. George Sand, *Correspondance,* ed. Georges Lubin (Paris, 1969), 5:699.
2. Frédéric Chopin, *Correspondance de Frédéric Chopin,* ed. Bronislas Sydow, Suzanne and Denise Chainaye, and Irène Sydow (Paris, 1960), 3:112–13.
3. Sand, *Correspondance,* 5:699.
4. Chopin, *Correspondance,* 3:114.
5. Fryderyk Chopin, *Selected Correspondence of Fryderyk Chopin,* ed. and trans. Arthur Hedley (London: Heinemann, 1962), p. 226.
6. George Sand, *Correspondance,* ed. Georges Lubin (Paris, 1964), 1:944.
7. *Ibid.,* 5:800.
8. Joseph Barry, *Infamous Woman: The Life of George Sand* (Garden City, N.Y.: Doubleday, 1977), p. 261.
9. George Sand, *Correspondance,* ed. Georges Lubin (Paris, 1969), 6:68.
10. Chopin, *Correspondance,* 3:137.
11. Sand, *Correspondance,* 6:296.
12. Chopin, *Correspondance,* 3:145.
13. Sand, *Correspondance,* 6:283.
14. Chopin, *Correspondance,* 3:153.
15. Sand, *Correspondance,* 6:556.
16. Chopin, *Correspondance,* 3:151.

CHAPTER TWENTY

1. George Sand, *Correspondance,* ed. Georges Lubin (Paris, 1969), 6:564.
2. George Sand, *Histoire de ma Vie* (Paris, 1928), 4:470.
3. Sand, *Correspondance,* 6:574.
4. Frédéric Chopin, *Correspondance de Frédéric Chopin,* ed. Bronislas Sydow, Suzanne and Denise Chainaye, and Irène Sydow (Paris, 1960), 3:166. Subsequent references to this work will appear in the text.
5. Sand, *Correspondance,* 6:565.
6. Chopin, *Correspondance,* 3:176.
7. Sand, *Correspondance,* 6:631.
8. Chopin, *Correspondance,* 3:192.
9. Sand, *Correspondance,* 6:869.

CHAPTER TWENTY-ONE

1. George Sand, *Correspondance,* ed. Georges Lubin (Paris, 1969), 6:906.
2. Frédéric Chopin, *Correspondance de Frédéric Chopin,* ed. Bronislas Sydow, Suzanne and Denise Chainaye, and Irène Sydow (Paris, 1960), 3:197.
3. George Sand, *Correspondance,* ed. Georges Lubin (Paris, 1970), 7:95.

4. Chopin, *Correspondance*, 3:200.
5. Sand, *Correspondance*, 7:159.
6. Chopin, *Correspondance*, 3:200.
7. Sand, *Correspondance*, 7:102.
8. Chopin, *Correspondance*, 3:206.
9. Sand, *Correspondance*, 7:147.
10. George Sand, *Histoire de ma Vie* (Paris, 1928), 4:472.
11. Sand, *Correspondance*, 7:151.
12. *Correspondance Général de Eugène Delacroix*, ed. André Joubin (Paris: Plon, 1936–38), 2:278.
13. Sand, *Correspondance*, 7:212.
14. Chopin, *Correspondance*, 3:227.
15. George Sand, *Oeuvres Choisies* (Brussels, 1851), 3:224.
16. George Sand, *Correspondance*, ed. Georges Lubin (Paris, 1968), 4:435.
17. Sand, *Oeuvres*, 3:232.
18. Franz Liszt, *Frédéric Chopin*, trans. Edward N. Waters (New York: Free Press of Glencoe, 1963), p. 90.
19. Sand, *Oeuvres*, 3:219.
20. Sand, *Correspondance*, 7:159.
21. Sand, *Oeuvres*, 3:217.
22. Sand, *Histoire*, 4:467.
23. Sand, *Oeuvres*, 3:298.
24. Sand, *Histoire*, 4:467.
25. Sand, *Oeuvres*, 3:217.
26. Liszt, *Chopin*, p. 85.
27. Sand, *Oeuvres*, 3:219.
28. Sand, *Correspondance*, 7:702.
29. Liszt, *Chopin*, p. 112.
30. Sand, *Oeuvres*, 3:243.
31. Sand, *Histoire*, 4:454–55.
32. Sand, *Oeuvres*, 3:215.
33. Sand, *Histoire*, 4:268.
34. Sand, *Oeuvres*, 3:304.
35. Sand, *Histoire*, 4:472.
36. Hortense de Méritens Allart, *Lettres Inédités à Sainte-Beuve*, ed. Pierre d'Alheim (Paris, 1908), p. 261.
37. Heinrich Heine, *Werke und Briefe* (Berlin, 1962), 9:364.
38. Franz Liszt, *Briefe an die Fuerstin Carolyne Sayn-Wittgenstein*, ed. La Mara (Leipzig, 1900), 4:7.
39. A. de Pontmartin, "Revue Littéraire," *Revue des Deux Mondes*, 18 (1847):575.
40. Chopin, *Correspondance*, 3:233.
41. Sand, *Correspondance*, 7:338.

CHAPTER TWENTY-TWO

1. George Sand, *Correspondance,* ed. Georges Lubin (Paris, 1970), 7:369.
2. George Sand, *Histoire de ma Vie* (Paris, 1928), 4:473.
3. Sand, *Correspondance,* 7:430.
4. Frédéric Chopin, *Correspondance de Frédéric Chopin,* ed. Bronislas Sydow, Suzanne and Denise Chainaye, and Irène Sydow (Paris, 1960), 3:237.
5. Sand, *Correspondance,* 7:455.
6. Chopin, *Correspondance,* 3:245.
7. Sand, *Correspondance,* 7:574.
8. George Sand, *Oeuvres Choisies* (Brussels, 1851), 3:280.
9. Chopin, *Correspondance,* 3:252.
10. Sand, *Correspondance,* 7:590.
11. Chopin, *Correspondance,* 3:261.
12. Sand, *Correspondance,* 7:682.
13. Eugène Delacroix, *The Journal of Eugène Delacroix,* ed. Hubert Wellington, trans. Lucy Norton (London: Phaidon, 1951), p. 71.
14. Chopin, *Correspondance,* 3:268.
15. Sand, *Correspondance,* 7:684.
16. Chopin, *Correspondance,* 3:272.
17. Sand, *Correspondance,* 7:682.
18. Arsene Houssaye, *Les Confessions* (Paris, 1891), 3:241.
19. Georges d'Heylli, *La Fille de George Sand* (Paris, 1900), p. 53.
20. Sand, *Correspondance,* 7:683.
21. Chopin, *Correspondance,* 3:274.
22. Sand, *Correspondance,* 7:691.
23. George Sand, *Journal Intime* (Paris, 1926), p. 219.
24. Sand, *Correspondance,* 7:701.
25. Chopin, *Correspondance,* 3:283. Subsequent references to this work will appear in the text.
26. Sand, *Histoire,* 4:472.

CHAPTER TWENTY-THREE

1. George Sand, *Correspondance,* ed. Georges Lubin (Paris, 1970), 7:720.
2. George Sand, *Correspondance,* ed. Georges Lubin (Paris, 1971), 8:26–27.
3. *Ibid.,* 7:720.
4. Frédéric Chopin, *Correspondance de Frédéric Chopin,* ed. Bronislas Sydow, Suzanne and Denise Chainaye, and Irène Sydow (Paris, 1960), 3:291.
5. Sand, *Correspondance,* 8:30.
6. *Ibid.,* 7:745–47.
7. *Ibid.,* 8:12.

8. Chopin, *Correspondance*, 3:294.
9. Eugène Delacroix, *The Journal of Eugène Delacroix*, ed. Hubert Wellington, trans. Lucy Norton (London: Phaidon, 1951), p. 80.
10. Chopin, *Correspondance*, 3:295.
11. Sand, *Correspondance*, 8:16.

CHAPTER TWENTY-FOUR

1. George Sand, *Correspondance*, ed. Georges Lubin (Paris, 1971), 8:66. Subsequent references to this work will appear in the text.
2. George Sand, *Oeuvres Choisies* (Brussels, 1851), 3:298.
3. Frédéric Chopin, *Correspondance*, ed. Bronislas Sydow, Suzanne and Denise Chainaye, and Irène Sydow (Paris, 1960), 3:299. Subsequent references to this work will appear in the text.
4. Sand, *Correspondance*, 8:153.
5. Chopin, *Correspondance*, 3:308.
6. Sand, *Correspondance*, 8:56.
7. Chopin, *Correspondance*, 3:312–14.
8. Sand, *Correspondance*, 8:173.
9. Chopin, *Correspondance*, 3:319.
10. M.S., "Concert donné par Chopin," *Revue et Gazette Musicale de Paris*, February 20, 1848, p. 58.
11. Chopin, *Correspondance*, 3:320.

CHAPTER TWENTY-FIVE

1. André Castelot, *The Turbulent City: PARIS* (New York: Harper and Row, 1962), p. 228.
2. George Sand, *Correspondance*, ed. Georges Lubin (Paris, 1971), 8:299.
3. Eugène Delacroix, *Correspondance Générale de Eugène Delacroix*, ed. André Joubin (Paris: Plon, 1936–38), 2:343.
4. Sand, *Correspondance*, 8:331.
5. Frédéric Chopin, *Correspondance de Frédéric Chopin*, ed. Bronislas Sydow, Suzanne and Denise Chainaye, and Iréne Sydow (Paris, 1960), 3:329.
6. George Sand, *Histoire de ma Vie* (Paris, 1928), 4:473.
7. Chopin, *Correspondance*, 3:331.
8. Sand, *Histoire*, 4:473.

CHAPTER TWENTY-SIX

1. George Sand, *Correspondance*, ed. Georges Lubin (Paris, 1971), 8:329–30.

2. Frédéric Chopin, *Correspondance de Frédéric Chopin,* ed. Bronislas Sydow, Suzanne and Denise Chainaye, and Irène Sydow (Paris, 1960), 3:335.
3. Sand, *Correspondance,* 8:359.
4. George Sand, *Souvenirs de 1848* (Paris, 1880), p. 91.
5. Sand, *Correspondance,* 8:423.
6. Sand, *Souvenirs,* p. 120.
7. Sand, *Correspondance,* 8:545.
8. Prosper Merimée, *Correspondance Générale,* ed. Maurice Parturier (Paris: Le Divan, 1946), 5:340.
9. Sand, *Correspondance,* 8:545.
10. George Sand, *Correspondance,* ed. Georges Lubin (Paris, 1964), 1:941.
11. George Sand, *La Petite Fadette* (Paris, 1958), p. 7.

CHAPTER TWENTY-SEVEN

1. Frédéric Chopin, *Correspondance de Frédéric Chopin,* ed. Bronislas Sydow, Suzanne and Denise Chainaye, and Irène Sydow (Paris, 1960), 3:341. Subsequent references to this work will appear in the text.
2. Frederick Niecks, *Frederick Chopin as a Man and Musician* (London and New York: Novello, Ewer, and Co., 1888), 2:292.
3. Chopin, *Correspondance,* (Paris, 1960), 3:398.
4. Franz Liszt, *Frédéric Chopin,* trans. Edward N. Waters (New York: Free Press of Glencoe, 1963), p. 172.
5. Chopin, *Correspondance,* 3:401.

CHAPTER TWENTY-EIGHT

1. George Sand, *Correspondance,* ed. Georges Lubin (Paris, 1971), 8:655.
2. George Sand, *Correspondance,* ed. Georges Lubin (Paris, 1972), 9:66.
3. *Ibid.* 8:659.
4. George Sand, *Histoire de ma Vie* (Paris, 1928), 4:474–75.
5. Frédéric Chopin, *Correspondance de Frédéric Chopin,* ed. Bronislas Sydow, Suzanne and Denise Chainaye, and Irène Sydow (Paris, 1960), 3:407.
6. Eugène Delacroix, *The Journal of Eugène Delacroix,* ed. Hubert Wellington, trans. Lucy Norton (London: Phaidon, 1951), p. 86.
7. Chopin, *Correspondance,* 3:408.
8. Delacroix, *Journal,* p. 86.
9. Chopin, *Correspondance,* 3:413.
10. Delacroix, *Journal,* p. 97.
11. Chopin, *Correspondance,* 3:409.
12. Sand, *Correspondance,* 9:220.

13. Chopin, *Correspondance,* 3:429.

14. Sand, *Correspondance,* 9:256.

15. Chopin, *Correspondance,* 3:439.

16. Frederick Niecks, *Frederick Chopin as a Man and Musician* (London and New York: Novello, Ewer, and Co., 1888), 2:316.

17. Chopin, *Correspondance,* 3:449.

18. Niecks, *Frederick Chopin,* 2:318.

19. Sand, *Correspondance,* 9:297.

20. Chopin, *Correspondance,* 3:442.

21. Niecks, *Frederick Chopin,* 2:321.

CHAPTER TWENTY-NINE

1. Frédéric Chopin, *Correspondance de Frédéric Chopin,* ed. Bronislas Sydow, Suzanne and Denise Chainaye, and Irène Sydow (Paris, 1960), 3:440.

2. George Sand, *Histoire de ma Vie* (Paris, 1928), 4:473.

3. George Sand, *Journal Intime* (Paris, 1926), p. 129.

INDEX